Step back in time, to the way it was... ...and is! Come visit!

NEVADA NORTHERN RAILWAY
NATIONAL HISTORIC LANDMARK
ESTABLISHED 1905
ELY, NEVADA

Unique Programs • Unique Opportunities

Take the Throttle - Operate a Steam Locomotive!*

Your hand on the throttle! - operate a steam locomotive! Instruction included.

Steam Locomotive Only - 14 mile trip....$795
Diesel Locomotive Only - 14 mile trip.....$595
Steam & Diesel - 2 routes - 28 mile trip...$995
*New for 2011 - Locomotive with Train***
Steam - 14 mile trip.............................$2,395
Diesel - 14 mile trip..............................$1,695
Steam & Diesel - 28 mile trip................$3,500

*Two people per rental **A day of railroading - includes training, rulebook, air brake class and a locomotive only rental for familiarization and locomotive rental with train. Steam & Diesel Locomotive with train requires two days. Full details on our website.

Railroad Reality Week

Work on the railroad! Learn, hands-on, what it takes to run a railroad! Includes working on track, in the shop and operations!
Adult Session
One week............................$845

Teen Session
One week............................$795

Not affiliated with NRHS

Winter Photo Shoots

Travel Time! Shoot award winning photos of century old original **operating** equipment in their original surroundings! Steam locomotives, steam crane, buildings and rolling stock.
Winter Photo Shoot
2 ½ days.............................$425
Winter Photo Shoot
Both weekends....................$725

(866) 407-8326 • www.nnry.com • (775) 289-2085

TOURIST TRAINS
GUIDEBOOK
✤ THIRD EDITION ✤

KALMBACH BOOKS

Kalmbach Books
21027 Crossroads Circle
Waukesha, Wisconsin 53186
www.Kalmbach.com/Books

Published in 2011
15 14 13 12 11   1 2 3 4 5

Manufactured in China

ISBN: 978-0-87116-430-8

Front cover photo: White Pass & Yukon Route by Karl Zimmermann
Back cover photo: Lehigh Gorge Scenic Railway by Jim Wrinn

Publisher's Cataloging-In-Publication Data
Tourist trains guidebook / [from the publisher of Trains magazine].
-- 3rd ed.

    p. : ill. (chiefly col.) ; cm.

   "Discover hundreds of fascinating train sites across the U.S. &
Canada."--Cover.
   "Trains books."--Cover.
   Includes index.
   ISBN: 978-0-87116-430-8

   1. Railroads--United States--Guidebooks. 2. Railroads--Canada--
Guidebooks. 3. Railroad museums--United States--Guidebooks.
4. Railroad museums--Canada--Guidebooks. 5. Railroad travel--
United States--Guidebooks. 6. Railroad travel--Canada--Guide-
books. I. Kalmbach Publishing Company. II. Title: Trains magazine.

HE2727 .T68 2011
917.304/025

Contributors

The following people provided reviews of the tourist train sites: Bryan Bechtold, Marvin Clemons, Dave Crosby, Andy Cummings, Steve Glischinski, John Godfrey, Martin Hansen, Scott Hartley, Patrick Hiatte, David Hoge, J. David Ingles, Tom Kline, Kathi Kube, G. Wayne Laepple, Robert LaMay, J. Parker Lamb, Elrond Lawrence, David Lustig, Rob McGonigal, Jackson McQuigg, Alexander Mitchell IV, Tom Murray, Don Nickel, Steve Patterson, Mark Perri, Mark Perry, Angela Pusztai-Pasternak, Ralcon Wagner, Bob Withers, Jim Wrinn, Karl Zimmermann

Contact us

To improve future editions of the guidebook, we would like to hear from you. Let us know about the sites you visited, your experiences, and if our descriptions were accurate. Please send your comments to Tourist Trains editor, Kalmbach Books, 21027 Crossroads Circle, PO Box 1612, Waukesha, WI 53187-1612.

Contents

Canada

Introduction

If you picked up this book, I hope you've come in search of an adventure that takes place with steel wheels on steel rails. Within these pages, you'll find historic trains across North America that will take you on a journey. Some are ready to take you to see tall timber or dazzling vistas. Others are there so you can enjoy a meal, a play, or music—on board or as a destination. You'll find museums that are the keepers of our rich railway history—from the days of steam to those having sleek streamliners. Historic sites mark where history was—and still is—made today. They're all found within the pages of this guide.

The *Tourist Trains Guidebook* is an essential tool that takes you into the exciting world of heritage railroading. This guide is designed to spur your imagination and spark your curiosity to go and explore. It's packed with useful information. You'll learn where to find real operating steam locomotives. You'll discover trains that run within sight of, or right through, some of our land's greatest national parks. You'll find trains that take you to see wildlife up close, relive history, or provide rafting or biking adventures.

You'll discover where you can step inside a genuine roundhouse, learn about narrow gauge trains that once went in search of riches, and find places that tell the story of man and machine vs. mountains. Some museums even have programs that allow you to run a locomotive.

So, pick a destination, flip through the pages, and learn about the exciting trains nearby. I encourage you to do as I do and let this book steer you to the tracks where adventure and excitement are always just around the next bend.

Jim Wrinn

Jim Wrinn, Editor
Trains

Using the guidebook

Tourist Trains Guidebook describes 477 excursion trains, dinner trains, trolley rides, railroad museums, and historical depots across the United States and Canada. Of those, 194 of the top attractions were reviewed by *Trains* magazine staff and contributors. In this edition, 24 additional sites have been reviewed and 30 new sites have been added as shorter listings.

The reviews provide an in-depth look at each attraction. They give you an idea of when to go for the best experience and what each site offers. They point out activities that are worth doing and what you shouldn't miss to make your visit enjoyable.

We have included the most up-to-date details possible for every attraction. However, due to the nature of the tourist train industry, we recommend that you contact any site before planning your visit. Steam engines may not be running, schedules and prices may change, and museums may be under renovation. In addition to websites, many of the museums and railways post upcoming events and their most current information on Facebook.

At the back of the book, you'll find a Railroad Discount Card that can be used at 70 different attractions found in the book. Each site's specific discount offer is found in its listing.

Finding a site

You can turn to the regional maps, beginning on page 305, to find a site's general location using the number next to its name. We divided the continental United States into seven regions, and states are color coded according to their region. (Canada is one region and one color.)

For each state, shorter entries come first and are followed by the full-page reviews. Each grouping is listed in alphabetical order. After each attraction's name, there is a number in a circle or a square. Squares represent train excursions, dinner trains, and trolley rides. Circles represent museums, depots, and other sites.

ALABAMA

Foley Railroad Museum ❶

Housed in a former Louisville & Nashville depot, the museum contains photos and artifacts relating to rail, the City of Foley, and Baldwin County history. It displays an L&N diesel switch engine, several boxcars, and a caboose. The museum is open Monday through Friday.

LOCATION: 125 E. Laurel Avenue, Foley
PHONE: 251-943-1818
WEBSITE: foleyrailroadmuseum.com
E-MAIL: foleymuseum@gulftel.com

Fort Payne Depot Museum ❷

Located in northeast Alabama, the museum is a former passenger station built in the late 1800s of pink sandstone, and it displays railroad artifacts in a caboose. It also includes local historical and military items. The museum is open Mondays, Wednesdays, and Fridays.

LOCATION: 105 Fifth Street NE, Fort Payne
PHONE: 256-845-5714
WEBSITE: fortpaynedepotmuseum.com
E-MAIL: depotmuseum@bellsouth.net

Huntsville Depot & Museum ❸

Built in 1860, the depot is the oldest in Alabama and is listed on the National Register of Historic Places. You can read graffiti left by Civil War soldiers and climb aboard several steam locomotives for an up-close look. The museum is open Tuesday through Saturday March through December. Norfolk Southern's busy Chattanooga to Memphis main line is adjacent to the depot.

LOCATION: 320 Church Street NW, Huntsville
PHONE: 256-564-8100
WEBSITE: earlyworks.com
E-MAIL: form on website

Heart of Dixie Railroad Museum ❹

LOCATION: 1919 Ninth Street, Calera
PHONE: 205-668-3435
WEBSITE: hodrrm.org
E-MAIL: form on website

Marvin Clemons

The museum features exhibits housed in a restored depot from Wilton, Ala. It operates two trains and displays a variety of locomotives and rolling stock. The Heart of Dixie has been designated as the official railroad museum for the state of Alabama.

CHOICES: The museum's Calera & Shelby Railroad operates over 5.5 miles of the Louisville & Nashville's former Alabama mineral railroad through the forested countryside. Two one-hour, diesel-powered excursions run every Saturday. On the first three Saturdays of each month, April through November, the two-foot gauge Shelby & Southern steam train operates 10-minute trips. The museum is open Tuesday through Saturday from mid-March through mid-December. Admission to the depot museum and outdoor exhibits is free (donations are welcome). A pavilion is available for picnics.

WHEN TO GO: With comfortable temperatures and lower humidity, spring and autumn are ideal seasons for a visit, as well as the best time to enjoy the colorful foliage along the heavily wooded Calera & Shelby right-of-way. For family outings, the museum regularly operates a number of theme-related excursions including the Cottontail Express, Day Out with Thomas, Steam Days, Pumpkin Patch Express, Santa Special, and the ever-popular Polar Express.

GOOD TO KNOW: In addition to regular excursion trains, the Ozan Winery offers wine-tasting train excursions on Saturday afternoons.

WORTH DOING: Located only a 15-minute drive from the museum, the American Village provides a delightful setting for a Revolutionary-era village, complete with special events and tours.

DON'T MISS: Housed in an early 20th century L&N freight house, the museum's Boone Library contains an extensive archive of books, periodicals, maps, and other local railroadiana. It is open on Thursdays and Saturdays.

GETTING THERE: The museum is located 30 miles south of Birmingham, just one mile off I-65 at Exit 228. Drive towards Calera and turn left onto Ninth Street to the museum.

North Alabama Railroad Museum ❺

LOCATION: 694 Chase Road, Huntsville
PHONE: 256-851-6276
WEBSITE: northalabamarailroadmuseum.com
E-MAIL: narm-mail@comcast.net

Ralcon Wagner

Combining a nicely restored country depot with a surprising variety of early diesel motive power and vintage rolling stock, the North Alabama Railroad Museum is a hidden jewel tucked away in the scenic Tennessee Valley.

CHOICES: The museum's depot and 30-piece collection of rolling stock is open for self-guided tours seven days a week. The museum also runs a diesel-powered, 10-mile round-trip excursion over its Mercury & Chase Railroad. Many trips have a special theme, and excursions operate primarily on select Saturdays April through December. One-hour guided tours are available when the excursion train runs.

WHEN TO GO: Anytime is a good time to take a self-guided tour of the museum. North Alabama's Tennessee Valley is at its scenic best in the early spring and late fall when the weather is typically ideal for taking one of the museum's themed excursions.

GOOD TO KNOW: The centerpiece of the museum is the Chase depot built by the Chase family in 1937 to serve its nursery business and the community that grew around it. The 1,000-acre nursery was once among the largest in the southeastern United States.

WORTH DOING: No trip to the Huntsville area is complete without a visit to the U.S. Space & Rocket Center. Located a short 10-minute drive from the museum, the center features a replica Saturn V rocket and other space exhibits.

DON'T MISS: The historic Huntsville Depot is located downtown. Built in the 1860s by the Memphis & Charleston Railroad, this building is steeped in Civil War history. It features exhibits on Alabama railroads and the Civil War and displays rolling stock and locomotives.

GETTING THERE: The museum is located near downtown Huntsville within a two-hour drive from Birmingham, Chattanooga, or Nashville. From Birmingham, take I-65 north (from Nashville, take I-65 south) to the I-565 east spur to the Moores Mill Road exit and then left onto Chase Road. From Chattanooga, take I-24 west to Highway 72 to Moores Mill Road and then left onto Chase Road.

DISCOUNT: $1 off each adult train ride, maximum four adults; excludes other offers.

ALASKA

Museum of Alaska Transportation & Industry ❶

The museum is home to the trains, planes, and other machines that helped develop the state. It features a train yard with locomotives, railcars, and a renovated section house. The museum is open daily May through September.

LOCATION: 3800 W. Museum Drive, Wasilla
PHONE: 907-376-1211
WEBSITE: museumofalaska.org
E-MAIL: form on website

Tanana Valley Railroad Museum ❷

The museum runs a restored 1899 Porter 0-4-0 steam locomotive around the perimeter of Pioneer Park on select days during the year. The museum is open daily Memorial Day through Labor Day, and visitors may see restoration activity as well as learn about the railroad. Pioneer Park contains several other interesting museums and operates a narrow gauge train through the site.

LOCATION: 2300 Airport Way, Fairbanks
PHONE: 907-459-7421
WEBSITE: ftvrr.org
E-MAIL: ftvrr.inc@gmail.com
DISCOUNT: One free train ride, up to two adults.

Alaska Railroad 🔳

LOCATION: 411 W. First Avenue, Anchorage
PHONE: 800-544-0552 or 907-265-2494
WEBSITE: alaskarailroad.com

Tom Murray

Completed in 1923, the Alaska Railroad was built to link the Pacific seaport of Seward with the resource-rich interior long before there were highways. Passenger service offers breathtaking excursions into rugged back-country terrain that is often inaccessible by car.

CHOICES: The flagship *Denali Star* operates daily between Anchorage and Fairbanks with stops at Talkeetna and Denali National Park. A local favorite, the *Coastal Classic*, goes to Seward, where boat tours provide access to Kenai Fjords National Park. Each of these trains includes a refurbished "lower 48" heritage dome car, coach, and bistro car, as well as a GoldStar (first class) dome car sporting open-air viewing decks. Adventure class (coach) passengers can watch the Alaskan landscape roll by from open Dutch doors. The *Hurricane Turn* provides flagstop service for campers and fishermen along the Susitna River. The *Glacier Discovery* train runs from Anchorage to Whittier for glacier cruises and to Spencer Glacier for canoeing, rafting, and hiking.

WHEN TO GO: Most trains operate mid-May to mid-September when the weather is warm and the days are long. Early in the season, when there is still snow on the mountains and little rain, is best. The Aurora winter train operates between Anchorage and Fairbanks on weekends from mid-September to mid-May, and various special trains also run during this time of year.

GOOD TO KNOW: The railroad works closely with major cruise lines, offering cruise passengers Grandview service (using former Florida Fun Train cars) to connect the ports of Seward and Whittier with the Anchorage airport. The cruise lines also operate their own double-decker domes on the *Denali Star*. However, the railroad's own equipment provides more flexibility, including the ability to move from car to car.

WORTH DOING: The *Hurricane Turn* provides an escape from sightseeing and tourism overload and a chance to visit with friendly Alaskans on their way to remote cabins.

DON'T MISS: Try either the *Coastal Classic* or *Glacier Discovery* trains. The scenery south of Anchorage is more varied and breathtaking than most of the Denali route.

GETTING THERE: Alaska Airlines has the most flights, but Anchorage is also served by other major airlines. Cruise ships from Vancouver and Seattle that dock at Seward, Whittier, and Anchorage are another option.

White Pass & Yukon Route ▪️4

LOCATION: 231 Second Avenue, Skagway
PHONE: 800-343-7373 or 907-983-2217
WEBSITE: wpyr.com
E-MAIL: info@whitepass.net

David Lustig

The White Pass & Yukon's 67.5 route miles make it the longest operating narrow gauge railroad in North America. More importantly, virtually every one of those miles is knock-out beautiful—a potpourri of lakes, rivers, and snow-capped mountains. Completed in 1900, the railroad was built to link the Yukon and other booming gold-mining districts with tidewater at Skagway.

CHOICES: There are many options for riding. The most popular is the half-day, 40-mile round trip to White Pass Summit. Other possibilities include going seven miles farther to Fraser. Even better are the six-hour trips along the full length of the line, Skagway to Carcross, that are available in either direction with motor-coach return.

WHEN TO GO: The White Pass & Yukon operates from early May to late September, and any time in that window is fine for a visit—though it is likely to be bracingly chilly early and late. As compensation, the snow-capped mountains will be more scenic.

GOOD TO KNOW: One of the railroad's two steam locomotives, either Mikado No. 73 or Consolidation No. 69, operates on Mondays and Fridays. Unique and colorful diesels—modernized, shovel-nose General Electric units and newer chop-nose road switchers built by Alco and then MLW—handle all the other trains.

WORTH DOING: The few hotels and handful of B&Bs in Skagway are best booked in advance. You can tour Skagway, the Yukon, and other scenic areas by Jeep, raft, horseback, or dogsled.

DON'T MISS: Though the entire line is spectacular, pay particular attention to the first 20 miles to White Pass Summit. Here the railroad uses grades of up to 3.9 percent to climb 2,865 feet. For the best views, grab seats on the left side of the train.

GETTING THERE: Most passengers arrive at Skagway by cruise ship, but the railroad successfully caters to independent travelers as well. You can get to Skagway from Bellingham, Wash., or Prince Rupert aboard the comfortable ferries of the Alaska Marine Highway. For motorists, Skagway is 110 miles south of the Alaska Highway, via the South Klondike Highway. A commuter airline serves Skagway directly from Juneau.

ARIZONA

Arizona Railway Museum ❶

The museum restores and displays railroad equipment of the Southwest and has more than 30 pieces of equipment including locomotives, freight cars, passenger cars, and a PCC trolley. It is open weekends September through May, with work sessions taking place on Saturdays. Passenger car tours are available by appointment. Caboose rides are offered on National Train Day.

LOCATION: 330 E. Ryan Road, Chandler
PHONE: 480-821-1108
WEBSITE: azrymuseum.org
E-MAIL: azrymuseum@cox.net

Southern Arizona Transportation Museum ❷

The centerpiece of the museum is steam locomotive No. 1673, which was built in 1900. You can learn more about No. 1673 on Locomotive Saturdays and tour the former Southern Pacific Railroad Depot Tuesday through Sunday. Guided tours are available by appointment. The museum is run by Old Pueblo Trolley, which also operates trolleys along Fourth Avenue.

LOCATION: 414 N. Toole Avenue, Tucson
PHONE: 520-623-2223
WEBSITE: tucsonhistoricdepot.org
E-MAIL: contactus@tucsonhistoricdepot.org

Grand Canyon Railway ❸

LOCATION: 233 N. Grand Canyon Boulevard, Williams
PHONE: 800-843-8724 or 928-773-1976
WEBSITE: www.thetrain.com
E-MAIL: form on website

Jim Wrinn

This train doesn't take passengers into the canyon, or even along the rim, except for a short distance, but what it does do is provide a unique way to reach one of the great scenic wonders of North America in style. Steam- and diesel-powered trains take riders from Williams on a 65-mile journey to the Grand Canyon's South Rim through high desert and pine forests. An exceptional ride, the trip is also a great value in that it saves you time in trying to find a parking space at the ever-popular South Rim.

CHOICES: Grand Canyon offers four levels of service: coach, first-class, dome, and parlor. Service and attention are hallmarks of this railroad. Coach passengers won't be disappointed with the strolling musicians and attentive service, while those in cars with higher levels of service will be pampered with extra room, private bars, and exceptional views.

WHEN TO GO: Traveling this area any time of the year is fascinating. The only two days the railroad doesn't run are December 24 and 25. The summer's heat is foiled by air-conditioned cars.

GOOD TO KNOW: You can ride from Williams, spend the night at South Rim, and return on the next day's train. The railroad has its own hotel, restaurant, RV park, and pet-sitting services available at Williams. Williams itself is a charming western town with plenty of shops and restaurants worth checking out. The Williams depot, built in 1908, was originally home to a Harvey Hotel and is listed on the National Register of Historic Places.

WORTH DOING: At South Rim, the train arrives at an old Santa Fe Railway depot. Walk up the hill to El Tovar, the historic railroad hotel, and you'll stand in awe of nature at its finest.

DON'T MISS: The railroad offers steam operations on selected days during the year behind Burlington Route 2-8-2 No. 4960. The engine uses recycled vegetable oil. Plan ahead and enjoy a steamy adventure.

GETTING THERE: Williams is 32 miles west of Flagstaff. Take I-40 to Exit 163 and follow Grand Canyon Boulevard to the depot.

Verde Canyon Railroad

LOCATION: 300 N. Broadway, Clarkdale
PHONE: 800-582-7245
WEBSITE: verdecanyonrr.com
E-MAIL: info@verdecanyonrr.com

Jim Wrinn

On the Verde Canyon Railroad, you'll ride a former copper mining spur down a lush green valley where eagles often soar. Ride across bridges, around rock formations, and through a 680-foot tunnel.

CHOICES: The four-hour, historic route from Clarkdale to the deserted Perkinsville Ranch travels between two national forests and into Verde Canyon, which is accessible only by rail. Narration describes the history, archaeology, geology, and wildlife of the area. Open cars offer canopies to protect riders from the intense sun, and air-conditioned cars are also an option to beat the heat. Special events on the Verde Canyon are too numerous to mention. Among our favorites are the Grape Train Escape, a wine tasting train, Throw Mama or Papa on the Train, and the Lucky Leprechaun Express.

WHEN TO GO: Trains run year-round, but summer can be exceptionally hot. In winter, you can view nesting bald eagles in their natural habitat.

GOOD TO KNOW: The railroad's pair of streamlined diesel locomotives from the 1950s features a special eagle paint scheme. Located in Clarkdale, the Verde Canyon Railroad depot opened in 1997 on the same site of two previous depots.

WORTH DOING: Visit the Tuzigoot National Monument, where an ancient Sinagua pueblo was built. The 42-acre site includes guided tours of the pueblo ruins and hiking trails.

DON'T MISS: Watch for the railroad trestle over a 175-foot-deep gorge and the Perkinsville covered bridge.

GETTING THERE: The railroad is about 40 minutes from Sedona and two hours from Phoenix. From Sedona, go southwest toward Cottonwood on Highway 89A to Mingus Avenue. Turn right on Mingus Avenue and go two miles to Main Street. Turn right on Main Street and travel through Old Town Cottonwood. Look for the sign and turn right on Broadway. From Phoenix, take I-17 north to Exit 287. Go west on Highway 260 and then turn left at Main Street through Old Town Cottonwood. Look for the sign and turn right on Broadway.

ARKANSAS

Eureka Springs & North Arkansas Railway ❶

This railway takes you on a 4.5-mile round trip through the Ozarks, complete with narration. You can chat with the conductor and crew as the train is switched. Dinner trains offer the chance for a relaxed meal. Around the depot, you can inspect a turntable, rolling stock, and other equipment. The railway is open Tuesday through Saturday April through October.

LOCATION: 299 N. Main Street, Eureka Springs
PHONE: 479-253-9623
WEBSITE: esnarailway.com
E-MAIL: form on website

Fort Smith Trolley Museum ❷

Visit this museum and you can see its growing collection of railroad, streetcar, and transportation exhibits. Board No. 224, a restored Fort Smith streetcar at the Fort Smith Museum of History on Rogers Avenue for an enjoyable trolley ride. The museum is open weekends, and trolleys run daily May through October and on weekends the rest of the year.

LOCATION: 100 S. Fourth Street, Fort Smith
PHONE: 479-783-0205
WEBSITE: fstm.org
E-MAIL: info@fstm.org

Frisco Depot Museum ❸

This restored Victorian depot was built in 1886 and operated by the Frisco Railroad. Take a self-guided tour and hear the stories of 14 figures representing passengers, station workers, and train crew. You can also take a guided tour, view several short films, and examine a caboose. Located in Mammoth Spring State Park, the depot is closed on Mondays.

LOCATION: Highway 9 and Highway 63, Mammoth Spring
PHONE: 870-625-7364
WEBSITE: www.arkansasstateparks.com/mammothspring
E-MAIL: mammothspring@arkansas.com

Arkansas & Missouri Railroad 4

LOCATION: 306 E. Emma Street, Springdale
PHONE: 800-687-8600 or 479-751-8600
WEBSITE: amrailroad.com
E-MAIL: brenda@amrailroad.com

David Hoge

From the highest point to down in the hollers, the Arkansas & Missouri operates excursion trains powered by its all-Alco roster of diesels. Rebuilt air-conditioned coaches transport riders through some of the most rugged terrain between the Appalachians and the Rockies. The A&M operates 139 miles of former St. Louis-San Francisco trackage from Monett, Mo., to Fort Smith, Ark., through the Boston Mountains of northwest Arkansas.

CHOICES: The longest ride is a 134-mile round trip from Springdale to Van Buren with a three-hour stop in Van Buren, where passengers can shop or dine near the 1901 Frisco depot. Another ride is a 70-mile round trip from Van Buren to Winslow with a ride over 100-foot trestles and through the 1,702-foot-long Winslow tunnel. A third trip takes you from Fort Smith over the Arkansas River to Winslow.

WHEN TO GO: With special events, trains run all year. Fall offers the best scenery, and fall trips sell out quickly, but spring is also popular because everything is blooming.

GOOD TO KNOW: Three classes—first-class, club, and coach—are offered on all trips, with lunch or snacks offered for first-class and club but not coach. Fares increase for trips during the fall foliage season. If you join the A&M fan club, members receive a 10 percent discount.

WORTH DOING: The A&M excursion fits in nicely with a trip to Branson or to the William J. Clinton Presidential Library in Little Rock. Eureka Springs offers shopping, and the nearby Buffalo and Mulberry Rivers provide camping, canoeing, and hiking opportunities. Two Civil War battlefields are nearby.

DON'T MISS: For a old-time railroading experience, you can purchase a ticket for the restored B&O cupola caboose, which holds about a dozen passengers.

GETTING THERE: Various airlines offer flights into Northwest Arkansas Regional Airport. Travel over I-540 and I-40 gives the area quick access, making the A&M easily accessible for a day of fun.

DISCOUNT: 10% off gift shop purchase; 10% off regular ticket price.

Arkansas Railroad Museum ❺

LOCATION: 1700 Port Road, Pine Bluff
PHONE: 870-535-8819
WEBSITE: arrailroadmuseum.com

David Hoge

The Arkansas Railroad Museum is the state's largest railroad museum. The museum is located in the machine shop built in the later part of the 19th century for the St. Louis Southwestern Railway, or Cotton Belt. The machine shop was part of a large complex of buildings and shops once located at Pine Bluff.

CHOICES: The museum's most famous tenant is the last steam locomotive built for the St. Louis Southwestern. No. 819 was assembled in the building that now houses the museum and was placed in service in early 1943. Along with No. 819, SSW No. 336 is also housed at the museum. Several diesel Alcos are also on display along with several passenger cars, a complete SSW work train, cabooses, and a Jordan snowplow. The museum features a large collection of memorabilia from the Cotton Belt and other Arkansas and East Texas railroads.

WHEN TO GO: The museum is open Mondays through Saturdays. Most exhibits are located inside, but much of the museum is not climate controlled and therefore subject to the heat and cold. Operating hours can be affected by extreme temperatures.

GOOD TO KNOW: Engines 819 and 336 are the only surviving Cotton Belt steam locomotives, and both are on the National Register of Historic Places.

WORTH DOING: While in Pine Bluff, you can take in the historical museum, which is located in a restored union station that is also listed on the National Register of Historic Places.

DON'T MISS: The museum holds an annual railroadiana show the first Saturday in April.

GETTING THERE: The museum is easily accessible from Little Rock, which has a daily Amtrak stop and an airport served by several airlines. The museum lies just a short distance off I-530, which connects Little Rock and Pine Bluff.

CALIFORNIA

Colma Depot ❶

This former Southern Pacific depot was built in 1865 and is part of the Colma Historical Association's museum, which also includes a blacksmith shop and freight shed. The second stop between San Francisco and San Jose, the depot was built to shelter passengers at Colma, where farmers and teamsters stopped on the way to San Francisco.

LOCATION: 1500 Hillside Boulevard, Colma
PHONE: 650-757-1676
WEBSITE: colmahistory.org
E-MAIL: colmahist@sbcglobal.net

Edward Peterman Museum of Railroad History ❷

A restored former Southern Pacific depot houses the museum's collection of artifacts that highlights Western railroads with a focus on signaling. Along with the depot, which dates to 1863, the site features a restored 1926 tower, a section tool house, and a speeder shed. The museum, operated by the South Bay Historical Railroad Society, is open Tuesday evenings and Saturdays.

LOCATION: 1005 Railroad Avenue, Santa Clara
PHONE: 408-243-3969
WEBSITE: sbhrs.org
E-MAIL: form on website

Fort Humboldt State Historic Park ❸

The park includes a logging museum that displays historic, steam-powered redwood-logging equipment, including two 0-4-0 locomotives and a steam donkey. On select summer Saturdays, the Timber Heritage Association steams up the equipment and provides short train rides. The park also includes a historical museum on the site where Ulysses S. Grant briefly served.

LOCATION: 3431 Fort Avenue, Eureka
PHONE: 707-445-6567
WEBSITE: parks.ca.gov/default.asp?page_id=665
E-MAIL: info@parks.ca.gov

History Park ❹

History Park contains 27 original and reconstructed historic buildings including a trolley barn. Operated by the California Trolley & Railroad Corporation, the barn contains trolleys, a horse-drawn streetcar, and other historic vehicles. Trolley rides take place on park grounds on weekends.

LOCATION: 1650 Senter Road, San Jose
PHONE: 408-287-2290
WEBSITE: www.historysanjose.org or ctrc.org

Lomita Railroad Museum ❺

This museum is a replica of the Boston & Maine station at Wakefield, Mass. You can climb into the cab of Southern Pacific No. 1765, a 2-6-0 Baldwin built in 1902, and look inside a 1910 UP caboose. Several freight cars and a wooden water tower are also displayed. The museum exhibits lanterns, china, and other artifacts. It is open Thursday through Sunday.

LOCATION: 2137 W. 250th Street, Lomita
PHONE: 310-326-6255
WEBSITE: lomita-rr.org
E-MAIL: f.bilyeu@lomita.com

Millbrae Train Museum ❻

The Millbrae Historical Society operates a museum containing photos, artifacts, and documents related to the railroad history of the Millbrae area. Housed in the former Southern Pacific train station, the museum displays a 1941 Pullman sleeper, with its original configuration and paint scheme, from the *City of San Francisco* streamliner. The museum is open on Saturdays.

LOCATION: California Drive and Murchison Drive, Millbrae
PHONE: 650-333-1136
WEBSITE: millbraehs.org

National City Depot ❼

Still in its original location, the National City Depot, built in 1882, is the oldest railroad-related structure in San Diego County. Operated by the San Diego Electric Railway Association, it exhibits several trolleys, railroad items, and local historical displays. The depot is open Thursday through Sunday.

LOCATION: 922 W. 23rd Street, National City
PHONE: 619-474-4400
WEBSITE: sdera.org/depot.php
E-MAIL: webmaster@sdera.org

Nevada County Narrow Gauge Railroad and Transportation Museum ❽

The museum's collection features NCNGRR engine No. 5. The 1875 Baldwin hauled timber, passengers, and freight. Other narrow gauge equipment and wooden railcars are on display as are a 1901 steam-powered carriage and other historic transportation pieces. Docent-led tours of the museum are available. It is open Friday through Tuesday during summer and on weekends in winter.

LOCATION: 5 Kidder Court, Nevada City
PHONE: 530-470-0902
WEBSITE: ncngrrmuseum.org
E-MAIL: contact@ncngrrmuseum.org

Niles Depot Museum ❾

The museum focuses on the Southern Pacific and Western Pacific, the early railroads of Fremont, Newark, and Union City. It also includes Union Pacific and Amtrak artifacts. Exhibits include railroad signals, model railroads, and a WP caboose. Housed in a passenger depot and a freight depot, the museum is open on Sundays.

LOCATION: 37592 Niles Boulevard, Fremont
PHONE: 510-797-4449
WEBSITE: nilesdepot.org
E-MAIL: tcsme@nilesdepot.org

Poway-Midland Railroad ❿

You can ride a variety of railroad equipment on this railroad. It operates a 1907 Baldwin 0-4-0 steam locomotive, a trolley car, and a speeder. You'll also see historic buildings, restored rolling stock, and a gallows turntable.

LOCATION: 14134 Midland Road, Poway
PHONE: 858-486-4063
WEBSITE: www.powaymidlandrr.org
E-MAIL: pmrr@att.net

Rail Journeys West ⓫

Take a luxurious rail vacation aboard the *Silver Solarium*, an original dome sleeper from the *California Zephyr*. Riding in a private railcar over Amtrak or VIA Rail routes, you can take a day trip from the San Francisco area or take longer trips to other destinations in the United States and Canada.

LOCATION: 3770 Flora Vista Avenue, Santa Clara
PHONE: 408-241-7807
WEBSITE: railjourneyswest.com
E-MAIL: info@railjourneyswest.com

Railway & Locomotive Historical Society, Southern California Chapter ⑫

Featuring classic gingerbread architecture, a former AT&SF depot was moved to the Los Angeles Fairplex. The museum includes indoor exhibits and outdoor displays of rolling stock and locomotives, including a Union Pacific Big Boy. You can visit the museum during the county fair in September or during open house weekends each month.

LOCATION: Fairplex Drive, Pomona
PHONE: 909-623-0190
WEBSITE: www.trainweb.org/rlhs
E-MAIL: rlhs-pomona@rrmail.com

Roots of Motive Power ⑬

Roots of Motive Power collects and restores rail and other equipment used for logging. The organization gets steamed up at various events during the year, both on and off the site, including the Roots of Motive Power Festival at the Roots facility and Frontier Days in Willits. Visitors can also tour the collection during scheduled work days each month.

LOCATION: 400 E. Commercial Street, Willits
WEBSITE: rootsofmotivepower.com
E-MAIL: wbromp@rootsofmotivepower.com

San Francisco Municipal Railway ⑭

The San Francisco Municipal Railway operates city transit services, historic streetcars and cable cars. Cable cars run on three lines: Powell and Hyde, Powell and Mason, and California. Streetcars run regularly on the F-Market and Wharves line that connects the downtown area with Fisherman's Wharf. At the F-line Steuart Street stop, just across from the Ferry Building is the San Francisco Railway Museum, which features a replica of a motorman's platform of a 1911 streetcar and other interactive exhibits.

LOCATION: 1145 Market Street, San Francisco
PHONE: 415-701-2311 or 311
WEBSITE: www.sfmta.com/cms/mhome/home50.htm

Society for the Preservation of Carter Railroad Resources ⑮

Visit this museum on a work day and you'll see restoration efforts of wooden cars completed using hand tools and 19th century techniques. Most cars the society preserves were built by Carter Brothers in Newark. For a one-of-a-kind experience, you can ride a train car pulled by Belgian draft horses. Special train rides and handcars operate several times a year.

LOCATION: 34600 Ardenwood Boulevard, Fremont
PHONE: 866-417-7277
WEBSITE: spcrr.org
E-MAIL: curator@spcrr.org

South Coast Railroad Museum ⑯

The museum's centerpiece is the historic Goleta depot, a Victorian-styled Southern Pacific country station. The museum features hands-on exhibits and a SP bay window caboose. Special events are scheduled throughout the year, and handcar rides are offered. In the Gandy Dancer Theater, you can view films on a variety of railroad topics. It is open Friday through Sunday.

LOCATION: 300 N. Los Carneros Road, Goleta
PHONE: 805-964-3540
WEBSITE: goletadepot.org
E-MAIL: form on website
DISCOUNT: Buy one miniature train ride ticket, get one free.

Waterfront Red Car Line ⑰

The Red Car line runs along the Port of Los Angeles waterfront as it did in the 1900s. It operates a restored car, No. 1058, as well as several replicas. You can board at World Cruise Center, Downtown, Ports O' Call, and Marina stations. Cars run Friday through Monday and on select weekdays when cruise ships are in port.

LOCATION: Sixth Street at Harbor Boulevard, San Pedro
PHONE: 310-732-3473
WEBSITE: portoflosangeles.org/recreation/waterfront_rcl.asp

Western America Railroad Museum ⑱

Housed in the restored Casa Del Desierto, a 1911 Harvey House, the museum features railroad art, artifacts, and memorabilia. Its outdoor displays include locomotives, rolling stock, cabooses, and other equipment, highlighted by Santa Fe No. 95 in classic warbonnet scheme. It is open Fridays, Saturdays, and Sundays.

LOCATION: 685 N. First Street, Barstow
PHONE: 760-256-9276
WEBSITE: barstowrailmuseum.org
E-MAIL: warm95@verizon.net

Cable Car Museum ⑲

LOCATION: 1201 Mason Street, San Francisco
PHONE: 415-474-1887
WEBSITE: cablecarmuseum.org

Jim Wrinn

Of all the transportation systems in the United States, one—the cable car—is forever linked to the City by the Bay, San Francisco. Here's a museum that tells the history of the cable car in the city, from its start in 1873. The museum houses several historic cable cars. Also on display are photos, tools, and models.

CHOICES: As part of the Washington-Mason line powerhouse and carbarn, the museum isn't static. You'll see cable cars come and go all day. Make sure to descend the steps from the museum deck into the winding room to see the cables that pull the cars along the city streets. You can also view three antique cable cars from the 1870s: the No. 46 grip car and the No. 54 trailer from the Sutter Street Railway and the Clay Street Hill Railroad No. 8 grip car.

WHEN TO GO: The museum is open every day (except New Year's Day, Easter, Thanksgiving, and Christmas). There is never a bad time to visit San Francisco, but be sure to take a jacket no matter what time of year it is!

GOOD TO KNOW: Admission to the museum is free. During the 1980s, the cable car system was completely overhauled. Track and cables were replaced on 69 city blocks. The powerhouse was rebuilt, and the cable cars were repaired and updated.

WORTH DOING: There is always plenty to see and do in San Francisco. You can walk through the Presidio, tour Alcatraz, visit Chinatown, or just hang out at Fisherman's Wharf.

DON'T MISS: Take in the cable car bell-ringing contest in Union Square, which has been an annual tradition since 1949.

GETTING THERE: No question about it—ride a cable car there! Both the Powell-Hyde and Powell-Mason lines stop right at the museum. From the California line, get off at Mason Street and walk three blocks north to the museum. Tickets can be purchased as you board the cable car.

California State Railroad Museum ⑳

LOCATION: 111 I Street, Sacramento
PHONE: 916-445-6645 or 916-323-9280
WEBSITE: csrmf.org
E-MAIL: form on website

Jeff Terry

This is among the best interpretive museums about railroading. The museum mixes a magnificent large-artifact collection with plenty of details and a sense of drama that bring them to life. Displays, hands-on exhibits, and human interaction all combine to produce an excellent experience for everyone, from those with a passing interest in railroads to those with a deep appreciation for railroading. And if you want the real thing, the museum operates its Sacramento Southern Railroad, a short train ride, in season.

CHOICES: Made up of several buildings, the museum offers guided tours. The Railroad History Museum, at 100,000 square feet, is the largest exhibit space and contains 21 restored cars and locomotives. Be sure to climb the stairs that take you into the cab of one of the largest preserved steam locomotives, a rare Cab Forward with its crew compartment in front of the boiler.

WHEN TO GO: Weekends, April through September, is when the museum offers its Sacramento Southern train rides behind Granite Rock No. 10, a rebuilt 1943 tank engine. The 40-minute, six-mile round trip travels over the levees of the Sacramento River. The museum also runs special events and excursions throughout the year. For photographers, watch for Trains & Tripods day, when tripods and handheld flashes are allowed.

GOOD TO KNOW: The museum is situated in the Old Sacramento district of the state capital near where the first transcontinental railroad was launched eastward in the 1800s. The district is a 28-acre National Historic Landmark District and state historic park.

WORTH DOING: The Old Sacramento State Historic Park contains a variety of museums, landmarks, and historical buildings. They include a military museum, a Central Pacific passenger station, and a Central Pacific freight depot.

DON'T MISS: Walk through the *St. Hyacinthe*, a 1929 heavyweight sleeper car. But this is no walk through a lifeless artifact. Inside the beautifully restored Canadian National Pullman car, sound, light, and motion combine to provide the sense that you are speeding through the night on this hotel on wheels.

GETTING THERE: When driving to Sacramento, take I-80 from San Francisco or I-5 from Reno. If you want the full rail experience, take an Amtrak train. The station is adjacent to Old Sacramento. The museum is at the corner of Second and I Streets.

Fillmore & Western Railway

LOCATION: 351 Santa Clara Street, Fillmore
PHONE: 800-773-8724 or 805-524-2546
WEBSITE: fwry.com
E-MAIL: info@fwry.com

Dale Bolms

Operating over a segment of a former Southern Pacific branch line, the Fillmore & Western Railway is a well-run combination of weekend scenic excursion trains, murder mystery dinner trains, and special trains. It is also one of the premier movie location sets. Billing itself as the "Home of the Movie Trains," from wrecks to shootouts, Hollywood has used this scenic little Southern California line to represent Washington D.C., Florida, the Pacific Northwest, and just about every place in between.

CHOICES: On some passenger runs, the F&W operates ex-Duluth & Northeastern 2-8-0 steam engine No. 14. On weekend excursion trains, you can ride in an open-air railcar or in restored vintage passenger coaches. For a full afternoon tour, the Museum or Murals Train offers a luncheon tour to Santa Paula with a choice of a walking tour of the city's murals or of the California Oil Museum. Mystery dinner trains offer a wide range of themes and can be combined with lodging options for weekend getaway packages.

WHEN TO GO: Any time is a good time in southern California, with summers obviously being hotter then other seasons. The rainy season, which is spotty at best, is from about November to March. The trains consist of vintage and antique pieces of rolling stock, which are not climate controlled, so wear weather-appropriate clothing.

GOOD TO KNOW: Fillmore is a suburb in a sea of suburbs north of Los Angeles. Lodging and dining can be found in Fillmore and nearby Santa Paula, Piru, Oxnard, and Ventura.

WORTH DOING: Farther north up the California coast is Santa Barbara, San Luis Obispo, and the Hearst Castle, the ultimate in opulence and home of the man who ran the Hearst newspaper and radio empire.

DON'T MISS: Explore the healthy roster of passenger and freight equipment in various states of repair found on the property.

GETTING THERE: Fillmore is about 60 miles northwest of downtown Los Angeles and about 25 miles east of Ventura. The nearest large-scale commercial airport is the Bob Hope Airport in Burbank. Flights also originate in Santa Barbara.

DISCOUNT: 10% off weekend scenic daytime rides; murder mystery discounts available.

Knott's Berry Farm 22

LOCATION: 8039 Beach Boulevard, Buena Park
PHONE: 714-220-5200
WEBSITE: www.knotts.com
E-MAIL: info@knotts.com

© Knott's

Knott's Berry Farm is a Southern California theme park that has morphed from its 1952 western-style operation to a world-class attraction with rides and events designed for every age. Part of the theme park is the original three-foot-gauge Ghost Town & Calico Railroad.

CHOICES: The railroad is just one part of this large theme park operation that rivals any other attraction in the United States. Most trains are powered by one of two Denver & Rio Grande Western 2-8-0s, either No. 41 (former Rio Grande Southern No. 41 and originally Denver & Rio Grande Western No. 409), and No. 340 (also a former D&RGW of the same number). There is also a Rio Grande Southern Galloping Goose and a number of authentic narrow gauge coaches, a parlor car, and a caboose.

WHEN TO GO: Southern California is enjoyable almost any time of the year. Summers can get very hot, so a hat comes in handy.

GOOD TO KNOW: If you're bringing the family, plan to stay all day. Like other theme parks in the area—Universal Studios and Disneyland—this is a kid-friendly destination with everything you need in one giant arena to tucker out even the hardiest person by the end of the day.

WORTH DOING: Southern California abounds in attractions, restaurants, and activities for everyone. Spend a week or a weekend.

DON'T MISS: In the park, be prepared to be overwhelmed by the amount of rides and sheer number of people. Good news for the railroad fan is that, by carefully selecting your photographic spots, you can come away with images that make it look like you snapped them in Colorado 60 years ago.

GETTING THERE: Buena Park is part of the greater Los Angeles area in Orange County and is near a number of local commercial airports. A vehicle is a must. Freeway exits are clearly marked.

Laws Railroad Museum ㉓

LOCATION: Silver Canyon Road, Bishop
PHONE: 760-873-5950
WEBSITE: lawsmuseum.org
E-MAIL: lawsmuseum@aol.com

Laws Railroad Museum

The 11-acre Laws Railroad Museum is home to the largest collection of equipment that operated on the Southern Pacific's narrow gauge empire. At one time, the line's narrow gauge rails stretched almost 300 miles from Nevada, near Carson City, to Keeler, Calif., in the Lone Pine area of Owens Valley.

CHOICES: Museum displays include SP 4-6-0 No. 9, one of the last three steam engines to operate on the line, various freight cars, a caboose, a turntable, and the original station. By the time the railroad was abandoned, Laws, four miles east of Bishop, existed pretty much in name only with the station being the only major building still standing. The museum has built a number of structures to show what Laws looked like in its heyday. A former Death Valley Railroad gas-electric doodlebug operates on summer holiday weekends and other select times.

WHEN TO GO: The museum is open all year with a few exceptions. It is closed on several major holidays such as New Year's Day, Easter, Thanksgiving, and Christmas. It also may close due to severe weather, and some buildings close during winter.

GOOD TO KNOW: The nearest city with restaurants and accommodations is Bishop. If you drive up from the south on Highway 395, there are numerous towns with hotels and eateries, starting with Lone Pine, Independence, and Big Pine. During the ski season, Highway 395 is the main route to and from the various resorts north of Bishop, so you might consider making reservations well in advance.

WORTH DOING: Owens Valley is known for the many motion pictures, mostly westerns, that have been filmed there over the years. A number of small nonrail museums dot the area. The remains of the Manzanar Relocation Center, one of the places where Japanese-Americans were interned during World War II is now part of the National Park Service and open to the public.

DON'T MISS: The area from Keeler to Laws is littered with narrow gauge artifacts, ranging from the remains of trestles and buildings to 4-6-0 No. 18 in Independence. The former SP standard gauge Lone Pine depot is intact as a private residence.

GETTING THERE: Laws is truly in the middle of nowhere, and the trip to the museum is half the fun. Locate Highway 395 on a California map and look about halfway between Reno, Nev., and Barstow, Calif. The highway is well traveled but consider bringing a cooler of refreshments for the long dry-spots between towns.

Napa Valley Wine Train 24

LOCATION: 1275 McKinstry Street, Napa
PHONE: 800-427-4124 or 707-253-2111
WEBSITE: winetrain.com
E-MAIL: form on website

Trenton McManus

When you think of Napa Valley, you think of wine. And if you want a unique wine experience, take this ride through one of the world's most famous grape-growing valleys. You'll ride in elegant style onboard a fashionable train on a three-hour, 36-mile round trip while enjoying gourmet food and a glass of wine while watching the vineyards roll by as you travel to St. Helena and back.

CHOICES: Ride in a heavyweight passenger car or a vista dome, each with a different dining experience. Dining in the dome offers great views and a four-course meal. Aboard the restored Pullman cars, the menu includes a large selection of gourmet offerings. You can also take part in many scheduled events such as onboard wine tastings, murder mysteries, vintner lunches, and moonlight escapes. Special trains also run around select holidays, and daily winery tours at several wineries are available.

WHEN TO GO: Any time of the year is good, but the September grape-harvesting season is among the most popular. On summer and early fall dinner trains, you'll be able enjoy fantastic sunsets as you dine.

GOOD TO KNOW: Attire is generally casual depending on the time of year or type of event. Dinner may be more dressy, and cocktail-party attire is acceptable. As Phil Collins might say, "No jacket required," but they are suggested for cool nights. One bit of advice: no blue jeans.

WORTH DOING: Napa Valley is filled with hundreds of wineries to visit as well as having numerous special events.

DON'T MISS: Enjoy the wine. The train's wine bar offers a selection of 40-50 wines for tasting. Its wine shop carries almost 300 different wines. All entrees are prepared in the kitchen cars, and you are welcome to sneak a peek inside to watch the action.

GETTING THERE: From San Francisco, take I-80 east to Exit 19. Follow Highway 29 north and exit at Napa/Lake Berryessa. Take Highway 221, which becomes Soscol Avenue, into Napa. Turn right on First Street and then turn left on McKinstry Street.

Niles Canyon Railway 25

LOCATION: 6 Kilkare Road, Sunol
PHONE: 925-862-9063
WEBSITE: ncry.org
E-MAIL: pla_ncry@ncry.org

Jim Wrinn

This museum railroad, a project of the Pacific Locomotive Society, provides a magnificent ride through a dramatic canyon at the edge of the San Francisco Bay area. An outstanding collection of equipment and beautiful scenery make this an excellent day trip in central California.

CHOICES: The railway runs 75-minute round trips through scenic Niles Canyon between Sunol and Niles. Departures are scheduled at both stations. On all trains, you can select from open cars, covered cars, or enclosed coaches. Trains are powered by either a diesel or a steam locomotive, when available, from the railway's impressive collection that also includes a variety of passenger cars, freight cars, and cabooses.

WHEN TO GO: The railroad operates every Sunday during summer and on the first and third Sundays of winter months. Spring and fall can be most pleasant. During April and May, the trains run more often for wildflower excursions. After Thanksgiving, a holiday schedule for the nighttime Train of Lights offers almost daily rides.

GOOD TO KNOW: Unlike other trips, the last daily train out of Niles is a one-way ride to Sunol, so make sure you have a ride back to Niles if needed. The line through Niles Canyon was the last completed link of the transcontinental railroad.

WORTH DOING: While in Fremont, you can visit the Niles Essanay Silent Film Museum and even take in a silent Saturday night flick. You can also visit the nearby Niles Depot Museum.

DON'T MISS: The restored Sunol depot was originally built in the 1880s, and the Niles depot, which features colonnade-style architecture and houses railroad exhibits, was built in 1901.

GETTING THERE: The Niles Canyon Railway is situated between Oakland and San Jose. From San Jose, you can take I-880 to Fremont and exit on Highway 84 east. Turn left onto Mission Boulevard and continue three blocks west to Sullivan Street, and the Niles station is on the left. To reach the Sunol depot from San Jose, just take I-680 to Highway 84. Travel west on Highway 84 one mile and turn right onto Main Street to Kilkare Road. From Oakland, take I-880 to Highway 84 east to get to either location.

Orange Empire Railway Museum ㉖

LOCATION: 2201 S. A Street, Perris
PHONE: 951-943-3020
WEBSITE: oerm.org
E-MAIL: info@oerm.org

Orange Empire Railway Museum

The Orange Empire Railway Museum was organized in 1956 by trolley and electric railway enthusiasts to preserve a fast disappearing way of transportation. Visitors can ride on classic trolleys, passenger trains, and other railroad equipment from Southern California's past.

CHOICES: Two trolleys run on a half-mile loop line, and one is usually an early Los Angeles streetcar. Another train, pulling freight or passenger cars, operates on the 1.5-mile standard gauge main line. On the freight train, you can ride in either a caboose or open gondola. The cars and locomotives are rotated from the museum's collection, which contains more than 180 vintage pieces. You also have the opportunity to ride in a locomotive cab or even run a locomotive.

WHEN TO GO: The museum is open 363 days a year and special events occur during the year. Trains run on weekends and some holidays. The weather is usually bearable during most of the year; however, summertime temperatures can reach triple digits.

GOOD TO KNOW: The museum, situated on 100 acres of land, is about 20 miles south of Riverside. It has preserved, and is restoring, an eclectic mix of more than 225 pieces of railroad equipment, which includes electric, steam, and diesel power as well as a variety of freight and passenger rolling stock.

WORTH DOING: The surrounding area, from Riverside to Temecula, is well developed with all the amenities a traveler would expect. For military aircraft fans, the March Field Air Museum has an extensive collection of aircraft adjacent to March Air Reserve Base in Riverside.

DON'T MISS: A 1922 steam engine, Ventura County Railway No. 2, operates excursions the third weekend of every month from September to May (except November).

GETTING THERE: Dozens of airlines serve Southern California. Besides Los Angeles International Airport, Ontario International Airport is 35 miles from the museum, and Palm Springs International Airport is 50 miles away. Perris is about an hour's drive from either San Diego or Los Angeles. In Perris, exit at Route 74. Follow Route 74 (Fourth Street) west for one mile and turn left onto A Street.

Pacific Southwest Railway Museum ㉗

LOCATION: 750 Depot Street, Campo
PHONE: 619-478-9937 or 619-465-7776
WEBSITE: psrm.org
E-MAIL: support@sdrm.org

John Wright

The Pacific Southwest Railway Museum operates in two locations near San Diego. The main collection is at Campo, just north of the U.S.–Mexican border. At Campo, visitors can enjoy a number of train-riding options. The other location is at La Mesa, about 10 miles east of downtown San Diego.

CHOICES: The museum has numerous pieces of equipment at Campo including a dozen diesel locomotives—among them, two rather rare EMD MRS-1 military road switchers—steam locomotives, freight cars, passenger cars, and cabooses. Train rides feature round-trip weekend excursions to the international border tunnel at Division, and locomotive cab rides are available on the trip.

WHEN TO GO: The Campo facility is open on weekends. The museum offers a variety of special events throughout the year, including some tailored to kids, such as pumpkin and North Pole trains.

GOOD TO KNOW: San Diego is a great tourist destination. Sea World is just north of the city, and the coastline is tourist friendly. Amtrak's *Pacific Surfliner* makes it easy to get up and down the coast to Los Angeles, and the city's efficient light-rail system can take you almost anywhere you wish to go.

WORTH DOING: The greater San Diego area is brimming with places to visit, including Old Town. If you have always wanted to tour a U.S. Navy aircraft carrier, the decommissioned USS *Midway* is open to the public, with many types of aircraft positioned on its flight deck.

DON'T MISS: The only surviving San Diego and Cuyamaca Railway station, the restored La Mesa depot includes a telegrapher's station and exhibit area. A steam engine and freight cars are also on display.

GETTING THERE: The Campo site is 50 miles east of San Diego. San Diego is served by many major airlines and Amtrak. Traveling to the Campo museum requires an automobile. The La Mesa depot is located at 4695 Nebo Drive in La Mesa.

DISCOUNT: Buy one adult fare, get one free on regular weekend excursion or doodlebug.

California

Railtown 1897 State Historic Park ㉘

LOCATION: Fifth Avenue at Reservoir Road, Jamestown
PHONE: 209-984-3953
WEBSITE: csrmf.org/railtown
E-MAIL: form on website

James Haney

Railtown 1897 State Historic Park is considered by many as the premier place for seeing California railroad history. It was originally part of the Sierra Railroad, arguably one of the best-known railroads in the world due to its extensive use in movies, television shows, and commercials. You can also enjoy a ride over these historic rails behind a steam locomotive.

CHOICES: The historic shops and roundhouse have been operating as a steam locomotive maintenance facility for more than 100 years. One of the highlights of any visit is taking the roundhouse tour and experiencing for yourself what a working facility looks, feels, and smells like. On the six-mile, 40-minute round trip through California's Gold Country, you can ride in coaches or open-air observation cars that were previously used in the Canadian Rockies. Special theme trains also run during the year.

WHEN TO GO: The park is open year-round. Tours of the roundhouse take place daily during the summer but have a more limited schedule during the rest of the year. Excursions run every weekend April through October. During the height of the tourist season, make reservations in the surrounding area well in advance.

GOOD TO KNOW: The state of California purchased the station, shops, and roundhouse facilities in 1982 to create Railtown 1897. Railtown is operated by the California State Railroad Museum and is part of the California State Parks System. With more than 200 credits, it is one of the most-filmed railroad locations. The first known filming was in 1919 for a silent movie, and scenes for *High Noon*, *Back to the Future Part III*, and *Unforgiven* were filmed here.

WORTH DOING: This area, up through Sutter's Mill, is where people settled during the gold strikes, so history abounds. If you like the outdoors and learning western history, this is a great place to explore.

DON'T MISS: On the guided tour of the roundhouse, be sure to examine the props that were used in the movies filmed on the railroad.

GETTING THERE: From any direction, you have to drive to get to the Jamestown area. but California's Gold Country is almost universally seductive, so you'll enjoy the trip. It is about a 90-minute drive from Stockton.

Roaring Camp Railroads 🔟

LOCATION: Graham Hill Road, Felton
PHONE: 831-335-4484
WEBSITE: roaringcamp.com
E-MAIL: form on website

Elrond Lawrence

Located in coastal wooded mountains, Roaring Camp Railroads has two unique rides that offer the best of California scenery and vintage railroading. Roaring Camp & Big Trees operates small but powerful steam locomotives over a narrow gauge line through redwood forests, while the Santa Cruz, Big Trees & Pacific travels down a scenic river gorge to the Pacific Ocean.

CHOICES: Each Roaring Camp railroad has a distinct personality. Roaring Camp & Big Trees operates a fleet of 1880s-era Shay, Heisler, and Climax locomotives on a winding route up Bear Mountain. The route passes directly through the Welch Big Trees Grove, the first land purchased expressly to preserve a redwood forest. The 75-minute excursions feature open-air coaches, perfect for viewing the redwoods, and passengers can detrain at the summit to visit the big trees. Santa Cruz boardwalk trains employ 1920s-era passenger coaches and open-air cars pulled by an ex-Santa Fe CF-7 diesel. The three-hour round trip runs through Henry Cowell Redwoods State Park, down the San Lorenzo River Gorge, and through an 1875 tunnel before arriving at the historic Santa Cruz boardwalk.

WHEN TO GO: While crowds may be thick, summer is still the best time to go, as several trains operate daily. The higher altitude and proximity to the ocean bring moderate temperatures. The marine climate can also bring chilly, foggy days, especially in summer. Less fog occurs during spring and fall. Special trains include moonlight dinner trains, a summer starlight train, a ghost train, and a popular holiday lights train.

GOOD TO KNOW: Only six miles away, Santa Cruz is a typical resort town. The century-old seaside boardwalk features a 1924 wooden roller coaster. Monterey, Pacific Grove, and Pebble Beach are only a short drive away on California Highway 1.

WORTH DOING: Roaring Camp re-creates an 1880s logging town and includes a steam-powered saw mill, period buildings, antique cabooses, and picnic grounds. Access to the grounds is free, and picnicking is encouraged, but there is a charge for parking.

DON'T MISS: Adventurous guests can ride the steam train up Bear Mountain and take a guided walk back to Roaring Camp.

GETTING THERE: Roaring Camp is located six miles north of Santa Cruz off Route 17. Take Mount Hermon Road which ends at Graham Hill Road. Turn left on Graham Hill Road and drive a half mile to Roaring Camp. It's less than an hour from the San Jose Airport.

Sacramento RiverTrain 30

LOCATION: E Street and Main Street, Woodland
PHONE: 800-866-1690
WEBSITE: sacramentorivertrain.com
E-MAIL: info@sierrarailroad.com

Sacramento RiverTrain

Twenty miles east of Sacramento, you'll find a uniquely scenic and relaxing train ride through rich farm country and a sprawling wildlife refuge. Operating over a 1911 electric interurban route, the Sacramento RiverTrain rolls east from the town of Woodland to West Sacramento, traveling along the banks of its namesake river and through the Yolo Wildlife Area, which covers 25 square miles and is home to nearly 200 species of birds.

CHOICES: The railroad operates dinner, brunch, and lunch trains year-round, mostly on weekends. Passengers board in Woodland and take a 28-mile trip that lasts over three hours. Powered by Sierra Northern No. 131, a mid-century GP9 diesel, the train features a combination of vintage coaches and diners, plus open-air cars. Interiors boast a relaxed, plantation-style décor.

WHEN TO GO: Trains run nearly every weekend of the year. Those who enjoy riding open-air cars might prefer to visit during the spring or fall, instead of the sweltering summer months that typically exceed 90 degrees. Special event trains include train robbery, murder mystery excursions, and sunset dinner trains. Seasonal trains include pumpkin trains, Valentine specials, a New Year's Eve express, and a popular Christmas train that runs daily through the second half of December.

GOOD TO KNOW: The former Yolo Shortline excursion train underwent an extreme makeover in recent years. It now sports a sparkling gold exterior that reflects the area's Gold Rush heritage, trimmed with blue waves that run the length of the train.

WORTH DOING: Woodland is a small Central Valley city with a charming historic downtown, surrounded by museums and wineries. Sacramento is home to the state capital, the California railroad museum, and many other historic attractions.

DON'T MISS: Look for the 8,000-foot Fremont Bridge over the Sacramento River, which the railroad bills as the longest wooden trestle in the western United States.

GETTING THERE: From San Francisco, drive I-80 east to Davis and take Highway 113 north. Exit at Main Street and turn left. Continue on Main to Industrial Way and turn right. Turn into the second driveway on the right.

Sierra Railroad Dinner Train 31

LOCATION: 330 S. Sierra Avenue, Oakdale
PHONE: 800-866-1690 or 209-848-2100
WEBSITE: www.sierrarailroad.com
E-MAIL: info@sierrarailroad.com

Sierra Railroad

The Sierra Railroad was formed in 1897 to connect the San Joaquin Valley to the Gold Country. Today, the Sierra carries passengers, hauls freight, and makes movies. The Sierra Railroad Dinner Train provides visitors an opportunity to travel on the historic Sierra Railroad while dining and enjoying the passing countryside.

CHOICES: There are many different types of trips to choose from, including those featuring romantic dinners, murder mysteries, lunches, Sunday brunches, and Wild West showdowns. Along the route, you'll pass through distinct western scenery and the scenes of various Hollywood westerns including *High Noon*, *Bad Girls*, and *Pale Rider*.

WHEN TO GO: The dinner train runs year-round, and any time is a good time to take a train ride through California's historic and fascinating Gold Country.

GOOD TO KNOW: The Sierra also offers a rail-and-raft trip that lets you float along the Stanislaus River on a trip that is appropriate for all ages.

WORTH DOING: Being way out west, you can visit the Cowboy Museum in Oakdale. The museum is housed in a historic Southern Pacific depot.

DON'T MISS: The Sierra Railroad is also a functioning freight operation, so railfans can view more then just passenger cars. To see an historic steam locomotive maintenance facility, you can take in Railtown 1897 Historic Park in nearby Jamestown.

GETTING THERE: The Sierra Railroad is located at the junction of Highway 108 and Highway 120 in the city of Oakdale, which is 90 minutes from Sacramento. The train station, which is made of railcars, is on Sierra Avenue.

Skunk Train 32

LOCATION: 100 W. Laurel Street, Fort Bragg
PHONE: 866-457-5865 or 707-964-6371
WEBSITE: skunktrain.com
E-MAIL: rjp@mcn.org

Skunk Train

One of the most amazing attributes of the Skunk Train is its ability to make you feel small. Ride the train from the coastal town of Fort Bragg and you'll quickly find out why. The route travels through a scenic wilderness filled with giant redwoods. As the train takes you through the mountain scenery, the giant trees will make your neck sore unless you move to an open car, where you can stand in wonder.

CHOICES: You can ride from either end of the 40-mile line, boarding at Willits or Fort Bragg. The line features 30 trestles, two tunnels, and a route that snakes its way up the redwood-covered mountainside. At Northspur, the mid-point on the railroad, you can enjoy a picnic lunch and watch the locomotive turn on a wye for the return trip. A summer overnight trip from either station allows you to spend one or more nights at the other end before returning. A barbecue dinner train is another option.

WHEN TO GO: Trains operate all year, but most excursions from Fort Bragg run March through September. Excursions from Willits take place during summer. Specials, limited runs, and a motor car also operate during the year.

GOOD TO KNOW: The railroad got its nickname from the yellow-painted, self-propelled gas-powered cars of the California Western Railway that provided service starting in 1925 and prompted people to say, "You can smell 'em before you can see 'em."

WORTH DOING: Along the coast between December and April, you have a good chance to see a California gray whale as they migrate south from Alaska and then return. For an up-close experience, you can find a whale-watching excursion operating out of Fort Bragg.

DON'T MISS: Ride the train on days when steam locomotive No. 45 is running. A 2-8-2 Mikado type built by Philadelphia's famous Baldwin Locomotive Works in 1924, the locomotive is among the largest in regular service today. If you're really into the experience, this railroad offers a ride in the cab of the steam locomotive.

GETTING THERE: Just over three hours north of San Francisco, the scenic drive to Fort Bragg starts on Highway 101. At Cloverdale, exit onto Highway 128 west, which turns into Highway 1, and continue north to Fort Bragg. The depot is at the foot of Laurel Street.

Travel Town Museum ㉝

LOCATION: 5200 Zoo Drive, Los Angeles
PHONE: 323-662-5874
WEBSITE: laparks.org/grifmet/tt or traveltown.org
E-MAIL: travel.town@lacity.org

David Lustig

Travel Town is a good place to enjoy a couple of hours looking at equipment that has been preserved nowhere else. The museum, part of the Griffith Park complex in Los Angeles County, has a collection of small- to medium-sized steam, diesel, and electric locomotives and rolling stock with a surprisingly diverse roster of equipment.

CHOICES: Operated by the Department of Recreation and Parks, the museum is free and kid-friendly, which sometimes takes its toll on the equipment. Nevertheless, the diversity of the saved equipment makes Travel Town worth stopping at if you're in the area. Steam equipment includes tank locomotives, 0-6-0s, 2-8-0s, a 2-6-2, a 2-8-2, a Shay, and a Heisler. Other equipment worth taking in includes an operating EMD Model 40 diesel, a Baldwin RS-12, a Santa Fe gas-electric, a Pacific Electric freight motor, plus various pieces of rolling stock.

WHEN TO GO: Summertime can get very hot in Southern California so bring a hat or other head covering.

GOOD TO KNOW: A food concession is inside, but eating and picnic areas are nearby in other parts of Griffith Park. If you would like to have lunch at a historic eatery, you can grab a chili dog at Pink's, which is 15 minutes away on La Brea Boulevard and has been operating since 1939.

WORTH DOING: Explore Griffith Park, a quiet oasis in busy LA, and especially take the time and visit the park's other sites including the famous observatory and world-class Los Angeles Zoo, which is right next to Travel Town.

DON'T MISS: If you want to take a break from walking, a rideable scale train encircles the collection.

GETTING THERE: Travel Town is near the confluence of I-5 and the 134 freeways. Freeway exits are clearly marked.

Western Pacific Railroad Museum ㉞

LOCATION: 700 Western Pacific Way, Portola
PHONE: 530-832-4131
WEBSITE: wplives.org
E-MAIL: info@wplives.org

Western Pacific Railroad Museum

Here at one of the Western Pacific's last diesel locomotive shops is a great collection of rolling stock. The focus is on one of the West's most beloved railroads, which traveled through beautiful mountain scenery and hosted the legendary *California Zephyr*. The setting couldn't be more appropriate.

CHOICES: This 37-acre site displays more than 100 pieces of equipment. Three former Western Pacific streamlined diesels call the museum home, as do locomotives from the Union Pacific and Southern Pacific. Western Pacific 0-6-0 No. 165, a steam switcher is the only steam locomotive in the collection. Rolling stock includes passenger cars, boxcars, cabooses, and maintenance-of-way equipment. The museum is hands-on, so you can climb into cabs and hop onto cars.

WHEN TO GO: The museum is open every day beginning in April until November. On summer weekends, caboose rides through a pine forest on a one-mile loop of track make for a fun train trip. In December, Santa trains run.

GOOD TO KNOW: Check in August for the annual Portola Railroad Days festival, which includes train rides, food, music, and a parade.

WORTH DOING: Close by is Lassen Volcanic National Park, where you can see hydrothermal features such as boiling mud pots, steaming ground, and roaring fumaroles.

DON'T MISS: Run a locomotive through the museum's program that puts you in the engineer's seat.

GETTING THERE: Portola is located in the Feather River Canyon between Sacramento and Reno. From the west, take I-80 to Highway 89 and go north to Highway 70, which runs into Portola. From the east, take I-80 to Highway 395 to Highway 70.

DISCOUNT: 10% off gift shop purchase.

Western Railway Museum ㉟

LOCATION: 5848 Highway 12, Suisun City
PHONE: 707-374-2978
WEBSITE: wrm.org
E-MAIL: form on website

Western Railway Museum

The Western Railway Museum gives visitors the opportunity to ride historic streetcars and interurban electric trains that once served California and other western states. There are more than 50 cars on display.

CHOICES: A trip to the Western Railway Museum begins in the mission-revival inspired visitor center. After purchasing admission tickets, explore Cameron Hall, a large display and exhibit hall designed in the grand railroad station style. The museum offers 15-minute, one-mile-long streetcar rides around the grounds and a 50-minute interurban ride over the re-electrified portion of the former Sacramento Northern Railway main line to Gum Grove. You can ride on recently restored San Francisco streetcar No. 1016 or Sacramento Northern interurban No. 1005.

WHEN TO GO: The Western Railway Museum is open Saturdays and Sundays from September to May. From Memorial Day through Labor Day, the museum expands its schedule and is open Wednesday through Sunday. It is closed on some holidays.

GOOD TO KNOW: The museum offers guided weekend tours of two of its car houses. It also features a shaded picnic area that is well suited for family or group outings.

WORTH DOING: During October, special Pumpkin Patch Trains take visitors on a scenic five-mile journey to a pumpkin patch, complete with a hay-bale fort, hay rides, live music, animals, and, of course, pumpkins. In April, the *Scenic Limited* also runs.

DON'T MISS: Visitors can stroll through the museum's large car house or take a guided tour of the building on weekends.

GETTING THERE: The museum is about 45 miles northeast of San Francisco, 12 miles east of I-80 on Highway 12. Public transportation is an option in reaching the museum by train and bus service.

Yosemite Mountain Sugar Pine Railroad 36

LOCATION: 56001 Highway 41, Fish Camp
PHONE: 559-683-7273
WEBSITE: yosemitesteamtrains.com

Jim Wrinn

The Yosemite Mountain Sugar Pine Railroad is a four-mile railroad excursion at Yosemite National Park's south gate. The ride allows you to see what it was like when steam locomotives hauled massive log trains through the Sierra Nevadas. It is a restored segment of the old narrow gauge Madera Sugar Pine Lumber Company Railroad, with a portion of the original right-of-way reconstructed using the same techniques as 100 years ago.

CHOICES: Two geared Shay steam locomotives, formerly used on the West Side Lumber Company, power the excursion trains. An unique experience is riding a Jenny railcar powered by Model A Ford automobile engines. The *Moonlight Special*, which operates Saturday nights in the spring and fall and Saturday and Wednesday nights during the summer, begins with a steak dinner and includes masked bandits, moonlight, and campfire sing-alongs.

WHEN TO GO: The Yosemite Mountain Sugar Pine Railroad operates daily from late-March through October and on select days during the winter months. At close to 5,000 feet elevation, it can get chilly at Fish Camp, even in the summertime. At the height of summer tourist season, Yosemite National Park can get extremely crowded.

GOOD TO KNOW: Refurbished railcars, once used to transport logging crews, now carry excursion passengers.

WORTH DOING: You can easily spend an entire day or longer in the area. Other activities in the Fish Camp area include fishing, backpacking, hiking, camping, and mountain biking. You can even try your hand at panning for gold.

DON'T MISS: For a fun and melodramatic evening, partake in Melodrama Evening, which starts with a steak dinner, continues with music and a steam train excursion, and finishes with a melodrama in the woods.

GETTING THERE: Fish Camp is 40 miles north of Fresno and 60 miles east of Modesto on Highway 41. The nearest big-time commercial airline service is at Fresno and Sacramento.

COLORADO

Cripple Creek & Victor Narrow Gauge Railroad **1**

The four-mile, 45-minute trip takes you through Gold Country over a portion of the old Midland Terminal Railroad. Running south from Cripple Creek, the steam train crosses a reconstructed trestle and passes historic mines near the deserted mining town of Anaconda. The railroad operates three narrow gauge locomotives, and trains operate May to October.

LOCATION: Fifth Street and Bennett Avenue, Cripple Creek
PHONE: 719-689-2640
WEBSITE: cripplecreekrailroad.com
E-MAIL: ccvngrr@aol.com

Limon Heritage Museum **2**

This museum focuses on local history and the Union Pacific and Rock Island Railroads. Located in a restored 1910 depot, it features a restored office and rail exhibits. A saddle boxcar, dining car, and UP caboose are on display in the adjacent rail park. It is open Memorial Day to Labor Day.

LOCATION: 899 First Street, Limon
PHONE: 719-775-8605
WEBSITE: townoflimon.com

Moffat Railway Car ❸

Tours of this 1906 Pullman car are available through the Moffat County Visitors Center, where it is on display. The car originally belonged to rail magnate David Moffat and was named for his daughter Marcia. The nearby Museum of Northwest Colorado (590 Yampa Avenue) contains a display of Moffat Road memorabilia.

LOCATION: 360 E. Victory Way, Craig
PHONE: 800-864-4405 or 970-824-5689
WEBSITE: craig-chamber.com
E-MAIL: info@craig-chamber.com

Pikes Peak Historical Street Railway ❹

Located in an 1888 Rock Island Railroad roundhouse, the Pikes Peak Historical Street Railway Foundation maintains a trolley museum with model displays and a restoration shop. A Southern Pacific baggage car holds a museum of Rock Island Railroad artifacts and models. The museum and grounds are open to the public on Saturdays.

LOCATION: 2333 Steel Drive, Colorado Springs
PHONE: 719-475-9508
WEBSITE: www.coloradospringstrolleys.org
E-MAIL: cstrolley@juno.com
DISCOUNT: $1 off museum admission; 15% off gift shop purchase of $5 or more.

Pueblo Railway Museum ❺

Concentrating on the golden age of railroading, the museum displays steam engines, diesel locomotives, and rolling stock in the yard behind Union Depot. Artifacts and rotating displays are housed in the Southeastern Colorado Heritage Center located across from the depot. Locomotive cab and caboose rides are offered during special events.

LOCATION: 132 W. B Street, Pueblo
PHONE: 719-251-5024
WEBSITE: pueblorailway.org
E-MAIL: info@pueblorailway.org

Ridgway Railroad Museum ❻

The Ridgway Railroad Museum focuses on local railroading history. It displays an assortment of restored railcars, and its indoor collection includes artifacts, photos, and tools. The museum holds several special events and monthly work sessions during the year. It is currently restoring Galloping Goose No. 4.

LOCATION: Highway 550 and Highway 62, Ridgway
WEBSITE: ridgwayrailroadmuseum.org
E-MAIL: ridgwayrailroadmuseum@ouraynet.com

Rio Grande Southern Railroad Museum ❼

The museum is located in a replica of the original Dolores depot. It is home to the restored Galloping Goose No. 5, which now operates several times during the year on the Cumbres & Toltec Scenic Railroad and the Durango & Silverton Narrow Gauge Railroad. The museum is open Mondays through Saturdays during summer and limited hours during winter.

LOCATION: 421 Railroad Avenue, Dolores
PHONE: 970-882-7082
WEBSITE: www.gallopinggoose5.com
E-MAIL: gghs5@centurytel.net

Windsor Museum ❽

Located in Boardwalk Park, a 1880s Colorado & Southern depot houses an exhibit of local steam-era railroading history. You can walk through a freight room, waiting room, and station agent's room. A caboose, schoolhouse, and church are also on site. The museum is open Tuesdays through Saturdays during summer.

LOCATION: Sixth Street and Ash Street, Windsor
PHONE: 970-674-2443
WEBSITE: ci.windsor.co.us
E-MAIL: form on website

Colorado Railroad Museum ❾

LOCATION: 17155 W. 44th Avenue, Golden
PHONE: 800-365-6263 or 303-279-4591
WEBSITE: coloradorailroadmuseum.org
E-MAIL: info@coloradorailroadmuseum.org

Jeff Terry

When you think of Colorado railroading, you think of mountain-climbing, narrow gauge trains of the Denver & Rio Grande Western. And that is exactly what you'll see at this museum just outside Denver in Golden. But that's not all—the museum has 100 pieces of equipment from many other Colorado railroads.

CHOICES: The museum features narrow gauge and standard equipment, from a steam locomotive once used on the Pikes Peak Cog Railway to a 317-ton Burlington Route steam locomotive and even a set of streamlined 1950s passenger diesels from the Rio Grande. You'll see examples of the famous Galloping Goose self-propelled rail buses that ran on the narrow gauge Rio Grande Southern in southwestern Colorado and the only preserved standard gauge Rio Grande steam locomotive, No. 687, a 2-8-0 built in 1890 and retired in 1955.

WHEN TO GO: The museum is open year-round, except for several holidays. Go during one of the special events when a vintage steam or diesel locomotive powers passenger trains on a short ride around the 15-acre property. Better yet, ride Galloping Goose No. 7 on a Saturday visit.

GOOD TO KNOW: Be sure to see the monument that once stood along the Rio Grande tracks to commemorate the creation of the dome car—a bubble-top passenger car that became famous in the 1950s and 1960s for its superb views.

WORTH DOING: The MillerCoors Brewery is adjacent to the museum and offers tours on most days throughout the year.

DON'T MISS: Visit the five-stall roundhouse that houses the museum's restoration shop, an operating turntable, and a viewing gallery that gives you a peek at the work.

GETTING THERE: The Colorado Railroad Museum is located 12 miles west of downtown Denver and is easily reached from I-70. Take Exit 265 westbound or Exit 266 eastbound and it is just off Highway 58 between I-70 and Golden.

DISCOUNT: $2 off adult train ticket; not valid for Day Out with Thomas.

Durango & Silverton Narrow Gauge Railroad ⑩

LOCATION: 479 Main Avenue, Durango
PHONE: 877-872-4607 or 970-247-2733
WEBSITE: www.durangotrain.com
E-MAIL: info@durangotrain.com

Ron Burkhard

The Durango & Silverton is one of the most spectacular narrow gauge steam train rides in North America. Traveling through the Rockies, coal-fired locomotives pull trains through the rugged Animas River Gorge on a railroad built in the 1880s to reach southwest Colorado silver mines.

CHOICES: The Durango & Silverton offers several options for passengers. During summer, you can live like a president with Presidential class service, which includes seating on one of the line's two private cars that feature plush seating and outdoor viewing platforms. For more legroom, try first-class service on the *Silver Vista*, a glass-roofed, open-air observation car. It has comfy oversized seats and an outdoor viewing platform. First-class service is also available aboard an 1881 parlor car. Deluxe service and standard service provide seating in a coach car or a gondola. If you can, when outbound from Durango, ride the right side of the train. It provides the best view of the Animas River Gorge at 350 feet above the water. The Cascde Canyon winter train travels 26 miles from Durango to the Cascade station and back, starting in late November until May.

WHEN TO GO: Winter provides incredible snowy vistas. Summer offers the excitement of up to four trains running each way, but it is also the busy season. September has the best nature show when Aspen trees turn a brilliant yellow and quiver in the autumn breeze. Various events, including photographer's specials, pumpkin patch trains, and cowboy poet trains, take place throughout the year.

GOOD TO KNOW: Durango is a well-developed city with every amenity available to tourists, including at least two historic hotels. Several restaurants in Silverton cater to passengers, providing a quick meal and a taste of the old West.

WORTH DOING: Take part in the other activities that abound near Durango, such as whitewater rafting, hiking, and fly-fishing. A visit to Mesa Verde National Park is a must.

DON'T MISS: There is a two-hour layover in Silverton, which gives you time to visit the freight yard museum in the depot.

GETTING THERE: The station is located in downtown Durango. The drive to the Four Corners area on Highway 550 is a scenic delight, as long as you don't mind heights.

Forney Museum of Transportation ⑪

LOCATION: 4303 Brighton Boulevard, Denver
PHONE: 303-297-1113
WEBSITE: forneymuseum.org
E-MAIL: museum@forneymuseum.org

Jeff Terry

An antique auto collection that began with one Kissel Kar is now a transportation museum that contains more than 500 artifacts in a 140,000 square-foot building.

CHOICES: In the museum's indoor train pit, you'll find a Big Boy locomotive, cabooses, trolleys, passenger cars, and a Forney locomotive. The showroom contains everything on wheels from buggies and bicycles to fire engines and Denver's only cable car.

WHEN TO GO: The museum is open Monday through Saturday year-round. It features special exhibits, family activities, and events related to different modes of transportation, including talks related to railroad topics. On Big Boy Weekend over Father's Day, you can go inside the cab of the world's largest articulated steam locomotive and walk through a 1920s dining car, 1890s coach, and 1905 caboose, which are open only once a year.

GOOD TO KNOW: A founder of the Forney Museum of Transportation, J. D. Forney was a second cousin to Matthais Forney, who designed the steam locomotive that bears his name. Forney-type tank locomotives operated primarily on narrow gauge railroads, elevated railways, and surface passenger lines.

WORTH DOING: There are plenty of things to do in Denver, within 15 minutes of the museum, such as touring the Capitol, the Firefighters Museum, the Botanic Gardens, and the Unsinkable Molly Brown's house.

DON'T MISS: One of eight remaining Big Boy locomotives, Union Pacific No. 4005 was wrecked in 1953 and rebuilt. Also view highlights of the auto collection such as Amelia Earhart's 1923 Kissel Speedster, a 1967 amphibious car from Germany, a 1911 electric car, a Staver, and a Nyberg.

GETTING THERE: The Forney Museum is located northeast of downtown Denver, a short distance off I-70 via exit 275B.

Fort Collins Municipal Railway 12

LOCATION: Roosevelt Street and Oak Street, Fort Collins
PHONE: 970-224-5372
WEBSITE: fortnet.org/trolley
E-MAIL: fcmrs@netzero.net

Bryan Bechtold

Fort Collins was the last city in the United States to operate the tiny four-wheel trolley cars known as Birneys, running its trolley system until 1951. A volunteer group of citizens rebuilt the original Mountain Avenue track and restored Car 21 to like-new condition, returning it to operation on its authentic tree-lined route in 1984.

CHOICES: The three-mile, round-trip trolley ride runs along Mountain Avenue from City Park to Howe Street, two blocks west of downtown. A round trip lasts 30 minutes. Other boarding stops are at Shields Street and Loomis Street. There are free rides on special days and for moms on Mother's Day and dads on Father's Day.

WHEN TO GO: The trolley operates on weekend afternoons and holidays from May to September.

GOOD TO KNOW: The original trolley barn is just two blocks north on Howe Street at the downtown end of the line. Long-range plans call for reconnecting track to the carbarn. Inside is Birney Car 25, which is undergoing restoration. Car 25 is one of five remaining cars that ran in Fort Collins.

WORTH DOING: Both ends of the route are family friendly. Downtown Fort Collins has an outstanding variety of restaurants and shopping just a short walk from the trolley. You can also pack a picnic and enjoy the City Park end of the line. For outdoor enthusiasts, Rocky Mountain National Park is less than two hours away by car.

DON'T MISS: BNSF freight trains run right down the center of nearby Mason Street for almost a mile, providing the best mainline street-running railroad action Colorado has to offer.

GETTING THERE: Fort Collins is 65 miles north of Denver on I-25. Exit I-25 at Colorado 14 and then drive west through town to City Park. A small depot is next to the tennis courts at Roosevelt and Oak Streets.

Georgetown Loop Railroad 🔟

LOCATION: Loop Drive, Georgetown
PHONE: 888-456-6777
WEBSITE: georgetownlooprr.com
E-MAIL: info@historicrailadventures.com

Chip Sherman

This railroad shows how engineering overcame mountains when it came to reaching precious minerals in the Colorado Rockies. As the name states, the railroad's highlight is a full loop, where the tracks cross over themselves to gain elevation. The reconstructed Devil's Gate viaduct stands no less spectacular than when it was built in the late 1800s.

CHOICES: You can board at the Devil's Gate station in Georgetown or at Silver Plume. Either way, you experience the same trip, but riding up grade first is always the better show. As you ride the train, scan the mountain slopes for bighorn sheep. Also look for the grade of the abandoned Argentine Central Railroad, which went even higher than Silver Plume.

WHEN TO GO: Beginning in May until mid-October, trains run on a daily schedule. Then, weekend operations and special events take place through the end of the year, weather permitting. Our favorite special is the Wisconsinesque Beer & Brats Day, featuring Tommy Knocker brews. Interstate traffic from Denver over the July 4th holiday can be a major headache.

GOOD TO KNOW: Steam locomotive No. 12, built in 1929, worked for the Kahului Railroad Co., hauling sugar cane, pineapples, and other freight. It came to Colorado via a theme park in Idaho.

WORTH DOING: The town of Georgetown is quaint and quiet with little influences of the modern world—with the exception of nearby I-70. Its National Historic Landmark District features unique shops, restaurants, and small museums in restored Victorian buildings.

DON'T MISS: After riding the train, travel on I-70 between Georgetown and Silver Plume and watch another train tackle the mountain, with not only the loop but also with a series of zigzags. At Silver Plume, you can take a guided walking tour through the 1870s Lebanon Silver Mine.

GETTING THERE: The railroad is about 50 miles west of Denver off I-70. Exit 226 takes you to Silver Plume and, a few miles away, Exit 228 takes you to Georgetown.

Leadville, Colorado & Southern Railroad 🖽

LOCATION: 326 E. Seventh Street, Leadville
PHONE: 866-386-3936 or 719-486-3936
WEBSITE: leadville-train.com
E-MAIL: form on website

Leadville, Colorado & Southern Railroad

In a state with many spectacular scenic railroads, this line doesn't disappoint. Leaving from the charming mining town of Leadville, the LC&S marches up the side of the Rockies near the tree line. Upon departure from the depot, the train leaves the 10,200-foot elevation for a 900-foot climb along the southern side of the upper Arkansas River Valley to a point close to Climax at Fremont Pass. The train passes through forests of lodgepole pine, spruce, and aspen.

CHOICES: On the 22-mile trip, you can ride in an open car or a car with a roof. Especially for train fans, there are several seats available in the locomotive or in the caboose. If it's a beautiful day in Colorado, as it often is, stick to the open cars for unobstructed views. Stay on the right side of the train for spectacular views of the mountains and the molybdenum mine at the end of the line. Along the way, the conductor provides narration and answers questions.

WHEN TO GO: The trains run late May into October, when the aspen trees put on a magnificent show of yellow. In mid-summer, the Wildflower Special lets you view alpine flowers at their peak.

GOOD TO KNOW: Incorporated in 1878, Leadville is the highest incorporated city in the continental United States at 10,152 feet above sea level. Downtown Leadville is home to many shops, galleries, restaurants, and lodging establishments and makes an easy base camp from which to explore the central Rockies.

WORTH DOING: Be sure to explore Leadville's National Historic Landmark District, which includes many buildings built between 1880 and 1905.

DON'T MISS: On the return trip, the train pauses for a break at French Gulch, where a wooden water tank that once supplied steam locomotives with water still stands.

GETTING THERE: From Denver, take I-70 west and then Highway 91 south to Leadville. From Vail, take I-70 west to Highway 24 and then Highway 24 south to Leadville.

DISCOUNT: Group discount given for every adult ticket.

Pikes Peak Cog Railway 15

LOCATION: 515 Ruxton Avenue, Manitou Springs
PHONE: 800-745-3773 or 719-685-5401
WEBSITE: cograilway.com
E-MAIL: info@cograilway.com

Jim Wrinn

The Pikes Peak Cog Railway offers a unique Swiss Alpine experience on rails. Diesel-powered, self-propelled passenger cars navigate unbelievably steep grades with the help of a cog to ascend the 14,110-foot high peak. The view at the top is beautiful, but the journey is awe inspiring as well with trains going beyond the timberline, passing herds of bighorn sheep, and arriving at a station that includes a high-altitude research center.

CHOICES: The railroad offers three-hour round trips that allow you 30 minutes at the summit. It also provides a one-way trip to the top for anyone who would like to hike back down (about six hours) or ride a mountain bike with an outfitter service. During the first part of the trip, the train travels through boulder fields, where you may see some interesting "faces" in the giant boulders. You'll also see some wildlife and a bristlecone pine forest with trees believed to be 2,000 years old.

WHEN TO GO: The railroad, unbelievably, operates year-round, thanks to a homemade snowplow that operates like a giant snow blower on rails. During summer, the railroad runs up to eight trains a day with departures every 80 minutes. During winter, November through March, the railway runs a limited schedule that is subject to a minimum number of passengers. A Santa train runs halfway up the peak in December.

GOOD TO KNOW: The railroad uses modern Swiss-built trains of a type used in the Alps. These units tackle grades of up to 25 percent—meaning the track rises 25 feet for every 100 feet of forward travel.

WORTH DOING: At the base of Pikes Peak, about an hour's drive away, lie the historic gold-mining towns of Cripple Creek and Victor. You may still find gold in Cripple Creek—at the town's casinos—or ride the Cripple Creek & Victor Narrow Gauge Railroad. In Colorado Springs, explore the many red sandstone formations in the Garden of the Gods.

DON'T MISS: At the peak, make sure to walk around the summit and look for Denver. Just be careful. On the north side is a drop-off called the Bottomless Pit.

GETTING THERE: Manitou Springs is six miles from Colorado Springs. Take Exit 141 off I-25 and go west (toward the mountains) on Highway 24 four miles to the Manitou Avenue (Manitou Springs) exit. Go west on Manitou Avenue for 1.5 miles to Ruxton Avenue. Turn left and go to the top of Ruxton Avenue.

Platte Valley Trolley 16

LOCATION: 15th Street and Platte Street, Denver
PHONE: 303-458-6255
WEBSITE: denvertrolley.org
E-MAIL: pvt@denvertrolley.org

Bryan Bechtold

The Platte Valley Trolley is often referred to as one of Denver's best-kept secrets. The trolley runs through the South Platte River Greenway Park linking several of the city's most popular attractions. The trolley is a faithful replica of a turn-of the-century, open-air breezer, which is ideally suited for enjoying the sightseeing trip.

CHOICES: The route starts at Confluence Park beside the REI store. The riverfront ride lasts 25 minutes. Stops are made at the Downtown Aquarium, Children's Museum, and Invesco Field at Mile High. The trolley only makes intermediate stops southbound, and runs end-to-end northbound.

WHEN TO GO: The trolley operates Friday, Saturday, and Sunday afternoons mid-April through October. It departs continuously every half hour from REI. During Denver Bronco home games, fans can catch a shuttle to the game.

GOOD TO KNOW: Confluence Park is the site of Denver's original settlement and is now a hub for paved bicycle trails that serve the city.

WORTH DOING: The Platte River area is a great place to take the family. Combine a trolley ride with nearby attractions, such as the Children's Museum, Elitch Gardens Theme Park, or the aquarium. You can also take a tour of Invesco Field and the Colorado Sports Hall of Fame.

DON'T MISS: The flagship REI store is housed in the former Denver Tramway powerhouse building. The Starbucks there has a collection of photos showing the interior as it looked in 1901, quite a difference from the three-story climbing rock there now. Give it a try!

GETTING THERE: The route is located in downtown Denver. By car, take I-25 to Exit 211 (23rd Street), turn east on Water Street, and follow the signs to the Children's Museum or continue straight to the REI store for your best parking options. RTD buses operate within a short walk. The trolley is about a 15-minute walk from Amtrak and RTD light rail service at Union Station.

Rio Grande Scenic Railroad 🔢

LOCATION: 601 State Avenue, Alamosa
PHONE: 877-726-7245 or 719-587-0520
WEBSITE: coloradotrain.com
E-MAIL: info@coloradotrain.com

Henry Koshollek

The Denver & Rio Grande built an incredibly scenic route into the San Luis Valley and its biggest city, Alamosa, in the late 1880s. The standard gauge line of today replaced a much more difficult narrow gauge line but lost nothing as far as its engineering marvels or trackside splendor.

CHOICES: The railroad offers four distinct excursion trains. On summer weekends, the *Fort Garland Limited* crosses famous La Veta Pass over the Sangre de Cristo Mountains. The *Toltec Gorge Limited* takes you through the San Luis Valley to Antonito, where a connection can be made to the Cumbres & Toltec Scenic Railroad. The *Potato Valley Explorer* is a unique rail experience. The diesel-powered train is made up of both freight and passenger cars and runs between Alamosa and Monte Vista. The *La Veta Mountaineer* winds through a variety of scenery, from flat farmland to mountains, on its trip from Alamosa to La Veta. It runs with steam on Fridays, Saturdays, and Sundays.

WHEN TO GO: The *Fort Garland Limited* and runs Memorial Day weekend through Labor Day. The *Toltec Gorge Limited* and *Potato Valley Explorer* operate through September. *La Veta Mountaineer* runs all year, providing passengers with wonderful winter vistas.

GOOD TO KNOW: Seating choices vary by route and train. They include dome, coach, and open-air cars. If you can, go for the dome for the best view of the mountains.

WORTH DOING: Explore the Spanish Peaks country. It is filled with hiking trails, scenic roads, and natural wonders, such as the tallest sand dunes in North America, which are found in Great Sand Dunes National Park.

DON'T MISS: During the summer, the railroad presents its summer music festival in a mountain setting that is accessible by the *Fort Garland Limited*. You can enjoy music under the stars, surrounded by aspen and pines, in a natural meadow amphitheater.

GETTING THERE: Located in south-central Colorado, Alamosa is about 200 miles south of Denver and 90 miles west of Pueblo. Highway 160 is the key route in and out of the San Luis Valley. The highway becomes Main Street in Alamosa, and the depot is just off Main Street on State Avenue.

Royal Gorge Route Railroad 18

LOCATION: 401 Water Street, Cañon City
PHONE: 888-724-5748 or 719-276-4000
WEBSITE: royalgorgeroute.com

Royal Gorge Route Railroad

Nowhere else in America can you ride a train through a very narrow mountain gorge with a fast-flowing river and look straight up at one thousand feet of cliff. The railroad offers a range of services on its 24-mile round trip through the Royal Gorge.

CHOICES: Service classes on the two-hour excursions begin with coach, which seats you in comfortable air-conditioned cars with access to an open-air car. Vista-dome class provides panoramic views under glass, food service, and a full-service bar. Parlor class puts you in the refurbished *Sunshine Falls* parlor car. A Lunch Train offers a three-course lunch. The three-hour Dinner Train has a three-course gourmet dinner, and the Wine Dinner Train adds wine to a five-course dinner. The popular Murder Mystery Train presents an entertaining whodunit while you enjoy dinner. Special events also take place during the year.

WHEN TO GO: Summer offers more schedule options and more dinner trains, sometimes running up to 13 cars in push-pull fashion with a locomotive on each end. While the scenery is gorgeous year-round, September is filled with brilliant yellow Aspen trees.

GOOD TO KNOW: After looking up at the world's highest suspension bridge, 1,053 feet above the river, you can go up to Royal Gorge Bridge Park (admission required) and drive, walk, or tram across the gorge.

WORTH DOING: In summer, raft-and-rail packages include a nine-mile raft trip down the Arkansas River in Bighorn Canyon. Rafting and kayak outfitters in the area that offer half- and full-day trips for beginners and experienced paddlers alike. If you make it through Satan's Suckhole, watch out for the deceptively named Puppy Rapids.

DON'T MISS: For would-be engineers, you can sign up for a cab ride in an F7 locomotive but space is limited to two passengers per trip.

GETTING THERE: Cañon City is 115 miles from Denver and 45 minutes from Colorado Springs via Highway 115. Colorado Springs has the nearest airport.

CONNECTICUT

Connecticut Antique Machinery Association ❶

The association features an operating three-foot-gauge railroad that is powered by a 1925 Baldwin locomotive that was used in the sugar cane fields of Hawaii. A variety of other locomotives and rolling stock fill out the collection. The site contains six other exhibits dedicated to antique industrial and agricultural machinery. It is open May through October.

LOCATION: Route 7, Kent
PHONE: 860-927-0050
WEBSITE: ctamachinery.com
E-MAIL: camainfo@ctamachinery.com

Connecticut Trolley Museum ❷

Founded in 1940, this museum offers a narrated three-mile, round-trip trolley ride. Its collection contains passenger and freight streetcars, interurban cars, elevated railway cars, service cars, and other rail equipment. A fire equipment museum is also on site. The museum is open April through October and schedules several special events during the year.

LOCATION: 58 North Road, East Windsor
PHONE: 860-627-6540
WEBSITE: ceraonline.org
E-MAIL: office@ceraweb.org

Danbury Railway Museum ❸

This museum contains 50 pieces of equipment representing 11 different northeastern railroads and includes unique pieces such as a New Haven Railroad Mack FCD railbus. Vintage train rides in the yard include a spin around an operating turntable. The 1903 station features displays and a model layout of the Danbury yard. It is open year-round except for holidays.

LOCATION: 120 White Street, Danbury
PHONE: 203-778-8337
WEBSITE: www.danbury.org/drm
E-MAIL: form on website
DISCOUNT: Receive $1 off each regular admission.

Shore Line Trolley Museum ❹

A visit to the museum is a unique sensory journey into the past as you hear trolley motors growl, smell the electric arc, and feel rattan seats. The museum operates a three-mile round trip along the scenic shore over the last remaining portion of Branford Electric Railway. It boasts a collection of almost 100 vintage vehicles.

LOCATION: 17 River Street, East Haven
PHONE: 203-467-6927
WEBSITE: www.bera.org

SoNo Switch Tower Museum ❺

This 1896 New Haven Railroad switch tower has been restored, complete with an original Armstrong 68-lever mechanical machine. Located next to the Northeast Corridor main line, the unique museum is open Saturdays and Sundays May through October.

LOCATION: 77 Washington Street, South Norwalk
PHONE: 203-246-6958
WEBSITE: www.westctnrhs.org/tower.htm
E-MAIL: info@westctnrhs.org
DISCOUNT: 10% off gift shop purchase.

Connecticut Eastern Railroad Museum ❻

LOCATION: 55 Bridge Street, Willimantic
PHONE: 860-456-9999
WEBSITE: cteastrrmuseum.org
E-MAIL: info@cteastrrmuseum.org

Robert LaMay

For anyone interested in seeing what takes place in a 1900s-era railroad village, this would be the place to visit. Located on the original site of the Columbia Junction freight yard and roundhouse, the Connecticut Eastern Railroad Museum is one of the few railroad museums to have a roundhouse complete with an operating standard gauge 60-foot Armstrong turntable.

CHOICES: The museum features a variety of restored buildings including a station, section house, freight house, and crossing shanties. Numerous working projects occur every week throughout the museum's operating season. It houses several diesel locomotives, various railcars, and a steam locomotive. Tour guides are also on hand to show and explain the Ghost Train story and other tales of railroad history.

WHEN TO GO: The museum is open weekends from May into October. A variety of events take place during the season, such as music concerts, night photo shoots, and Metal Fest in May—a full day of blacksmithing events and demonstrations.

GOOD TO KNOW: Kids of all ages can operate a replica 1850s-style pump car along a section of rail. You can also pretend that you are the engineer and sit in the engineer's seat of a New Haven Railroad FL9 passenger diesel locomotive. Volunteers are repairing damage from vandalism prior to the 2010 season.

WORTH DOING: Willimantic is situated in the "Last Green Valley," designated as Quinebaug and Shetucket Rivers Valley National Heritage Corridor. The valley contains seven state forests and five state parks. During Walktober, there are more than 100 guided walks and special events, including one at the Connecticut Eastern Railroad Museum.

DON'T MISS: Watch, usually in early afternoon, as a locomotive or rail bus is turned on the museum's turntable and then put into the Columbia Junction six-stall roundhouse.

GETTING THERE: Located about 30 miles east of Hartford in downtown Willimantic, the museum can be easily reached via numerous state roads such as Routes 6, 66, 32, 195, and 2. Once downtown, turn onto Bridge Street (Route 289 South), take a quick right, and follow the railroad tracks down a dirt road to the museum entrance.

DISCOUNT: $2 off adult admission.

Essex Steam Train & Riverboat 7

LOCATION: 1 Railroad Avenue, Essex
PHONE: 800-377-3987 or 860-767-0103
WEBSITE: essexsteamtrain.com
E-MAIL: valley.railroad@snet.net

Valley Railroad Company, Jody Dole

The Essex Steam Train is unusual in offering a train ride that can be combined with a riverboat excursion, providing scenic views of the Connecticut River from both rail and water. The 12-mile rail round trip from Essex station to Deep River takes about an hour while the rail-water package lasts more than two hours.

CHOICES: The Essex Steam Train is hauled by steam locomotive No. 40 while the *Becky Thatcher*, a replica of a three-deck Mississippi-style riverboat, handles the water excursion. Beyond basic train and train-and-riverboat tours, the Valley Railroad Company offers a number of special events, including the annual Hot Steamed Jazz Festival and a dinner train. On some weekends, a caboose is available for riding.

WHEN TO GO: The railroad operates late May through October, with Day Out with Thomas weekends in May and the Santa Special (afternoons) and North Pole Express (evenings) in November and December. Spring and fall are fine times to visit, with the leaves either a new green or brilliant autumn colors.

GOOD TO KNOW: Essex is a historic seaport village, with lots of white-clapboard New England charm. The charmingly Victorian Goodspeed Opera House in nearby East Haddam presents productions of classic musical comedies.

WORTH DOING: Nearby Gillette Castle is a whimsical faux-medieval mountaintop estate built of local fieldstone and completed in 1919 for actor and playwright William Gillette, most famous for his portrayal of Sherlock Holmes. Visit it on your own or as a train-ferry-hiking package offered by the railroad.

DON'T MISS: The diesel-hauled Essex Clipper Dinner Train, which operates seasonally and offers a four-course dinner, actually makes the longest run of any of the trains, going beyond Deep River and up to Haddam. One of its two dining cars is a special treat: the heavyweight Pullman parlor car *Wallingford*, built in 1927 for the New York, New Haven & Hartford Railroad.

GETTING THERE: Essex is located on Route 9 just three miles from I-95. The nearest major airports are in New Haven and Hartford, roughly equidistant.

Naugatuck Railroad 🔳

LOCATION: 242 E. Main Street, Thomaston
PHONE: 860-283-7245
WEBSITE: rmne.org
E-MAIL: form on website

Scott Hartley

Today's Naugatuck Railroad runs over 19.6 miles of former New Haven Railroad, between Waterbury and Torrington, a line built by the original Naugatuck in 1849. The tracks follow the railroad's namesake river for the entire route. The Naugatuck Railroad, part of the Railroad Museum of New England, offers regularly scheduled train service over a nine-mile portion of its line, and periodic special excursions over other segments.

CHOICES: Departing the 1881 Thomaston station aboard 1920s heavyweight coaches built for Canadian National, you cross two trestles over the Naugatuck River, see century-old New England brass mills, and roll high across the face of giant Thomaston Dam. Operating locomotives include U23B 2203 (the last domestic U-Boat built by General Electric), Alco RS3 New Haven 529, and EMD FL9 New Haven 2019 (the only FL9 still operating on original NH trackage).

WHEN TO GO: Excursions run on Sundays and Tuesdays from Memorial Day through September, with Saturday departures added in October. The fall colors peak in early to mid-October, and this is the most popular time to ride the Naugatuck's trains. Northern Lights Limited and Santa Express trains run weekends late November through December, and wine-tasting trains run throughout the year.

GOOD TO KNOW: Built in 1881 by the original Naugatuck Railroad, the brick Thomaston station is being restored. The station features a display track of historic New England railroad rolling stock.

WORTH DOING: Thomaston offers a pleasant New England downtown with historic mills, a picturesque opera house, and restaurants. Nearby Litchfield has shops and restaurants as well. Waterbury's Mattatuck Museum shows visitors the history of Connecticut's brass industry.

DON'T MISS: In 2010, for the first time in more than 60 years, steam returned to the railroad when Flagg Coal No. 75 pulled excursions. Check with the railroad to see if No. 75 will return for another opportunity to ride behind live steam.

GETTING THERE: Take I-84 to Waterbury and then Route 8 north to Exit 38.

DELAWARE

Wilmington & Western Railroad ❶

LOCATION: 2201 Newport-Gap Pike, Wilmington
PHONE: 302-998-1930
WEBSITE: wwrr.com
E-MAIL: schedule@wwrr.com

Jim Wrinn

The Wilmington & Western is one of the premier tourist railroads on the East Coast. Attractive equipment, historic steam locomotives, and a scenic route through Delaware's Red Clay Valley make this line a must-see when visiting the mid-Atlantic.

CHOICES: The Wilmington & Western offers two basic trip options from Greenbank Station: a 90-minute round trip to the Mount Cuba picnic grove or a 2.5-hour round trip covering the entire 10-mile line to Hockessin. The train is comprised of vintage steel coaches with adjustable windows, and an open-air car is available during the warmer months. Special trains offer onboard dining, murder mysteries, train robberies, and holiday-themed events.

WHEN TO GO: The W&W is open almost year-round, but steam operates on only select dates for much of the season. Doodlebugs and diesels power other trips. Fall foliage and winter holidays see steam excursions nearly every weekend. Mid-October through early November is prime season for autumn leaves in the Red Clay Valley. December is Santa Claus Express time, with the focus on families and fun.

GOOD TO KNOW: Built by the American Locomotive Company in 1909 for the Mississippi Central, 4-4-0 American No. 98 is one of the few American Standard types operating.

WORTH DOING: Nearby attractions include a tall ship, Longwood Gardens, and Winterthur, a 1,000-acre estate featuring a 175-room house that showcases collections of antiques and Americana amidst meadows, woodlands, and an expansive garden.

DON'T MISS: On Pufferbelly Days, the railroad's two steam locomotives, 4-4-0 No. 98 and 0-6-0 No. 58, operate double-headed. On Track Car Weekend, you can ride a vintage track inspection vehicle in addition to the train.

GETTING THERE: Greenbank Station is about four miles southwest of downtown Wilmington on Route 41, close to I-95. Amtrak's Northeast Corridor provides service to downtown Wilmington, and Philadelphia International Airport is 35 miles away.

DISCOUNT: $1 off each adult ticket, up to four adults; excludes specials.

DISTRICT OF COLUMBIA

Smithsonian National Museum of American History ❶

LOCATION: 14th Street and Constitution Avenue, Washington, D.C.
PHONE: 202-633-1000
WEBSITE: americanhistory.si.edu
E-MAIL: info@si.edu

National Museum of American History

The National Museum of American History features the landmark transportation exhibition America on the Move. Eighteen multimedia dioramas, each recreating a specific time and place using artifacts, images, and sound, demonstrate how road and rail transportation shaped America, from before 1876 to 2000.

CHOICES: Must-see exhibits include the massive Southern Railway No. 1401, a 280-ton passenger locomotive built in 1926; *Jupiter*, a Baldwin-built narrow gauge 4-4-0; and a 19th century streetcar. The museum also displays *John Bull*, one of the oldest surviving steam locomotives in North America. This 1831 English-made locomotive is displayed on a vintage iron truss bridge that once served the Philadelphia and Reading Railroad.

WHEN TO GO: The museum is open every day of the year except Christmas Day. Spring sees the renowned cherry trees in bloom at the nearby Tidal Basin. The Smithsonian Folklife Festival, a huge outdoor exposition of living cultural heritage, takes place each year around Independence Day on the National Mall.

GOOD TO KNOW: The National Museum of American History is one of a dozen Smithsonian museums located on or near the National Mall, exhibiting everything from art to aviation and natural history. All Smithsonian museums feature free admission.

WORTH DOING: Explore the National Mall. In this national park, you can visit the Washington Monument, Lincoln Memorial, Jefferson Memorial, and several war memorials.

DON'T MISS: Listen to the re-created conversation between the fireman and engineer of Southern No. 1401 as they discuss their upcoming run. Take a full-immersion multimedia journey around Chicago's famous loop as it was in 1959 aboard "L" car 6719.

GETTING THERE: Public transportation is the best option. Washington's Metrorail subway offers convenient access to the museum from its Smithsonian and Federal Triangle stations. A DC Circulator bus loops around the museums on spring and summer weekends.

FLORIDA

Boca Express Train Museum ❶

Guided tours take you through two restored 1947 Seaboard Air Line streamlined rail cars, both of which are listed on the National Register of Historic Places. The museum also includes a 1930 restored Florida East Coast depot, a 1940s Atlantic Coast Line caboose, and a Baldwin steam engine.

LOCATION: 747 S. Dixie Highway, Boca Raton
PHONE: 561-395-6766 ext. 100
WEBSITE: www.bocahistory.org
E-MAIL: programs@bocahistory.org

Central Florida Railroad Museum ❷

Located in a former 1913 Tavares & Gulf Railroad station, the museum features a Clinchfield caboose and a 1938 Fairmont motor car. Exhibits focus on central Florida railroads. The museum is operated by the Winter Garden Heritage Foundation which also operates the nearby Heritage Museum. That museum is housed in a 1918 Atlantic Coast Line depot and exhibits some railroad memorabilia, a Chessie caboose, and local historical items. Both museums are open daily.

LOCATION: 101 S. Boyd Street, Winter Garden
PHONE: 407-656-0559
WEBSITE: wghf.org
E-MAIL: museum@wghf.org

Flagler Museum ❸

The home of Henry Flagler, who developed the Florida East Coast Railway, is now a museum of the Gilded Age. Docent-led tours are offered, or you can tour the 55-room Whitehall on your own. The Flagler Kenan Pavilion, designed in the style of a 19th century Beaux Arts railway palace, houses Henry Flagler's private railcar.

LOCATION: 1 Whitehall Way, Palm Beach
PHONE: 561-655-2833
WEBSITE: flaglermuseum.us
E-MAIL: mail@flaglermuseum.us

Naples Depot Museum ❹

Recently renovated, the museum is housed in a former Seaboard Air Line passenger station and listed on the National Register of Historic Places. It features restored railcars, interactive exhibits, and a model railroad. Miniature train rides are also offered.

LOCATION: 1051 Fifth Avenue South, Naples
PHONE: 239-262-6525
WEBSITE: www.colliermuseums.com

Southwest Florida Museum of History ❺

Housed in the former Atlantic Coast Line Railroad depot, the museum displays a 1929 Pullman railcar. You can tour the *Esperanza* and get a glimpse of travel aboard a private car. The museum features exhibits from prehistoric times to modern day that showcase southwest Florida. It is open Tuesdays through Saturdays.

LOCATION: 2031 Jackson Street, Fort Myers
PHONE: 239-321-7430
WEBSITE: swflmuseumofhistory.com

Florida Railroad Museum ◎

LOCATION: 12210 83rd Street East, Parrish
PHONE: 941-776-0906
WEBSITE: frrm.org
E-MAIL: form on website

Scott Hartley

The Florida Railroad Museum operates diesel-powered trains on a 13-mile round trip in southwest Florida. Leisurely rides on air-conditioned and open-air coaches through farmland, piney woods, and palmetto flats give riders a glimpse of Florida before Disney and interstate highways.

CHOICES: Variety is the order for the day with the Florida Railroad Museum's equipment. Passenger equipment comes from a wide range of railroads, including the Lackawanna, Union Pacific, and Louisville & Nashville. Regardless of the time of year, you'll want to opt for the air-conditioned rolling stock instead of open air—after all, air-conditioning was invented by Florida physician John Gorrie in 1851 for good reason! Get there well before train time to get a cool seat. Special events include a World War II reenactment, a train robbery, and Halloween and Christmas trains.

WHEN TO GO: The Florida Railroad Museum operates weekends year-round. Mid-December through Easter is Florida's high season. The Florida Railroad Museum is at its busiest then, but this season also boasts Florida's mildest weather, making it the perfect time to combine a ride on the railroad with a canoe trip or a picnic at nearby Little Manatee River State Park.

GOOD TO KNOW: The Florida Railroad Museum's locomotive rental program allows you to operate a diesel-electric from the 1950s.

WORTH DOING: Other area attractions include Manatee Village Historical Park, which displays a variety of historic buildings and a steam locomotive, the South Florida Museum that also includes an aquarium and planetarium, and the Gamble Plantation Historic State Park.

DON'T MISS: Packing a lunch for the museum's picnic area makes for an enjoyable break, where a Porter 0-6-0T steam locomotive is on display.

GETTING THERE: You have plenty of choices. Tampa International Airport and Sarasota Bradenton International Airport are fairly close by. Amtrak serves Tampa by train and Sarasota and Bradenton by dedicated connecting motor coach. By car, take I-75 for speed or Highway 301 to see more of the real Florida.

Gold Coast Railroad Museum ❼

LOCATION: 12450 SW 152nd Street, Miami
PHONE: 888-608-7246 or 305-253-0063
WEBSITE: gcrm.org
E-MAIL: webmaster@gcrm.org

Gold Coast Railroad Museum

With its impressive collection of rolling stock and locomotives—featuring the *Ferdinand Magellan*, a Pullman office car used by Presidents Roosevelt, Truman, Eisenhower, and Reagan—and its historic location on the site of a World War II airship base, the Gold Coast Railroad Museum is a fascinating place to visit.

CHOICES: Interested in former Florida East Coast Railway or *California Zephyr* passenger equipment? You'll find it here, along with diesels and steam locomotives from other railroads. On weekends, the Gold Coast offers a 20-minute standard gauge train ride using a diesel-electric (either an EMD E9 or GP7) and either a former Florida East Coast stainless coach or a caboose. Also on weekends, the Gold Coast runs a two-foot gauge children's steam train.

WHEN TO GO: The Gold Coast Railroad Museum is open daily year-round, except for some holidays. The museum offers special events around holidays and days out with Thomas the Tank Engine.

GOOD TO KNOW: Florida East Coast Railway 4-6-2 steam locomotive No. 153, like the *Ferdinand Magellan*, is a National Historic Landmark. Used on "the railroad that died at sea," No. 153 pulled a rescue train that delivered evacuees safely to Miami just before a hurricane destroyed the Key West line in 1935.

WORTH DOING: Consider combining your trip to the Gold Coast with a visit to Zoo Miami, which is located next to the railroad museum.

DON'T MISS: The Gold Coast offers cab rides on its weekend diesel-hauled passenger trains for an additional fee. Make sure, however, you call ahead for reservations. Also look for free admission days, evening hours, and free children's train ride offers.

GETTING THERE: Miami is served by all major airlines, Amtrak, and major highways. The museum is located between Miami and Homestead, off the Florida Turnpike.

Seminole Gulf Railway 8

LOCATION: 2805 Colonial Boulevard, Fort Myers
PHONE: 800-736-4853 or 239-275-8487
WEBSITE: semgulf.com
E-MAIL: reservations@semgulf.com

Scott Hartley

Seminole Gulf is a regional railroad with about 118 miles of track that operates a murder mystery dinner train as well as providing freight service to Gulf communities in the Fort Myers area.

CHOICES: Throughout the year, the railroad offers a variety of themed murder mysteries aboard a dinner train. Along the 3.5-hour entertaining journey, the train takes you across the Caloosahatchee River over a railroad drawbridge. The views from this and other numerous bridges you cross are especially scenic, not that you'll be able to watch the scenery. You will be busy enjoying a five-course meal and trying to solve a mystery. If you do and are a super sleuth, you may even win a prize.

WHEN TO GO: The mystery dinner train operates Wednesday through Sunday evenings year-round, but of course, Florida is always best enjoyed in winter! Several specials occur around various holidays.

GOOD TO KNOW: The railroad operates on the tracks of the former Atlantic Coast Line and Seaboard Air Line, which joined in 1967 to become Seaboard Coast Line. Seminole Gulf has previously offered daytime excursions, and the railway may again in the future as well.

WORTH DOING: Before your dinner, you can walk along Fort Myers Beach or a beach on a nearby barrier island, such as Sanibel or Captiva, and go shelling. For more adventure, Everglades National Park is 90 minutes away. You can visit the park's Gulf Coast Visitor Center at Everglades City, where you can take a boat tour or rent a canoe. You can enter the heart of the park from the east, which is about a three-hour drive.

DON'T MISS: A Christmas rail-boat event combines a train trip, dinner, and a boat ride through Punta Gorda Isles' lighted holiday festivities.

GETTING THERE: The railway is located in suburban Fort Myers, which is on the western Florida coast 40 miles north of Naples. The depot is located 1.5 miles from Highway 41 and three miles from I-75.

TECO Line Streetcar System ▣

LOCATION: St. Pete Times Forum Drive, Tampa
PHONE: 813-254-4278
WEBSITE: tecolinestreetcar.org

Scott Hartley

Nostalgic-looking streetcars take passengers along a 2.7-mile route that connects downtown Tampa, Channelside, and the Ybor City entertainment district.

CHOICES: With a new extension along Franklin Street to Whiting Street, you can ride a streetcar to the heart of downtown Tampa, across from the Poe Plaza esplanade. You can also board anywhere along the line's other 10 stops. Get off, enjoy the neighborhood, and catch a later car. Five stops are located in Tampa's Channel District, four are in historic Ybor City, and another is downtown at the Dick Greco Plaza. The TECO fleet includes a restored original Birney streetcar, replicas of Birney safety streetcars, and an open-air streetcar. Fares are charged per person per trip, but one-day unlimited ride cards are also available. The streetcar system also offers guided group tours.

WHEN TO GO: Cars operate year-round. They run every 15 to 20 minutes from morning through the evening with extended hours on Saturdays.

GOOD TO KNOW: Tampa's streetcar line dates back to 1892 when it carried workers between downtown and the cigar factories on the city's west side. The line peaked in the 1920s with some 24 million riders and then closed in 1946.

WORTH DOING: In Ybor City, within walking distance of the streetcar line, you can visit a cigar maker and even see craftsmen roll fresh cigars by hand. The Florida Aquarium and the Ybor City Museum are accessible from the line.

DON'T MISS: Check out the annual Streetcar Fest, which takes place in November with food, music, and streetcar rides.

GETTING THERE: If starting in Ybor City, which is east of downtown Tampa, take I-4 and follow the signs to Ybor City. At the Dick Greco Plaza downtown, you can connect to trolleys, buses, and taxis.

GEORGIA

Agrirama Museum of Culture & Historic Village ➊

At Agrirama, Georgia's Museum of Agriculture, you can tour 35 buildings that represent the state's past, including a railroad depot and sawmill. A ride aboard a steam train takes you around the historic site. The living museum is open Tuesday through Saturday year-round. Special events are scheduled throughout the year.

LOCATION: 1392 Whiddon Mill Road, Tifton
PHONE: 800-767-1875 or 229-386-3344
WEBSITE: agrirama.com
E-MAIL: director@agrirama.com

Okefenokee Heritage Center ➋

This regional art and history museum displays Old Nine, a restored 1912 Baldwin 2-8-2 steam locomotive. The rail exhibit also includes a baggage car, REA Express car, passenger coach, caboose, and an early Waycross depot that describes regional rail history. Music fans may be interested in the exhibit of Waycross native Gram Parsons.

LOCATION: 1490 N. Augusta Avenue, Waycross
PHONE: 912-285-4260
WEBSITE: okefenokeeheritagecenter.org
E-MAIL: sbean@wayxcable.com

River Street Streetcar 🔢

Savannah's River Street Streetcar makes seven stops along the historic riverfront between Montgomery Street and the Waving Girl Landing, where passengers can connect with the *Savannah Belles* ferry. Built in Melbourne, Australia, during the 1930s, the W5 class streetcar now runs on battery power and biodiesel. It operates Thursdays through Sundays.

LOCATION: River Street, Savannah
PHONE: 912-447-4026
WEBSITE: www.connectonthedot.com
E-MAIL: comments@connectonthedot.com

Stone Mountain Scenic Railroad 🔢

A 1940s locomotive with open-air cars takes you on a five-mile, 30-minute excursion around Stone Mountain. Narration provides a look at rail history, beginning in the mid-1800s when the rail line was first built, and provides interesting facts about the mountain. And tune up your singing voice, as sing-alongs take place during the ride. The park has plenty of other fun events and attractions including a mini golf course themed around the Great Locomotive Chase.

LOCATION: Highway 78 East, Stone Mountain
PHONE: 800-401-2407 or 770-498-5690
WEBSITE: stonemountainpark.com
E-MAIL: form on website

Thronateeska Heritage Center 🔢

The Thronateeska Heritage Center contains several historic railroad structures including an original 1857 freight depot and Railway Express Agency building, and its history museum is located in the 1912 Union Depot. Its transportation annex displays a variety of railcars and Georgia Northern Railway steam locomotive No. 107. The complex also includes a planetarium and science center.

LOCATION: 100 W. Roosevelt Avenue, Albany
PHONE: 229-432-6955
WEBSITE: heritagecenter.org
E-MAIL: info@heritagecenter.org

Blue Ridge Scenic Railway ▣

LOCATION: 241 Depot Street, Blue Ridge
PHONE: 877-413-8724 or 706-632-8724
WEBSITE: brscenic.com
E-MAIL: brscenic@tds.net

Ron Huster

The Louisville & Nashville's original route from Knoxville to Atlanta covered some rugged territory, and today it makes for a scenic ride into the wilderness. Following the unspoiled Toccoa River, this 26-mile round trip takes riders between the depot at Blue Ridge and McCaysville near the Tennessee border.

CHOICES: Trains depart downtown Blue Ridge from the depot, which was constructed in 1906 and is listed on the National Register of Historical Places. You can ride in either a closed-window car or an open-air car. As the diesel-powered train climbs through the north Georgia mountains, commentary is piped into the cars, and a conductor may add his own perspective to the trip.

WHEN TO GO: Trains run March through December, and spring and fall are great seasons for travel in the Southeast. The region's lush vegetation has a tendency to create a tunnel effect. During spring and autumn, you have the chance to see into the forest as well as take in the scenery. Pumpkin pickin' and Santa trains offer family fun.

GOOD TO KNOW: This railroad started out as a narrow gauge line in the late 1880s with the tracks being three feet wide. Later investors changed it to standard gauge. The railway is the only mainline railroad excursion service based in Georgia.

WORTH DOING: The railroad offers a combination rail-and-raft package that is good for the Toccoa River, which the railroad crisscrosses, or for the nearby Ocoee River. The Toccoa is a slow run, while the Ocoee is a wild whitewater ride. Both options include return transportation to Blue Ridge.

DON'T MISS: During your layover, take the opportunity to walk around McCaysville, have lunch, and visit some of the town's antique shops.

GETTING THERE: Blue Ridge is about 90 miles north of Atlanta and about 80 miles from Chattanooga, Tenn. From Atlanta, take I-75 north to I-575, which turns into Highway 515, and continue on Highway 515 to Blue Ridge. The depot is on the left side of Depot Street.

Roundhouse Railroad Museum ❼

LOCATION: 601 W. Harris Street, Savannah
PHONE: 912-651-6823
WEBSITE: chsgeorgia.org
E-MAIL: info@chsgeorgia.org

Roundhouse Railroad Museum

Part of the multi-site Coastal Heritage Society museum complex, Savannah's Roundhouse Railroad Museum is a must-see for those interested in early American railroading technology. Located on the edge of Savannah's renowned historic district, the museum encompasses 13 structures from the original Central of Georgia shops site, several of which date back to the early 1850s.

CHOICES: The 1926 roundhouse contains a collection of Georgia steam locomotives, passenger cars, and freight cars, including the 1886 0-6-0 shop switcher No. 8 and a rare 1878 wooden business car. A self-guided tour provides information about the history and technology of the site. The operating turntable in the roundhouse is a must-see. Special events, including family happenings, take place throughout the year. On select weekends, the museum offers diesel- or steam-powered train rides.

WHEN TO GO: The museum is open year-round. Savannah's near-tropical climate offers a welcome relief from northern cold throughout the winter months.

GOOD TO KNOW: A variety of additional options are available at the roundhouse for a fuller rail experience. For an added fee, you can take a locomotive cab ride and interact with the engineer, ride a handcar, or tour an executive car.

WORTH DOING: The Savannah Historic District, a National Historic Landmark, is one of America's premier urban historic neighborhoods. You'll find fine examples of buildings in the Georgian, Greek Revival, and Gothic styles.

DON'T MISS: Expand your tour with a visit to the other sites in the complex. The Savannah History Museum is housed in the 1850s Central of Georgia passenger station and train shed one block north of the roundhouse. Old Fort Jackson, a brick fort built before the War of 1812, presents cannon-firing demonstrations. Battlefield Park commemorates a Revolutionary War battle.

GETTING THERE: Amtrak's station is three miles away. A number of major airlines or their regional affiliates serve Savannah International Airport. Highways 16 and 17 lead to Martin Luther King, Jr. Boulevard, which takes you to the museum.

SAM Shortline 🗉

LOCATION: 105 E. Ninth Avenue, Cordele
PHONE: 877-427-2457 or 229-276-0755
WEBSITE: samshortline.com

SAM Shortline

The SAM Shortline offers a relaxing trip through the small towns of southwest Georgia. The train leaves from Cordele, and the main objective is to reach Archery. Along the way, you travel through Georgia Veterans State Park and the towns of Leslie, Americus, and Plains, the home of President Jimmy Carter.

CHOICES: There are six different excursion trains, each one laying over in different towns on the route. If you would like to explore a location longer, you may be able to catch the train on its return trip. You can board at any of the depots along the route. SAM offers coach, premium, and adult-only seating. Premium seating is in the Americus car and features tables and chairs. Adult-only seating is in the *Samuel H. Hawkins* car, and it offers loungers, booths, and an observation area.

WHEN TO GO: Trains run Fridays and Saturdays as well as on select Thursdays March through December. Days out with Thomas take place in October, and numerous special excursions operate throughout the season.

GOOD TO KNOW: Why SAM? The original railroad was the Savannah, Americus & Montgomery Railroad built during the 1880s and headed by Col. Samuel Hugh Hawkins of Americus.

WORTH DOING: In Americus, you can visit Habitat for Humanity's Global Village, and if you want to make a longer trip, the Andersonville National Historic Site and National POW Museum is 11 miles northeast.

DON'T MISS: Many of the excursions, such as the Peanut Express, stop in Plains and Archery, where you can visit Jimmy Carter's childhood home. In Plains, the Seaboard Coast Line depot was his campaign headquarters during the 1976 election. While you're there, make sure to buy a bag of peanuts.

GETTING THERE: Cordele is about 140 miles south of Atlanta. From I-75, take Exit 101 and go west on Highway 280. At Highway 41, turn north to Cordele.

Southeastern Railway Museum ⑨

LOCATION: 3595 Buford Highway, Duluth
PHONE: 770-476-2013
WEBSITE: srmduluth.org
E-MAIL: admin@southeasternrailwaymuseum.org

Jim Wrinn

The museum showcases railroading in Georgia and the Southeast with exhibits and more than 90 pieces of rolling stock. Among the highlights are a business car used to help convince leaders to bring the 1996 Olympics to Atlanta, a private car once used by President Warren G. Harding, and one of the famous green and gold *Southern Crescent* passenger diesels. It also offers short train rides.

CHOICES: The 34-acre museum features a variety of buildings and displays. Building One, the main exhibit hall, contains Southern Railway E8 passenger diesel-electric No. 6901 and the 1911 Pullman private car *Superb*, which was used by President Harding and is on the National Register of Historic Places. The museum's collection includes passenger coaches, private cars, trolleys, baggage cars, freight cars, cabooses, and maintenance-of-way equipment. A diesel-powered train ride takes you around the museum's site aboard vintage cabooses.

WHEN TO GO: The museum is open Thursdays, Fridays, and Saturdays all year (second Thursdays January through March). In summer, it is also open on Wednesdays. Train rides are offered in season, and special days take place during the year including Caboose Days and days with Santa.

GOOD TO KNOW: Restoration of the Southern Railway depot in Duluth is underway, and when completed, it will house exhibits. The museum is also working on adding a miniature train ride to the grounds.

WORTH DOING: From professional sports to botanical gardens and the zoo, take a few days and see all that the Atlanta area has to offer.

DON'T MISS: View famous excursion engines Savannah & Atlanta Pacific type No. 750 and Atlanta & West Point Pacific type No. 290, the latter well known for appearing in the movie *Fried Green Tomatoes*.

GETTING THERE: The museum is located in Duluth, a northeast suburb of Atlanta. It is just south of downtown Duluth. From Atlanta, take I-85 to Exit 104 and take Pleasant Hill Road to Buford Highway. Turn right on Buford Highway and then left onto Peachtree Road to the museum.

Southern Museum of Civil War and Locomotive History ⑩

LOCATION: 2829 Cherokee Street, Kennesaw
PHONE: 770-427-2117
WEBSITE: www.southernmuseum.org

Southern Museum of Civil War and Locomotive History

A museum of high-caliber exhibits and static displays, the Southern Museum of Civil War and Locomotive History displays the famed steam locomotive *General*. The *General*, a Western & Atlantic Railroad 4-4-0 built in 1855, was the star in one of the Civil War's greatest acts of intrigue—the Great Locomotive Chase. The museum, part of which is located in a former cotton gin, is a must-see attraction.

CHOICES: While the story of the Andrews Raid and the *General* is still the biggest offering at the museum, additional railroading and Civil War displays are featured. It also chronicles the story of Georgia locomotive manufacturer Glover Machine Works. The Glover Machine Works manufactured steam locomotives, locomotive parts, and other industrial products from 1902 until the 1930s. Patterns from the casting shop are artfully displayed, and extensive exhibits cover the story of the locomotive manufacturer. The facility also features special railroad exhibits and events.

WHEN TO GO: The museum is open daily year-round, except for major holidays, and the weather is generally mild. The Atlanta area has lots of modern railroad action, and other museums, such as the Atlanta History Center, help tell the story of the Civil War and railroading in Atlanta.

GOOD TO KNOW: The story of the Andrews Raid was thrilling and unique enough to attract the attention of the Walt Disney Company, which released the film *The Great Locomotive Chase* in 1956.

WORTH DOING: Take a walking tour of historic Kennesaw (once known as Big Shanty) after exiting the front door of the museum and view a 1908 Western & Atlantic Railroad depot, numerous 19th century residences, and an 1887 grocery store.

DON'T MISS: The Atlanta Cyclorama, located in Grant Park, houses the *Texas*, the Western & Atlantic Railroad locomotive used by Confederates to hunt down Andrews Raiders.

GETTING THERE: Kennesaw is located off I-75 and Highway 41, about a 45-minute drive from Hartsfield-Jackson Atlanta International Airport, the world's busiest. Amtrak's *Crescent* also serves the city twice daily.

HAWAII

Laupahoehoe Train Museum ➊

The musem is located on the Big Island along the Hamakua Heritage Coast. It is housed in a station agent's home, which has been restored and furnished to its early 1900s appearance. The museum contains photos and artifacts of the Hilo Railroad and displays a standard gauge caboose, narrow gauge boxcar, and diesel switcher.

LOCATION: 36-2377 Mamalahoa Highway, Laupahoehoe
PHONE: 808-962-6300
WEBSITE: thetrainmuseum.com
E-MAIL: laupahoehoetrainmuseum@yahoo.com
DISCOUNT: Buy one adult admission, get one free.

Hawaiian Railway 2

LOCATION: 91-1001 Renton Road, Ewa
PHONE: 808-681-5461
WEBSITE: hawaiianrailway.com
E-MAIL: info@hawaiianrailway.com

Robert Pisani

The Hawaiian Railway is the only active railroad on the island of Oahu. It offers regularly scheduled 90-minute, fully narrated rides over 6.5 miles of track. Along the way, you'll pass a variety of interesting and historical sites, including Fort Barrette. The train stops at Kahe Point, so you can take in the extraordinary ocean views.

CHOICES: Regular excursions take place twice each Sunday afternoon. On the second Sunday of each month, parlor car No. 64 is added to the regular train of open cars, and reservations (and an additional fare) are necessary for riding in this beautifully restored car. Three side-rod diesel locomotives have been restored to operation, and several steam locomotives have been cosmetically restored. The railway also has a collection of railcars and other equipment.

WHEN TO GO: The railway's train yard is open year-round. A haunted Halloween train, complete with ghost stories, runs in October.

GOOD TO KNOW: Parlor car No. 64 is the luxurious parlor car that Benjamin Dillingham, founder of the Oahu Railway & Land Company, had built for his personal use in 1900. Restored by the Hawaiian Railway Society, No. 64 is worth the ride, and the fare for riding the car goes toward its upkeep.

WORTH DOING: No trip to Oahu would be complete without a heart-rending visit to Pearl Harbor. You can also wander over Oahu and other islands and literally discover pieces of Hawaii's railroading past, which included sugar plantation, military, and common carrier railways.

DON'T MISS: The railway, which is situated on what was part of the Oahu Railway & Land Company main line, is north of Pearl Harbor. The scenery is incredible. Wear comfortable shoes and wander through the train yard and then relax with lunch in the picnic area.

GETTING THERE: The railway is minutes from Honolulu by bus or car. If you drive, take H1 west and exit on 5A Ewa. Then take Highway 76 south for 2.5 miles, turn right at Renton Road, and continue for 1.5 miles to the entrance.

DISCOUNT: $3 off adult ticket (off a $10 fare) for 3 p.m. Sunday ride.

Kauai Plantation Railway ▣

LOCATION: 3-2087 Kaumualii Highway, Lihue
PHONE: 808-245-7245
WEBSITE: kauaiplantationrailway.com
E-MAIL: train@hawaiilink.net

David Lustig

The Kauai Plantation Railway operates daily on a genuine Hawaiian plantation. Experience plantation life and learn about Kauai agriculture as the train travels through more than 100 acres of unspoiled Hawaii on a three-foot-gauge train. Passengers enjoy a 40-minute journey through fields of sugar cane, pineapple, banana, papaya, coffee, tropical flowers, and hardwood trees.

CHOICES: Train rides leave from a Hawaiian train depot, and you can ride in a reproduction of a railway car from the time of King Kalakaua or an open-sided excursion car. In addition, there is a ride-hike-lunch-orchard tour. Currently, motive power is a pair of small diesels, including a restored 1939 Whitcomb engine. Two Baldwin steam locomotives are being rebuilt to power excursions. These engines were built for plantation service on the Island of Oahu and are some of the few Hawaiian engines that remain.

WHEN TO GO: The train operates daily, and any day is a beautiful day in Hawaii, and there are up to five runs a day. Hawaii is in the tropics, and that suggests suntan lotion, a hat, and comfortable clothing.

GOOD TO KNOW: The three-foot-gauge railway was the first railroad built on Kauai in almost 100 years. More than 2.5 miles of roadbed was constructed with rails hand-spiked onto 6,000 wooden ties. More than 50 varieties of fruits and vegetables can be found on the plantation, from avocado and bananas to rambutan and sugar cane. The plantation also features a restaurant and shops.

WORTH DOING: Public luaus are scheduled on Tuesday and Friday evenings, and a special train can take you there.

DON'T MISS: On the tour package, after riding the train, you can hike in the rain forest and sample fresh fruit picked right off the tree. You also have the opportunity to feed goats, sheep, and pigs.

GETTING THERE: The Kauai Plantation is just off Route 50 (Kaumualii Highway) approximately one mile south of Lihue, which is the main city on Kauai. The railway is located at Kilohana Plantation next to Kauai Community College. Just look for the white picket fence.

Lahaina Kaanapali Railroad 🔳

LOCATION: 975 Limahana Place, Lahaina
PHONE: 808-661-0080
WEBSITE: sugarcanetrain.com
E-MAIL: form on website

David Lustig

The Sugar Cane Train travels between the historical whaling town of Lahaina to the lush Kaanapali Resort on the Hawaiian island of Maui. Narrow gauge steam engines transport visitors in open-air cars through the Kaanapali golf courses, along the ocean, and across a scenic railroad trestle.

CHOICES: You can board the Sugar Cane Train from either the Lahaina station or the Puukolii station. On the round trip, the conductor entertains you with narration about the history of the train and the sugar cane industry as well as fun Hawaiian facts. Don't miss the beautiful views of the Pacific Ocean and of the neighboring islands, Molokai and Lanai, from the 325-foot curved wooden trestle.

WHEN TO GO: Steam trains operate daily, all year round. While the most popular time is summer, if you visit between December and April, you just might see a breaching humpback whale from the train. During this time, many whales are active off the west Maui coast.

GOOD TO KNOW: While few Hawaiian railroads remain today, for more than 100 years, they hauled sugar cane to the mills and transported workers. You can learn more about the industry at the Alexander & Baldwin Sugar Museum.

WORTH DOING: There are a variety of luaus offered on the island, and you should experience at least one of these unique Hawaiian activities. West Maui is a premier Hawaii tourist destination, featuring five-star hotels and exquisite dining and shopping experiences. You'll be able to take a glass-bottom boat cruise, snorkel, try assorted water sports, and even dive into a tank of sharks at the Maui Ocean Center.

DON'T MISS: By sitting in the same seat, you will be able to experience both an ocean view and a mountain view. The views alternate depending on the direction of the train.

GETTING THERE: Many large airlines offer direct flights to Maui from mainland, West Coast cities. Once on Maui, both of the railroad's stations are located off Honoapiilani Highway (Highway 30), the coast's main, and only, highway.

IDAHO

Nampa Train Depot Museum ❶

Built in 1903, the building served as the Oregon Short Line depot and was then used as offices for the Union Pacific. The building now houses artifacts relating to local history. Outside, a UP caboose is available for group tours. The museum is open year-round. Depotfest takes place in August.

LOCATION: 1200 Front Street, Nampa
PHONE: 208-467-7611
WEBSITE: canyoncountyhistory.com
E-MAIL: info@canyoncountyhistory.com

Northern Pacific Depot Railroad Museum ❷

Listed on the National Register of Historic Places, this building served as a station until the 1980s. The elegant chateau-style depot was built at the turn of the 20th century from brick transported from China and concrete panels made from mine tailings. It now serves as a railroad museum that features exhibits on railroading in the area's mining district. Depot Day takes place in May.

LOCATION: 219 Sixth Street, Wallace
PHONE: 208-752-0111
WEBSITE: wallace-id.com/business.html#tourist

Thunder Mountain Line Railroad ▣

LOCATION: 120 Mill Road, Horseshoe Bend
PHONE: 877-432-7245 or 208-331-1184
WEBSITE: thundermountainline.com
E-MAIL: shari@thundermountainline.com

Thunder Mountain Line Railroad

This is one of the most scenic trips in the northern part of the Rocky Mountains. The train parallels the Payette River for most of the journey through sagebrush-covered hills, fir trees, and mountain meadows. Often visible are fox, deer, elk, blue heron, osprey, and bald eagles. Much of the river is excellent for whitewater rafting, so you not only get entertainment from the scenery but from the rafters as well.

CHOICES: On this line, you have almost 50 choices for a train ride aboard open-air or coach cars. In addition to the *Horseshoe Bend Express* excursion, there are more than 40 special theme trains. The *Horseshoe Bend Express* travels along an old wagon road on its three-hour round trip between Horseshoe Bend and Banks. Along the way, the train winds through a narrow canyon, passes through Boise National Forest, and offers a variety of scenic views. Special events trains also run west from Horseshoe Bend to the town of Montour. They include Hawaiian luaus and train robberies and everything in between.

WHEN TO GO: The countryside is rugged and beautiful to travel through any season. Trains operate Friday through Sunday beginning in March and run through the end of the year. There are also some weekday trains scheduled during summer.

GOOD TO KNOW: The history of this line goes back more than 100 years when a railroad was planned to transport gold prospectors. It was completed in 1914. Eventually, it supported the timber industry and carried vacationers.

WORTH DOING: Experience the scenic Payette River and Boise National Forest up close. You can raft or kayak through Class IV rapids or just float along the river. The forest offers over 1,300 miles of hiking trails and more than 70 camping and picnic spots.

DON'T MISS: The Thunder Mountain Line offers a summer kickoff in June and a special event for everyone. You might want to avoid (or ride in an open-air car) the Beno Limited, which is a chili cook-off that tastes better than it sounds.

GETTING THERE: The Horseshoe Bend depot is located about 25 minutes north of Boise. Take Highway 55 from Boise to Horseshoe Bend and once there turn right on Mill Road. Cascade is about another 40 miles north of Horseshoe Bend on Highway 55, and the Ashley Inn is on Main Street (Highway 55).

ILLINOIS

Amboy Depot Museum ❶

Built in 1876, this former Illinois Central division headquarters building has been restored, inside and out. It is now a museum that presents the history of Amboy and contains artifacts of the Illinois Central Railroad. The museum also contains a freight house with additional artifacts, an 0-8-0 Baldwin steam engine, a wooden caboose, and a schoolhouse. It is open year-round.

LOCATION: 50 S. East Avenue, Amboy
PHONE: 815-857-4700
WEBSITE: amboydepotmuseum.org
E-MAIL: information@amboydepotmuseum.org

Galesburg Railroad Museum ❷

The Galesburg Railroad Museum displays a Chicago, Burlington & Quincy Hudson steam locomotive, a Railway Post Office car, a 1930 caboose, a Pullman parlor car, and various pieces of rail equipment and artifacts. The museum is open April to September.

LOCATION: 211 S. Seminary Street, Galesburg
PHONE: 309-342-9400
WEBSITE: galesburgrailroadmuseum.org

Great Western Railroad Depot Museum ❸

This depot museum displays artifacts of the Chicago Great Western Railway. The depot serviced the nearby Winston Tunnel, the longest railroad tunnel in Illinois. The museum features a Milwaukee Road caboose, a working telegraph, and operating model railroads. It is open weekends.

LOCATION: 111 E. Myrtle Street, Elizabeth
PHONE: 815-858-2343
WEBSITE: elizabeth-il.com
E-MAIL: elizabethhistoricalsociety@yahoo.com

Greenup Depot ❹

The historic Greenup Depot is a museum that displays artifacts of railroad and telegraph history. The preserved 1870 Vandalia Line depot also maintains a collection of audio, visual, and written materials related to these subjects. It is open year-round. Just west of the town is a 200-foot reconstructed covered bridge; Abraham Lincoln helped construct the original bridge.

LOCATION: 216 Cumberland Street, Greenup
PHONE: 217-923-9306
WEBSITE: greenupdepot.org
E-MAIL: historic@rr1.net

Historic Pullman Foundation ❺

The Historic Pullman Foundation operates the Pullman Visitor Center, which features artifacts, photos and a video that informs visitors about George Pullman, the Pullman Company, and Pullman's 1880s model industrial town. You can take a self-guided tour of the historic area or a guided walking tour, which are offered the first Sunday of the month from May through October.

LOCATION: 11141 S. Cottage Grove Avenue, Chicago
PHONE: 773-785-8901
WEBSITE: pullmanil.org
E-MAIL: foundation@pullmanil.org

Kankakee Railroad Museum ❻

Kankakee's restored train depot displays railroad memorabilia and a model train layout of Kankakee in the 1950s. Also on display are a 1947 Pullman coach, caboose, and trolley. Tours of the restored trolley are available by appointment. The museum is open Friday through Sunday.

LOCATION: 197 S. East Avenue, Kankakee
PHONE: 815-929-9320
WEBSITE: kankakeerrmuseum.com

Trolley Car 36 ❼

Departing from downtown's Riverview Park, a 45-minute trolley ride transports you along Rockford's historic riverfront, with a 10-minute stopover at Sinnissippi Gardens and Lagoon. Excursions on the newly refurbished trolley take place during the summer. Riverboat cruises are also available.

LOCATION: 324 N. Madison Street, Rockford
PHONE: 815-987-8894
WEBSITE: www.rockfordparkdistrict.org
E-MAIL: rpdmail@rockfordparkdistrict.org

Union Depot Railroad Museum ❽

The railroad museum is housed in an 1888 depot building. It contains displays related to the Chicago, Burlington & Quincy, Illinois Central, and Milwaukee Road. You can view a 1923 Mikado type 2-8-2 steam locomotive, a Milwaukee Road combine car, and other railcars. Grab a bite at the nearby Whistle Stop restaurant in the renovated Illinois Central freight house.

LOCATION: 683 Main Street, Mendota
PHONE: 815-539-3373
WEBSITE: mendotamuseums.org
E-MAIL: mmhs@mtco.com

Fox River Trolley Museum 9

LOCATION: 361 S. LaFox Street, South Elgin
PHONE: 847-697-4676
WEBSITE: foxtrolley.org
E-MAIL: info@foxtrolley.org

Donald MacBean

Tucked away in the western suburbs of Chicago is the Fox River Trolley Museum, where young and old can take a nostalgic trolley ride along the scenic Fox River.

CHOICES: The museum operates a four-mile round trip over the last remaining section of the original Aurora, Elgin & Fox River electric line that once linked Carpentersville, Elgin, Aurora, and Yorkville. The trolley ride travels from South Elgin to the Jon J. Duerr Forest Preserve just north of St Charles. A variety of trolleys run including Car 20, which could be the oldest operating interurban trolley in the country. It entered service in 1902. Also look for Car 304, which is one of the last cars to operate on the Aurora, Elgin & Fox River electric line back in 1935. Car 304 returned to the line in 2009. The trolleys board at the Castlemuir depot. A caboose and occasionally some of the museum's other cars are on display. And when the carbarn doors are open, you can sneak a peek at the cars inside.

WHEN TO GO: The museum is open on weekends and summer holidays as well as for several special events. It is open on Sundays Mother's Day through early November and on Saturdays beginning the last Saturday in June through Labor Day weekend. Trolleys depart every 30 minutes. On October weekends, families can enjoy the Pumpkin Trolley or Halloween Haunted Ghost Story Train.

GOOD TO KNOW: Picnic tables are available around the depot, and in the Jon J. Duerr Forest Preserve, there are covered shelters with grills that can be reserved.

WORTH DOING: For a unique look at the trolleys in action, hike or bike along the Fox River Bike Trail, which parallels the trolley line and crosses the Fox River on a bridge built on old railway piers and abutments.

DON'T MISS: The Village of South Elgin celebrates Riverfest for four days in August with live entertainment, carnival rides, food, fireworks, a craft show, and a car show. In conjunction, the museum runs Trolleyfest with trolley rides and railcar displays.

GETTING THERE: The museum is 40 miles west of Chicago. From Chicago, take I-90 or Highway 20 west to Elgin. Exit on Highway 31 (State Street which becomes LaFox Street) and go south two miles to the museum.

Illinois Railway Museum ⑩

LOCATION: 7000 Olson Road, Union
PHONE: 800-244-7245 or 815-923-4000
WEBSITE: www.irm.org

Kathi Kube

Just 90 minutes northwest from downtown Chicago, and about half an hour from Union Pacific's Geneva Subdivision, lies the Illinois Railway Museum, which prides itself on running more diesel trains than other comparable museums. The museum also pays homage to its beginnings as an electric railway museum by operating streetcars and interurban cars daily.

CHOICES: As an operating museum, there are many trains to ride, including streetcars, interurbans, and other commuter cars pulled by vintage diesels. You can even ride a trolley or electric bus from one equipment barn to another. When you're not riding trains, explore the 80 acres of land and 400 pieces of equipment, including almost 90 freight cars, plus signals, tools, signage, and other artifacts. Six barns contain rail equipment, and another has bus equipment. Admission includes unlimited rides.

WHEN TO GO: The museum is open daily Memorial Day through Labor Day, weekends May through October, and Sundays in April. During July and August, remember that not all the cars and none of the barns are air-conditioned. The museum operates numerous special events including Terror on the Railroad, Happy Holiday Railway, two Day Out with Thomas Weekends, and a Take-the-Throttle experience.

GOOD TO KNOW: IRM's signature piece, the Chicago, Burlington & Quincy *Nebraska Zephyr*, runs at least six to eight times a year, including all major holidays and Diesel and Showcase weekends.

WORTH DOING: Union is centrally located between Rockford and suburban Chicago. It also offers tourists Donley's Wild West Town with gunslinger shows, pony rides, and gold panning. Nearby Marengo has several restaurants, and about a dozen hotels are within a half-hour drive from the museum.

DON'T MISS: Diesel Days in July and Museum Showcase Weekend in September are great times to see a lot of equipment running. Typically, 14 vintage locomotives are put to work pulling freight and commuter trains on Diesel Days. On Museum Showcase Weekend, the staff operates less-frequently run equipment.

GETTING THERE: If driving from Chicago, take I-90 to Highway 20, the Marengo exit. Drive northwest about 4.5 miles to Union Road and then take Union Road north.

DISCOUNT: $1 off each adult, 50 cents off each child; not valid for Day Out with Thomas.

Monticello Railway Museum ⓫

LOCATION: 992 Iron Horse Place, Monticello
PHONE: 877-762-9011 or 217-762-9011
WEBSITE: mrym.org
E-MAIL: info@mrym.org

Jim Wrinn

In the midsection of Illinois, this museum offers one of the best collections of rolling stock and a good train ride to boot. All decked out in their original attires, two streamlined diesel locomotives of the 1950s, one from Canadian National and the other from the Wabash Railroad, are among the most popular locomotives.

CHOICES: Although the museum has several steam engines, it has one of the Midwest's premier diesel locomotive collections. The collection features a Milwaukee Road NW2 and a former Illinois Central RS3, as well as more than 80 pieces of rolling stock. You can board the eight-mile round trip over former Illinois Central and Illinois Terminal trackage from two historic depots, one at the museum and the other in downtown Monticello. At either location, you can make a layover for additional exploration and then catch a later return trip.

WHEN TO GO: The museum is open on weekends and holidays May through October. Special events, including Railroad Days in September, are scheduled throughout the year for train buffs and families alike.

GOOD TO KNOW: After a 15-year restoration process, Southern Railway steam engine No. 401 begun pulling excursions for the museum. The Baldwin engine was built in 1907.

WORTH DOING: Just a short drive away, on Allerton Road, is one of the Seven Wonders of Illinois. The Allerton Park and Retreat Center was once a private mansion. And you can now walk through 14 miles of wooded trails and gardens that contain 100 sculptures.

DON'T MISS: For a fee, you can operate a locomotive for 30 minutes under the supervision of a regular member of the train crew during spring and fall throttle times.

GETTING THERE: The museum is located between Champaign and Decatur, just off I-72. At Exit 166, take Market Street to Iron Horse Place and follow the frontage road to the end. The town of Monticello is just a few miles away via Highway 105.

Museum of Science and Industry ⑫

Illinois

LOCATION: 57th Street and Lake Shore Drive, Chicago
PHONE: 800-468-6674 or 773-684-1414
WEBSITE: msichicago.org
E-MAIL: contact@msichicago.org

Scott Brownell

One of the Windy City's premier attractions, the Museum of Science and Industry provides an enjoyable, interactive, and educational experience for everyone. You can "ride" the famous *Pioneer Zephyr*, take a coal mine adventure, and view a railroad journey from Chicago to Seattle in miniature.

CHOICES: The museum has many railroad-themed exhibits, highlighted by the *Pioneer Zephyr*, which completed a record-setting 13-hour run from Denver to Chicago in 1934. You can tour the locomotive cab, and a tour guide takes you through an observation car, a baggage car, and several other cars. You'll also want to take the coal mine tour, where you can see coal loaded onto a train, and then board a work train and learn about mining techniques.

WHEN TO GO: The museum is open daily with extended hours on select days throughout the year. The museum offers free admission days and opens new exhibits throughout the year. Special exhibits cost extra.

GOOD TO KNOW: You won't be able to see everything the museum has to offer in one visit. There's a lot to see, so plan your day around the coal mine tour and the *Pioneer Zephyr*. You can bring a lunch or grab sandwiches at the Brain Food Court. (The museum is not within walking distance of restaurants.) When exiting the food court, watch the Swiss Jolly Ball, where a metal ball rides a locomotive, while navigating around a pinball-type contraption.

WORTH DOING: The museum is home to the only German submarine in the United States, which is a popular tour. Also, take a look at silent film star Colleen Moore's Fairy Castle, a miniature dollhouse made in the 1930s using real gold and jewels.

DON'T MISS: The world's largest model railroad, called The Great Train Story, runs on 1,425 feet of track with 30 trains making their way through Midwest farm fields, around mountains, and over 28 bridges. Railroad artifacts surround the layout, including a Pennsylvania Railroad locomotive cab.

GETTING THERE: Take a train. Amtrak offers free rides to kids on the *Hiawatha* on summer weekends. Chicago's Metra Electric District and Indiana's South Shoreline trains stop two blocks from the Museum's north entrance (the 57th Street Station).

Rochelle Railroad Park ⑬

LOCATION: 124 N. Ninth Street, Rochelle
PHONE: 815-562-7031
WEBSITE: rochellerailroadpark.org
E-MAIL: tourism@rochelle.net

Erik Bergstrom

With nearly 100 trains passing through daily, the Rochelle Railroad Park is one of the most popular railroad-watching destinations in North America thanks to a perfect blend of heavy railroad action and a safe, well-appointed place to watch the passing trains.

CHOICES: BNSF Railway and Union Pacific double-track main lines cross right in the middle of Rochelle. The railroad park adjacent to the tracks features picnic tables and a scanner tuned to railroad radio frequencies, and it is an excellent place to watch trains around the clock. A re-created hobo jungle in the park gives a glimpse into these travelers' lifestyle and gives children a place to play. A Whitcomb locomotive, which was manufactured in Rochelle, is also on display.

WHEN TO GO: Since the park is always open, you can visit at any time of the day or any time of the year. Braving the cold winter months provides special viewing opportunities. Rochelle Railroad Days takes place in June and features equipment displays, hobo stories, and a watermelon seed spitting contest.

GOOD TO KNOW: If you'd like a preview of the action in Rochelle, visit *Trains* magazine's website and watch from a live Web cam perched above the park's pavilion. Go to www.trainsmag.com and click on the Web cams link.

WORTH DOING: Roberts Armory World War II Museum conducts an armored reenactment during Railroad Days and is open several days during the year. The Rochelle Firehouse museum and Flagg Township Museum are other local attractions.

DON'T MISS: If you are interested in shooting photos or videos, the sun at Rochelle can be troublesome at times. At those times, you can venture out to other railroad hot spots in the area like the BNSF Mendota Subdivision in Mendota or the heavily trafficked BNSF Trancon at Toluca.

GETTING THERE: Rochelle is conveniently located at the junction of I-88 and I-39 in north central Illinois, a little more than an hour from Chicago's O'Hare International Airport. Once off the Interstate, Highway 38 or Highway 251 will take you to the railroad park.

Silver Creek & Stephenson Railroad 🔢

LOCATION: 2954 S. Walnut Road, Freeport
PHONE: 815-232-2306 or 815-235-2198
WEBSITE: thefreeportshow.com

Jeff Terry

This railroad offers a four-mile ride behind a 1912 geared Heisler steam engine. Trains leave from a reproduction of the original Illinois Central depot in Elroy, and the building houses a large collection of railroad memorabilia.

CHOICES: A Heisler steam locomotive pulls several cabooses and an open-air car through farmlands and across Yellow Creek on a 30-foot-high cement and stone pier bridge. The Silver Creek depot houses the ticket office and railroad displays.

WHEN TO GO: The train ride operates on various weekends and holidays between Memorial Day and the end of October. The Train of Terror operates in October.

GOOD TO KNOW: Volunteers created this railroad on the abandoned right of way of the Chicago, Milwaukee, St. Paul & Pacific Railroad. Because rails and ties were removed prior to purchase, members had to haul rail in from as far away as Minnesota, and ties were salvaged from across Illinois. Members of the Stephenson County Antique Engine Club laid their first tracks in May 1985.

WORTH DOING: While in Freeport, visit the Silver Creek Museum. It contains 28 rooms of historical displays. It is open the same days as the railroad.

DON'T MISS: Give the 36-ton Heisler a close inspection. Unlike most steam locomotives, it is driven with a V-2 arrangement of the cylinders on either side of the boiler; they run a crankshaft that moves a gearbox and wheels. Fewer than 1,200 of these locomotives were built, and only a handful remain in operation today.

GETTING THERE: Freeport is about 20 miles west of Rockford on Highway 20, and the museum is on the corner of Walnut and Lamm Roads.

DISCOUNT: $1 off each adult ticket on all open dates.

INDIANA

Carthage, Knightstown & Shirley Railroad 🔳

After departing from the old New York Central station, the CKS takes you on a 10-mile, 75-minute round trip from Knightstown to Carthage. When you pull back into the station, you can look over the railroad's assortment of antique railroad equipment. The CKS offers special events, including train robberies, during its season. It operates Fridays, Saturdays, and Sundays May through October.

LOCATION: 112 W. Carey Street, Knightstown
PHONE: 765-345-5561
WEBSITE: cksrail.com
E-MAIL: cksrrinc@netzero.net

Depot Railroad Museum ❷

A replica of Salem's former Monon depot, this depot was built by high school students. It features a Monon caboose, artifacts, and model railroad. The museum is open Tuesdays through Saturdays April through December and Saturdays only the rest of the year. The depot is part of the John Hay Center museum complex, which also contains a pioneer village and several other museums.

LOCATION: 206 S. College Avenue, Salem
PHONE: 812-883-1884
WEBSITE: salemdepot.com
E-MAIL: info@salemdepot.com

Linden Depot Museum ❸

The Linden Depot Museum contains memorabilia from the two railroads it served, the Nickel Plate Road and the Monon Railroad. It displays a caboose from the NKP, several railcars, and other pieces of equipment. Built in 1907, it is listed on the National Register of Historic Places. It is open May through October.

LOCATION: 520 N. Main Street, Linden
PHONE: 765-339-7245
WEBSITE: lindendepot.com
E-MAIL: information@lindendepot.com

Madison Railroad Station ❹

This restored 1895 Pennsylvania Railroad station is known for its unique octagon waiting room with stained glass windows. Exhibits describe the Madison railroad station and the Madison railroad incline. You can visit an agent's office, try the functional telegraph key, and walk through a restored, wooden caboose.

LOCATION: 615 W. First Street, Madison
PHONE: 812-265-2335
WEBSITE: www.jchshc.org
E-MAIL: form on website

Monon Connection Museum ❺

The museum features a completely furnished, full-size replica of an Illinois Central depot and outdoor displays. Exhibits include a large collection of dining car china, hundreds of hand-held lanterns, and restored brass steam locomotive bells and whistles. It is open Tuesday through Sunday. The Whistle Stop restaurant adjoins the museum.

LOCATION: 10012 N. Highway 421, Monon
PHONE: 219-253-4101
WEBSITE: mononconnection.com
E-MAIL: info@mononconnection.com

National New York Central Railroad Museum ❻

You begin your journey through the history of the New York Central by entering through a 1915 passenger coach. In the main gallery, which is a 100-year-old freight house, hands-on exhibits let you construct track and operate a steam locomotive. Outside, the museum's collection of locomotives and rolling stock includes an NYC Mohawk 4-8-2 and a Pennsylvania Railroad GG1.

LOCATION: 721 S. Main Street, Elkhart
PHONE: 574-294-3001
WEBSITE: nycrrmuseum.org
E-MAIL: info@nycrrmuseum.org
DISCOUNT: Buy one adult admission, get one of equal or lesser value free.

Princeton Depot Museum ❼

The Princeton Depot Museum features artifacts of the railroads that served the area and displays a caboose. It is located in the restored Chicago & Eastern Illinois passenger depot, which was built in 1875. The museum shares the depot with the Gibson County Visitors Bureau and is open Monday through Friday.

LOCATION: 702 W. Broadway Street, Princeton
PHONE: 812-385-0999
WEBSITE: gibsoncountyin.org
E-MAIL: info@gibsoncountyin.org

Wabash Valley Railroaders Museum ❽

The museum features two interlocking towers with operating machines, a depot, and a viewing platform adjacent to CSXT main lines. Haley Tower was one of the last manned interlocking towers in the Midwest, and the 1910 Spring Hill Tower was the last lever interlocking machine on the Canadian Pacific. It is open weekends May through October.

LOCATION: 1316 Plum Street, Terre Haute
PHONE: 812-238-9958
WEBSITE: haleytower.org
E-MAIL: president@haleytower.org

Hesston Steam Museum ⑨

Indiana

LOCATION: 1201 E. County Road 1000 North, La Porte
PHONE: 219-778-2783 or 219-872-5055
WEBSITE: hesston.org
E-MAIL: form on website

Jim Wrinn

This museum runs steam trains of two narrow gauges, two-foot and three-foot, in a parklike setting. It also offers miniature live steam operations and other steam-powered attractions including a sawmill and a steam crane.

CHOICES: Ride a steam locomotive, in your choice of gauges, through the museum's 155-acre site. Each train travels over a different route. Wander through a unique collection of steam equipment. Be sure to look for an 1889 Scottish-built locomotive and a Czech 0-4-0 built in 1940. On special days, watch the 92-ton, steam-powered log crane feed logs to the steam-powered lumber mill.

WHEN TO GO: Trains run weekends and holidays Memorial Day through Labor Day and then on several Sundays in October, when you can enjoy apple cider made from an antique press. On Memorial Day weekend and over the July 4th holiday, additional steam equipment runs, the sawmill operates, and other activities take place. In fall, ride the ghost train if you dare, and in December, try the Candy Cane Express. Several other special days are planned during the season.

GOOD TO KNOW: Keep an eye out for a Kiddieland train ride. The museum operates two of the locomotives from the now-closed suburban Chicago amusement park. The locomotives are coal-powered steam engines.

WORTH DOING: You can visit the La Porte County Historical Society Museum, which contains 80,000 artifacts. Among them are more than 800 antique firearms and weapons. If you visit in July, you can attend the La Porte County Fair, which features Pioneerland and its collection of historic buildings that include a log home, blacksmith shop, and barns.

DON'T MISS: The annual Hesston Steam & Power Show takes place over Labor Day weekend. Beside train rides, the event features the operation of antique farm equipment, tractors, and other machinery.

GETTING THERE: The museum is in northern Indiana near the Michigan border and is about a 90-minute drive from Chicago. It is easily accessible from either I-94 (Exit 1) or the Indiana toll road (Exit 49) on County Road 1000.

94

Hoosier Valley Railroad Museum ⑩

LOCATION: 507 Mulberry Street, North Judson
PHONE: 574-896-3950
WEBSITE: hvrm.railfan.net
E-MAIL: hvrm@yahoo.com

Don Nickel

What better location is there for a railroad museum than where four major rail lines crossed? North Judson hosted the Chesapeake & Ohio, Erie, Pennsylvania, and New York Central railroads in its glory days. Today, at the Hoosier Valley Railroad Museum, trains still journey down portions of the former C&O and Erie track on 10- and 20-mile excursions.

CHOICES: If you like cabooses, then the Hoosier Valley Railroad Museum should be high on your list. A vintage diesel engine pulls cabooses of Erie Lackawanna, Elgin, Joliet & Eastern, Nickel Plate Road, and other lines through rural Indiana scenery. The round trips take you to either English Lake (45 minutes) or La Crosse (2 hours). An open-air car is also available for seeing the sights on the train trip. Motive power includes an Alco S1 in Erie Lackawanna paint, an EMD Model 40, and a unique GE 95-ton switcher, freshly restored and repainted for the Interlake Iron Corporation. Museum displays include freight and passenger equipment, as well as C&O No. 2789, the last 2-8-4 acquired by the railroad.

WHEN TO GO: The Hoosier Valley Railroad Museum depot is open on Saturdays and during special events such as pumpkin and Halloween trains. Trains run from May to October currently, and plans are being made to expand into the holiday season.

GOOD TO KNOW: World War II reenactments occur on the museum grounds, as do a variety of other events.

WORTH DOING: Celebrate one of the area's crops during the annual Mint Festival, which takes place on Father's Day weekend with train rides, music, mint farm tours, and a mint cooking competition.

DON'T MISS: The Fort Wayne Railroad Historical Society's former Nickel Plate Road No. 765 has previously journeyed to North Judson and pulled excursions and special trains. Look for its return for a ride on a steam train.

GETTING THERE: North Judson is located on Highways 10 and 39 in northern Indiana. Signs on Highway 10 direct you to the museum site or just follow the tracks to the museum grounds.

Indiana Railway Museum ⑪

LOCATION: 1 Monon Street, French Lick
PHONE: 800-748-7246 or 812-936-2405
WEBSITE: indianarailwaymuseum.org
E-MAIL: info@indianarailwaymuseum.org

Jim Wrinn

For many years, the Southern Railway and the Monon Railroad brought scores of vacationers to the mineral spring baths in the southern Indiana hill country. Today, the museum offers a 20-mile round trip that leaves from the historic 1907 depot that served both railroads and travels through beautiful forested country and the 2,200-foot Burton tunnel.

CHOICES: Located in a historic passenger depot, the museum operates the French Lick, West Baden & Southern Railway. Two-hour excursions through the Hoosier National Forest travel along lakes and limestone cuts. Train robbery specials occur throughout the season, and Santa trains and haunted trains also run. The museum features an impressive collection of equipment with exhibits housed in the depot as well. The collection includes steam and diesel locomotives and more than 65 passenger and freight cars.

WHEN TO GO: The museum is open year-round Monday through Friday and also on weekends April through November. Trains operate weekends April through November and on several holidays. During summer, excursions also run Tuesday through Thursday, as well as Tuesday and Thursday trips in other months. Trips in October feature beautiful fall colors of the scenic Hoosier National Forest.

GOOD TO KNOW: French Lick is on Eastern Standard Time, which is good to remember when visiting from the Central time zone. You are still able to soak in the sulfer-rich spring water with 25-minute baths at the spas of the French Lick Springs Hotel and the West Baden Springs Hotel.

WORTH DOING: Southern Indiana is home to a variety of caves ready for exploring, such as Squire Boone Caverns, Wyandotte Caves, and Marengo Cave.

DON'T MISS: Be sure to check out the former Louisville, New Albany & Corydon Railroad boxcar No. 14023 repainted as a Pluto water car that shipped Pluto mineral water that was bottled by the French Lick Springs Hotel.

GETTING THERE: French Lick is in southern Indiana, easily accessible from Bloomington (60 miles), Columbus (90 miles), and Indianapolis (110 miles). From Indianapolis or Bloomington, take Highway 37 to Highway 56. Take Highway 56 west to French Lick and the museum. From Columbus, take I-65 to Highway 56.

DISCOUNT: $1 off regular adult ticket, up to four adults.

Indiana Transportation Museum ⑫

LOCATION: 825 Park Drive, Noblesville
PHONE: 317-773-6000 or 317-776-7887
WEBSITE: itm.org
E-MAIL: info@itm.org

Don Nickel

Located in Forest Park in Noblesville, the Indiana Transportation Museum offers visitors an excellent assortment of historic operating equipment, static displays, and excursions over a wide range of segments of a former Nickel Plate Road line.

CHOICES: Regular train rides on Saturdays and Sundays use either a vintage 1930s stainless steel passenger consist or a caboose train, depending on the length of the trip. The caboose trains are used on shorter rides. The *Hamiltonian* dinner train, using L&N dining car *Cross Keys Tavern*, operates from Fishers to Noblesville, while Dinner in the Diner departs from Noblesville and travels to different locations along the line. For a more casual meal, the Pizza Plus Express, operating on select Saturday evenings, offers pizza or other dining options. During summer months, ITM offers a weeknight getaway with Dinner or a Movie. The month of August brings the Indiana State Fair, and ITM operates the FairTrain and delivers passengers from Fishers to the fairgrounds.

WHEN TO GO: Indiana Transportation Museum's operating season begins in mid-April, continues through October, and then resumes with holiday trains in December. During the operating season, the museum grounds are open on Saturday and Sunday except during FairTrain operation.

GOOD TO KNOW: Tickets purchased for any excursion serve as an entry to the museum grounds, allowing riders to enjoy the displays located at Noblesville.

WORTH DOING: Make an entire day of your trip to the museum. Forest Park offers a wide assortment of opportunities for family fun. These include an aquatic center, carousel, miniature golf, and a playground area. Picnic areas are also available.

DON'T MISS: By making advance arrangements, you can tour several exhibits with a museum docent including an 1898 Florida East Coast business car and Nickel Plate Road No. 1, a 1929 Pullman heavyweight business car.

GETTING THERE: The museum is located in Forest Park, which is just north of Highway 32 on Highway 19 in Noblesville. Just 20 miles north of Indianapolis, the museum is easily accessed from I-69 and Highway 31.

TrainTown ⑬

LOCATION: 15808 Edgerton Road, New Haven
PHONE: 260-493-0765
WEBSITE: fortwaynerailroad.org
E-MAIL: contact@fortwaynerailroad.org

Don Nickel

TrainTown, operated by the Fort Wayne Railroad Historical Society, is home to one of the nation's largest operating steam locomotives, Nickel Plate Road 2-8-4 No. 765, which runs occasionally on tourist railroads around the country.

CHOICES: On weekends, you can tour TrainTown and check out the 400-ton No. 765, when it is not on tour, and other pieces of historic rail equipment. Make sure to visit the shops and talk with the volunteers who restore everything from baggage carts to locomotives. Excursions on Nickel Plate Road No. 765 take place on tourist railroads, such as the Cuyahoga Valley in Ohio, Steam Railroading Institute in Michigan, and Hoosier Valley Railroad in Indiana.

WHEN TO GO: Several times a year, the society conducts operating days with rides aboard a vintage caboose, and Santa trains running in December.

GOOD TO KNOW: No. 765, a 1944 Berkshire type, is one of the most modern and powerful steam locomotives still capable of operation. You can view the locomotive during several open houses the society holds during the year.

WORTH DOING: In September, take in the Johnny Appleseed Festival in honor of the folk hero, who is buried in Fort Wayne. It features music, crafts, food, and apples, of course.

DON'T MISS: The group offers an Engineer-for-an-Hour program with a 44-ton diesel. For a fee, you can operate the engine under supervision.

GETTING THERE: TrainTown is just east of Fort Wayne in the village of New Haven. From Fort Wayne, take I-469 to Exit 21. Turn right on Harper Road, then right on Ryan Road, and left on Edgerton Road.

Whitewater Valley Railroad 🔢

LOCATION: 455 Market Street, Connersville
PHONE: 765-825-2054
WEBSITE: whitewatervalleyrr.org
E-MAIL: form on website

Jim Wrinn

This surprising 19-mile line travels from Connersville to Metamora with much of the trip near the Whitewater Canal. The scenic route features excellent views of area forests and farms.

CHOICES: The railroad offers standard, open-window coaches as well as caboose rides on its 32-mile, five-hour round trip. A two-hour layover gives you a chance to tour Metamora, a restored canal town.

WHEN TO GO: Regular excursion trains operate on Saturdays and Sundays from May through October. During the year, watch for special event trains, such as the one to Metamora Canal Days, the Wild West Train, a dinner train, and fall foliage trains. Other events are themed around holidays and children's activities.

GOOD TO KNOW: The railroad has an ongoing restoration program and has recently completed a variety of projects including a Nickel Plate caboose.

WORTH DOING: Metamora is a popular getaway spot with plenty of art galleries, shops, and restaurants. Take time to explore the city's historic buildings. You can also watch its water-powered grist mill in action and take a boat ride along the canal.

DON'T MISS: Inspect the operating diesel built by the Lima Locomotive Works of Lima, Ohio. Believed to be the last of its kind in operation today, locomotive No. 25 was one of only 174 diesels built by this company, one of the most famous steam locomotive manufacturers of all time. The museum also owns three others from this builder.

GETTING THERE: Connersville is about 65 miles southeast of Indianapolis and is accessible from all directions. If coming from the north, take Highway 1 off I-70 into Connersville. The depot is on your left between Fourth and Fifth Streets.

IOWA

Marquette Depot Museum ❶

Housed in a renovated Milwaukee Road depot, the museum contains Milwaukee Road exhibits and general railroad artifacts. A restored caboose is on display. The museum is open daily May through October, and the depot also contains a travel information center.

LOCATION: 216 Edgar Street, Marquette
PHONE: 563-873-1200
WEBSITE: mcgreg-marq.org

Oelwein Railway Museum ❷

This museum consists of a former Railway Express Agency building, Chicago Great Western yard office, and tower with a display of locomotives, railcars, and artifacts. Climb the yard tower for a great view of the area. During Oelwein's annual Railroad Days weekend, you can ride on one of the museum's handcars.

LOCATION: 26 Second Avenue SW, Oelwein
PHONE: 319-283-1939
WEBSITE: cgwo.org
E-MAIL: info@cgwo.org

RailsWest Railroad Museum ❸

This former Chicago, Rock Island & Pacific passenger depot was built in 1899. Open year-round, the museum displays a Chicago, Burlington & Quincy 4-6-0 locomotive, Union Pacific 4-8-4 (Northern) locomotive, Plymouth locomotive, and Rock Island caboose. While in Council Bluffs, be sure to visit the one-of-a-kind Squirrel Cage Jail with its three floors of revolving cells.

LOCATION: 16th Avenue and S. Main Street, Council Bluffs
PHONE: 712-323-5182
WEBSITE: thehistoricalsociety.org
E-MAIL: Info@thehistoricalsociety.org

Boone & Scenic Valley Railroad ▪

LOCATION: 225 10th Street, Boone
PHONE: 800-626-0319 or 515-432-4249
WEBSITE: www.scenic-valleyrr.com
E-MAIL: info@bsvrr.com

Jeff Terry

Iowa isn't known for rolling terrain, but this fascinating railroad provides a scenic ride with interesting landscape through the Des Moines River Valley. The railroad runs across two impressive bridges, with the 156-foot-tall Bass Point Creek High Bridge being the highlight of a 15-mile round trip. The railroad's dinner, dessert, and picnic trains run on a slightly longer route.

CHOICES: The railroad is among the few in the country that offer steam-, diesel-, and electric-powered trains. You can ride a 1920s excursion in coach class or opt for the *Valley View* car, an open-air car that was formerly a C&NW transfer caboose. There is also limited seating in the train's caboose. Hop the restored 1915 Charles City & Western electric trolley for an interurban run through downtown Boone. And browse the railroad equipment displayed on the grounds and inside the depot's museum. Picnic trains travel the same route as the dinner or dessert trains, you just have to supply the lunch.

WHEN TO GO: Between Memorial Day and the end of October, excursion trains run daily, with steam locomotives on Saturdays. Dinner trains are scheduled on Fridays and Saturdays, and dessert and picnic trains on Saturdays. Trolleys operate on weekends. The museum grounds are open year-round. The indoor museum is open daily during the summer season and weekdays November through May.

GOOD TO KNOW: The railroad's Chinese steam engine, built in 1989, is one of two built at that time and imported to the United States for tour and excursion service.

WORTH DOING: The city of Boone celebrates its railroad heritage during Pufferbilly Days, an annual September event with train rides, a model train display, a parade, and a spike-driving contest.

DON'T MISS: On the dinner, dessert, and picnic trains, step outside on the *City of San Francisco*'s rear observation deck to experience the sights and smells.

GETTING THERE: The railroad is in central Iowa, an hour's drive northwest of Des Moines. Take I-35 to Ames and travel west on Highway 30 to Boone. Go north on Story Street through the business district to 10th Street and then go west six blocks to the depot.

DISCOUNT: $2 off each adult ticket, up to two adults, coach class tickets only.

Iowa

Midwest Central Railroad 5

LOCATION: 405 E. Threshers Road, Mount Pleasant
PHONE: 319-385-2912
WEBSITE: mcrr.org or oldthreshers.org

Jeff Terry

The Midwest Central Railroad was established when volunteers built a 1.25-mile loop of track around the Midwest Old Threshers Reunion site and acquired several steam locomotives and cars. Later, to bring visitors and exhibitors into the grounds, a counter-clockwise trolley loop line was built, dubbed the Midwest Electric Railway. On this loop line, streetcars from Iowa and Illinois and several countries operate, often with standing room only.

CHOICES: Both the railroad and the electric railway are in full operation during the Old Threshers Reunion. During the reunion, the trains haul approximately 35,000 to 40,000 passengers. In addition to rides, the railroad offers numerous seminars explaining how steam engines, track signals, and other railroad systems function.

WHEN TO GO: The Midwest Old Threshers Reunion begins the Thursday before Labor Day and ends on Labor Day. In addition, both the railway and the electric line operate trips over haunted rails each October, and the railroad runs a diesel-powered train for the 4th of July and a steam-powered North Pole Express.

GOOD TO KNOW: The Old Threshers Reunion is the largest of its kind in the United States. Farmers and tractor enthusiasts gather for fun and demonstrations of steam tractors, early gas tractors, and other period farm implements. There are tractor pulls, a steam-powered merry-go-round, and much more. It's like an old-fashioned state fair, but its emphasis is on living agricultural history. Several museum buildings on the grounds display everything from a family farmhouse to farm implements.

WORTH DOING: If you're a camper, stay at the Old Threshers campground and take the trolley into the grounds and then ride the train. You can take in the whole show without the hassle of parking and enjoy the sights and sounds of steam as you camp. Just be sure to make campground (or hotel) reservations early.

DON'T MISS: Take an international trolley ride. Midwest Electric Railway international streetcars include cars from Rio de Janeiro, Brazil, and Milan, Italy.

GETTING THERE: Probably the best way to visit Mount Pleasant is by driving. Located in southeastern Iowa, Mount Pleasant is south of Iowa City on Highway 218. The city is also served daily by Amtrak trains 5 and 6, the *California Zephyr*.

Union Pacific Railroad Museum ❻

LOCATION: 200 Pearl Street, Council Bluffs
PHONE: 712-329-8307
WEBSITE: uprrmuseum.org
E-MAIL: cajohnso@upcontractor.up.com

Union Pacific Railroad

Few railroads have gone to the great lengths of the Union Pacific to preserve and document their past. The Union Pacific Railroad Museum houses one of the oldest corporation collections of any kind in the country. Visitors will not find lines of steam locomotives, diesels, or rolling stock. Rather, they will be inundated with a tasteful display of artifacts, photographs, and documents that trace the development of the UP and the role it played in American West.

CHOICES: The museum can be taken in whole or digested by specific eras depending on your interests. The Union Pacific's history is a history of the American West. The collection dates from the mid-1800s and features original manuscripts such as reports from survey teams searching for the best route for laying track. Surveying equipment, early rail equipment, and nonrail artifacts from outlaws and Native Americans fill the building.

WHEN TO GO: With the exception of a raging snowstorm, even winter is a good time to visit the museum. It is open Tuesdays through Saturdays. Exhibits are changed and special events occur periodically during the year.

GOOD TO KNOW: One of the museum's most recent permanent exhibits is devoted to passenger service. It features cutaway coach, lounge, and dining cars as well as multimedia exhibits and thousands of artifacts.

WORTH DOING: Take time to tour both Council Bluffs and Omaha. Both are culturally rich cities with much to offer visitors. Council Bluffs has several casinos and is Iowa's leading gaming spot. The Henry Doorly Zoo in Omaha is a world-class zoo that appeals to adults as well as children.

DON'T MISS: The museum has a combination of static and interactive displays. The working locomotive simulator is educational as well as a lot of fun.

GETTING THERE: Omaha is an important regional airline hub with numerous flights from all directions daily, and Amtrak serves Omaha. Located on the east side of Council Bluffs, the museum is easily accessible for motorists from I-80 or I-29.

KANSAS

Atchison Rail Museum and Depot ❶

Adjacent to the Santa Fe depot, the Atchison Rail Museum features an outdoor collection of railcars. On summer weekend, the cars are open for viewing and a miniature railroad operates. The AT&SF freight depot was built in 1880 and renovated in 1989. It houses the county's historical society museum and its exhibits on Amelia Earhart and Lewis and Clark.

LOCATION: 200 S. 10th Street, Atchison
PHONE: 913-367-2427
WEBSITE: www.atchisonkansas.net

Great Overland Station ❷

The elegant and ornate former Union Pacific station is the setting for a museum, which features exhibits on the Union Pacific, Santa Fe, Kansas rail history, and Harvey Houses. It was designed by Gilbert Stanley Underwood, who also designed Omaha's Art Deco station. A rail park is also being developed.

LOCATION: 701 N. Kansas Avenue, Topeka
PHONE: 785-232-5533
WEBSITE: greatoverlandstation.com
E-MAIL: info@greatoverlandstation.com

Great Plains Transportation Museum ❸

The museum features an outdoor display of locomotives, cabooses, and cars, including Santa Fe steam locomotive No. 3768 and Santa Fe FP45 diesel No. 93. Indoor exhibits feature railroad signs, lanterns, tools, and other artifacts. It is open year-round on Saturdays and also on Sundays from April to October.

LOCATION: 700 E. Douglas Avenue, Wichita
PHONE: 316-263-0944
WEBSITE: gptm.us
E-MAIL: info@gptm.us

Santa Fe Depot ❹

Dating to 1911, the former Santa Fe depot is on the National Register of Historic Places. It contains railroad memorabilia, some that was found in the depot, and a model train display. The stylish brick building also houses the Cannonball Welcome Center. It is open year-round Monday through Friday.

LOCATION: 201 E. Sherman Avenue, Kingman
PHONE: 620-532-2142
WEBSITE: skyways.lib.ks.us/towns/Kingman/depot
E-MAIL: sfdepot@sbcglobal.net

Abilene & Smoky Valley Railroad ⑤

LOCATION: 200 S. Fifth Street, Abilene
PHONE: 888-426-6687 or 785-263-1077
WEBSITE: www.asvrr.org
E-MAIL: asvrail@gmail.com

Patrick Hiatte

A 90-minute, 10-mile round trip takes you through the Smoky Hill River Valley from historic Abilene to Enterprise. Along the way, you'll cross the Smoky Hill River on an early steel truss bridge, see stone houses and barns built by German settlers, and enjoy America's agricultural heartland.

CHOICES: You have a choice of steam or diesel power. Trains are pulled by a Santa Fe Pacific steam engine or an Alco S1 diesel. Recently restored, after sitting in an Abilene park for more than 40 years, steam engine No. 3415 operates on a limited schedule. Most often the diesel engine leads the train, which consists of a restored Katy Railroad coach and a pair of open-air (but shaded) gondola cars. An extra fare will get you on board the caboose or in the cab of the steam or diesel locomotive. On select Saturdays, you can extend your trip on the Silver Flyer railbus, which meets the train in Enterprise and continues to Woodbine for lunch.

WHEN TO GO: Trains run Wednesday through Sunday June through August and on weekends in May, September, and October. No. 3415 typically operates on Memorial Day, Independence Day, and Labor Day weekends and for the Central Kansas Fair the first weekend in August. Dinner trains catered by local restaurants also run.

GOOD TO KNOW: The Dwight D. Eisenhower Presidential Library and Museum site, including Ike's boyhood home, is across the tracks from the ASV depot.

WORTH DOING: Enjoy a cold bottle of sarsaparilla in Old Abilene Town, which is just south of the depot. It features replica buildings, gunfights, and dancing girls. Other nearby attractions include a 100-year-old operating carousel, the Greyhound Hall of Fame (dogs not buses), and museums for dolls, fashion, and patent medicine.

DON'T MISS: In addition to the ASV's restored Rock Island depot, a Santa Fe depot and Union Pacific depot and freight house are still standing. The UP depot is open to the public and houses the Abilene Visitors Center, where you can enjoy a sugar cookie made from Mamie Eisenhower's recipe.

GETTING THERE: Abilene is on I-70 about 150 miles west of Kansas City and about 90 miles north of Wichita. The ASV depot is about two miles south of I-70 off Highway 15 (Buckeye Avenue), just south of the Eisenhower complex.

Midland Railway 6

Deek Deitrick

LOCATION: 1515 W. High Street, Baldwin City
PHONE: 913-721-1211 or 785-594-6982 (depot)
WEBSITE: midland-ry.org

Deek Deitrick

Kansas

The Midland Railway offers 20-mile round trips in the pleasant Kansas countryside between Baldwin City and Ottawa. The Midland has a roster of first-generation diesels including an Alco RS3 in its original New York Central livery and an EMD NW2 in Midland Railway green. It uses several passenger coaches, cabooses, and a transfer caboose on its excursions.

CHOICES: Regular service includes one-hour excursions from Baldwin City to Norwood that cross two 200-foot trestles and two-hour trips to the end of the line at Ottawa Junction, where the line meets BNSF's Transcon. Midland also offers Thomas the Tank Engine, Halloween, and other specials.

WHEN TO GO: The Midland operates primarily on weekends from June to October, with Thursday trains added for summer. The Midland also participates in a variety of community festivals, including the Maple Leaf Festival, the third weekend in October.

GOOD TO KNOW: Baldwin City has a motel and B&B, plus a host of restaurants, all within two miles of the Midland station. More extensive offerings can be found 30 minutes away in Lawrence, Ottawa, or Olathe.

WORTH DOING: Visit the bridge near the Douglas-Franklin County line, which is a favorite photo location. Ask for directions at the depot. The Maple Leaf Festival occurs during the optimal leaf-viewing time and features craft displays, a carnival, and, of course, food.

DON'T MISS: Look through the Midland's 1906 Baldwin City depot, which is on the National Register of Historic Places.

GETTING THERE: The closest Amtrak stops are in Lawrence and Kansas City, Mo., and the closest major airport is in Kansas City. Baldwin City is 45 miles southwest of Kansas City on Highway 56. The Midland depot is on High Street, just west of the town square.

KENTUCKY

Historic Railpark and Train Museum ❶

A Louisville & Nashville depot has been transformed into a museum featuring two floors of interactive exhibits about railroading and the L&N. In the railpark, visitors can explore a passenger train that includes a post office car, diner, sleeper, and office car. The site is open year-round, and its Festival of Trains takes place in December.

LOCATION: 401 Kentucky Street, Bowling Green
PHONE: 270-745-7317
WEBSITE: historicrailpark.com
E-MAIL: form on website

Paducah Railroad Museum ❷

Operated by the Paducah Chapter of the National Railway Historical Society, the museum displays equipment and memorabilia from railroads including the three that served Paducah. It features replicas of a waiting room and freight office as well as section cars, tools, and an operating signaling system. A steam engine, caboose, and baggage car are displayed a block away.

LOCATION: 200 Washington Street, Paducah
PHONE: 270-519-7377
WEBSITE: paducahrr.org

Railway Museum of Greater Cincinnati ❸

The museum collects, restores, and displays equipment that belonged to the seven railroads then served Cincinnati. The outdoor yard contains more than 70 cars and locomotives. It includes a large number of Pullman cars, several switchers, and a Pennsylvania Railroad E8A diesel locomotive. It is open Wednesdays and Saturdays year-round.

LOCATION: 315 W. Southern Avenue, Covington
WEBSITE: cincirailmuseum.org
E-MAIL: questions@cincirailmuseum.org

Big South Fork Scenic Railway ▪

LOCATION: 100 Henderson Street, Stearns
PHONE: 800-462-5664 or 606-376-5330
WEBSITE: bsfsry.com
E-MAIL: info@bsfsry.com

Big South Fork Scenic Railway

In the 20th century, short lines and branches brought forth coal for use nationwide, and one of the primary locations was Stearns, home of the Kentucky & Tennessee short line. The coal is gone now, but the K&T has been reborn as a scenic railroad.

CHOICES: The railway offers three-hour trips through the Daniel Boone National Forest and Big South Fork National River and Recreation Area on the former Kentucky & Tennessee Railway. The train follows mountain streams, passes through a tunnel, and crosses a bridge as it descends 600 feet to the floor of the river valley. The ride includes a layover at the restored mining camp of Blue Heron.

WHEN TO GO: The railroad runs regular excursions on a varied schedule from April through October. During November, excursions run to the Big South Fork gorge. Several special events take place during the season, and Halloween and Christmas trains also run. Spring is especially beautiful in this part of the Appalachians because of all of the blooming plants that inhabit the mountains.

GOOD TO KNOW: The bridge over Roaring Paunch Creek is unique. It was constructed in 1937 from a used railroad bridge. The bridge girders needed to be offset because the line crossed the creek at an angle. The bridge's girders were offset in the opposite direction, so it was placed upside down, and the ties and track then added.

WORTH DOING: The McCreary County Museum, which is housed in the Stearns Coal and Lumber Company headquarters that was built in 1907, exhibits many facets of Appalachian life including the coal and lumber industries.

DON'T MISS: Take the walking tour of the Blue Heron Mine at the end of the run. Built in 1937, this mine and coal tipple operated until it was abandoned in 1962. It was restored with ghost structures (representations of where the actual buildings stood) and oral history exhibits by the National Park Service as part of the Big South Fork River and Recreation Area. You can also camp, hike, fish, and raft the river.

GETTING THERE: Stearns is 70 miles from Knoxville, Tenn., and 120 miles from Lexington. From Knoxville, take I-75 north to Exit 141. Take Route 63 west to the junction with Route 27. Take Route 27 north to Stearns. Turn left on Route 92 and travel west one mile to the depot.

DISCOUNT: $2 off each regular adult admission April-October; excludes specials.

Bluegrass Scenic Railroad 5

LOCATION: 175 Beasley Road, Versailles
PHONE: 800-755-2476 or 859-873-2476
WEBSITE: bgrm.org
E-MAIL: form on website

Bluegrass Scenic Railroad

The railroad offers one-hour excursions over three miles of former Southern Railroad track through the heart of Kentucky's Bluegrass region.

CHOICES: The railroad's museum operates a diesel-powered train made up of vintage coaches from the 1920s and 1930s, and many trips have a special theme. They include a Civil War train robbery, a mystery train, haunted trains, Santa specials, and the annual Trains (model), Planes & Automobiles Festival. Locomotive cab rides are also offered. You can view outdoor displays of railcars, equipment, and a rare watchman's shanty. Inside, museum exhibits showcase artifacts, including a working telegraph set, from Kentucky's railroad history.

WHEN TO GO: The grounds of the museum are open every day so you can inspect or photograph equipment when you like. Excursions operate on Saturdays and Sundays from mid-May through October.

GOOD TO KNOW: While in Bluegrass Country, you can tour its noted horse farms and bourbon distilleries.

WORTH DOING: Minutes away from the museum are several other local attractions that include the Woodford County Historical Society, the Aviation Museum of Kentucky, and the Wildside Winery and Vineyard. If you like smaller trains, visit the Nostalgia Station Toy Museum in downtown Versailles. It is housed in a restored 100-year-old Louisville & Nashville Railroad depot and contains numerous antique toy trains.

DON'T MISS: The museum has a large collection of locomotives and rolling stock in various stages of restoration. Interesting cars include U.S. Army boxcars, a Seaboard safety training car, and a Louisville & Nashville bay window caboose.

GETTING THERE: From Versailles, proceed south and west on Highway 62 for approximately 1.5 miles. Turn right onto Beasley Road into Woodford County Park. The museum is on the left after you cross the tracks.

Kentucky Railway Museum ⑤

LOCATION: 136 S. Main Street, New Haven
PHONE: 800-272-0152 or 502-549-5470
WEBSITE: kyrail.org
E-MAIL: info@kyrail.org

Alex Moss

Housed in a replica of the original New Haven station, the Kentucky Railway Museum has more than 50,000 items in its collection and more than 120 pieces of rolling stock and engines. The museum also operates excursions on 17 miles of former Louisville & Nashville track.

CHOICES: The museum's excursion trains take you on a 22-mile, 90-minute round trip through the scenic and historic Rolling Fork River Valley between New Haven and Boston. The museum operates a steam locomotive, ex-L&N 4-6-2 No. 152, on various steam weekends during the year. Diesel operating power includes ex-Monon BL2 No. 32 and ex-AT&SF CF-7 No. 2546. You can ride in open-air or air-conditioned coaches.

WHEN TO GO: The museum is open year-round, and excursions take place April through December. Trains run on weekends throughout the season with several Tuesday and Friday runs added during summer. Spring and fall scenery is nice, with temperatures in the 70s and low 80s.

GOOD TO KNOW: Steam engine No. 152 was built in 1905, is listed on the National Register of Historic Places, and was designated the official steam locomotive of the Commonwealth of Kentucky.

WORTH DOING: Abraham Lincoln was born nearby, and historical sites to visit include his birthplace, boyhood home, and the Lincoln Museum. Mammoth Cave National Park, Fort Knox, the Patton Museum of Cavalry and Armor, and My Old Kentucky Home State Park are also close by.

DON'T MISS: The museum offers special excursions that include dinner trains, murder mystery trains, locomotive cab rides, train holdups, Santa trains, and days out with Thomas the Tank Engine.

GETTING THERE: The museum is about 45 miles from Louisville and 65 miles from Lexington. If driving from Louisville, take I-65 south to Exit 105, Route 61 to Boston, and then Route 52 to New Haven. From Lexington, take Highway 60 west to the Martha Layne Collins Parkway. Take the parkway to Exit 21 and then Route 31E to New Haven.

My Old Kentucky Dinner Train 7

LOCATION: 602 N. Third Street, Bardstown
PHONE: 866-801-3463 or 502-348-7500
WEBSITE: www.kydinnertrain.com
E-MAIL: form on website

R. J. Corman

My Old Kentucky Dinner Train operates in 1940s dining cars on 16 miles of former Louisville & Nashville track between Bardstown and Limestone Springs. The passenger waiting room is located in Bardstown's former limestone freight house, which dates from 1860 and is on the National Register of Historic Places.

CHOICES: The train offers both lunch and dinner trips, as well as murder mystery, Halloween, North Pole and other special events trains. It offers 2.5-hour lunch excursions on Saturdays. Other lunch and dinner excursions run Tuesday through Sunday on a varied schedule. Trains are pulled by two ex-Southern FP7s. The Budd-built lightweight cars are of AT&SF, C&O, and PRR ancestry, including the former C&O No. 1921 that operated on President Dwight Eisenhower's funeral train. Two restored depots, Deatsville and Limestone Springs, can be seen on the line.

WHEN TO GO: The train operates year-round, and the scenery is especially nice in spring and fall, with temperatures in the 70s and low 80s. Tobacco is grown from June through August and can be viewed along the route.

GOOD TO KNOW: Founded in 1780, Bardstown is Kentucky's second-oldest city and features a mix of old and new inns, restaurants, and shops. Several local distilleries give tours, and the Kentucky Railway Museum is 15 minutes away.

WORTH DOING: The area is rich in history and includes Abraham Lincoln's birthplace and his boyhood home. The Civil War Museum at Old Bardstown Village is dedicated to the war's western theater. The village also contains 11 historic log cabins. The Women of the Civil War Museum and several other museums are also nearby.

DON'T MISS: The train passes through part of the Bernheim Forest, a private 14,000-acre nature preserve, a habitat for a variety of trees, vegetation, and wildlife. While in the forest, the train passes slowly over the 310-foot-long, 60-foot-high Jackson Hollow timber trestle built for predecessor Bardstown & Louisville Railroad in 1860.

GETTING THERE: Bardstown is about 40 miles south of Louisville and 55 miles southwest of Lexington. When driving from Louisville, take I-65 south to Exit 112 and then Route 245 east. From Lexington, take Route 60 west and then the Martha Layne Collins Parkway.

LOUISIANA

DeQuincy Railroad Museum ❶

Home to the DeQuincy Railroad Museum, the former Kansas City Southern depot is an outstanding example of Mission Revival architecture and is on the National Register of Historic Places. It displays a 1913 Alco steam locomotive, a caboose, and a passenger coach as well as artifacts and memorabilia. The annual Louisiana Railroad Days Festival is held here in April.

LOCATION: 400 Lake Charles Avenue, DeQuincy
PHONE: 337-786-2823
WEBSITE: cityofdequincy.com

New Orleans Streetcars ❷

Streetcars are a great way to see New Orleans, and if you have the desire, you can ride three different streetcar lines. The St. Charles line features the oldest continuously operating streetcar in the world. It passes antebellum mansions, historic monuments, universities, and other sights. The Canal Street line takes passengers from the French Market through the central business district to City Park Avenue. The Riverfront line travels the downtown area along the Mississippi River.

LOCATION: Carrolton Avenue and Claiborne Avenue, New Orleans
PHONE: 504-248-3900
WEBSITE: neworleansonline.com/tools/transportation/gettingaround/streetcars.html

Southern Forest Heritage Museum ❸

At this museum, a guided tour takes you around a 57-acre historic sawmill complex, where you'll see a roundhouse and other industrial structures, three early logging locomotives, two McGiffert loaders, a Clyde skidder, and other steam equipment. Motor-car rides on original Red River & Gulf Railroad track are also available. An exhibit also highlights the history of the railroad.

LOCATION: 77 Long Leaf Road, Long Leaf
PHONE: 318-748-8404
WEBSITE: forestheritagemuseum.org
E-MAIL: longleaf@centurytel.net

MAINE

Belfast & Moosehead Lake Railway ❶

Excursion trains depart from the historic Brooks railroad station (which is being restored to its 1940s appearance), run to Waldo, and return. You can enjoy the 70-minute trip aboard a coach or open-air car led by a former Belfast & Moosehead Lake Railroad locomotive. Special fall and pizza trains also operate. For a unique perspective, and some exercise, try pedaling a rail bike along the tracks for four miles.

LOCATION: 31 Veterans Highway, Brooks
PHONE: 207-722-3899
WEBSITE: brookspreservation.org
E-MAIL: information@brookspreservation.org

Boothbay Railway Village ❷

Powered by one of three operating engines, a two-foot-gauge steam train takes you around a re-created historic village with several stations and an engine house. Exhibits show the history of Maine narrow gauge railroads, and various pieces of rolling stock and equipment are on display, as are more than 50 antique or classic automobiles and other vehicles.

LOCATION: 586 Wiscasset Road, Boothbay
PHONE: 207-633-4727
WEBSITE: railwayvillage.org
E-MAIL: staff@railwayvillage.org

Cole Land Transportation Museum ❸

The museum houses 200 antique land transportation vehicles and 2,000 photographs of life in early Maine. Its railroad collection includes one of the first Bangor & Aroostook diesels, a Canadian Pacific section shack, a Maine Central caboose, and a relocated station.

LOCATION: 405 Perry Road, Bangor
PHONE: 207-990-3600
WEBSITE: colemuseum.org
E-MAIL: mail@colemuseum.org

Downeast Scenic Railroad ▨

This scenic railroad travels from Ellsworth to Ellsworth Falls and Washington Junction and then returns to Ellsworth over the historic Calais branch line. For the 90-minute weekend excursions, passengers may ride in a restored vintage passenger car, open-air car, or an 1918 Reading caboose.

LOCATION: 32 Main Street, Ellsworth
PHONE: 866-449-7245 or 207-667-7819
WEBSITE: downeastscenicrail.org
E-MAIL: info@downeastscenicrail.org

Oakfield Railroad Museum ❺

Exhibits in the restored Oakfield station include hundreds of photographs dating to the beginning of the Bangor & Aroostook Railroad in 1891, vintage signs, signal lanterns, railroad maps, and telegraph equipment. A restored caboose, handcar, and motor car are also displayed. It is open summer on Saturday and Sunday afternoons.

LOCATION: 40 Station Street, Oakfield
PHONE: 207-757-8575
WEBSITE: oakfieldmuseum.org
E-MAIL: oakfieldmuseum@pwless.net

Seashore Trolley Museum ❻

The museum offers a 25-minute ride through the countryside aboard a restored early 1900s electric streetcar. There are more than 50 streetcars on display in three carbarns. Almost every state is represented as well as Canada, Japan, and several European countries. Special events, including a sunset ride with ice cream, are scheduled throughout the year.

LOCATION: 195 Log Cabin Road, Kennebunkport
PHONE: 207-967-2712
WEBSITE: trolleymuseum.org
E-MAIL: form on website

Maine Eastern Railroad 7

LOCATION: 4 Union Street, Rockland
PHONE: 866-637-2457
WEBSITE: maineeasternrailroad.com
E-MAIL: info@maineeasternrailroad.com

Alex Mayes

The Maine Eastern offers scenic coastline views from big-windowed, stainless steel coaches pulled by former New Haven Railroad FL9 locomotives. The railroad operates on a 57-mile branch line between Brunswick and Rockland. Along the line, there are 33 bridges and more than 100 curves.

CHOICES: The Maine Eastern's season runs from May through October, with two daily round trips Wednesday through Saturday between Rockland and Brunswick and one round trip on Sundays. All trains include air-conditioned coaches and a café-dining car. Extra fare parlor accommodations are also offered.

WHEN TO GO: Ride to Rockland to attend the North Atlantic Blues Festival or the Maine Windjammer Parade in July, or enjoy the Maine Lobster Festival in August. There are numerous special events in the fall during the color season, and the train is a great way to avoid the traffic jams on Route 1.

GOOD TO KNOW: In addition to the train trip, Maine Eastern offers an array of travel packages to suit every taste, including train and sail options, stop-offs to explore the quaint towns of Bath and Wiscasset, lighthouse tours, and multi-day offerings. Trips on sailing vessels and even working lobster boats can be arranged.

WORTH DOING: There is plenty to do in the mid-coast area, including whale-watching trips, antique shops, museums, and historic sites. Well-known Acadia National Park is further up the coast, and ferries from Rockland carry visitors to several offshore islands. Scenic beaches, quaint villages, and fabulous views are everywhere.

DON'T MISS: Nearby attractions include the Owl's Head Transportation Museum, the Wiscasset, Waterville & Farmington Railway Museum, and Boothbay Railway Village.

GETTING THERE: Brunswick is just off I-295, about half an hour north of Portland and 2.5 hours from Boston, while Rockland is another 90 minutes north. Traffic on Route 1 between Brunswick and Rockland is heavy and slow-moving, especially on summer and fall weekends.

Maine Narrow Gauge Railroad & Museum **8**

LOCATION: 58 Fore Street, Portland
PHONE: 207-828-0814
WEBSITE: mngrr.org
E-MAIL: mngrr@maine.rr.com

Arthur Hussey II

The Maine Narrow Gauge Railroad & Museum operates along the Eastern Promenade fronting Casco Bay. Excursions offer spectacular views of ferries, sailboats, cruise ships, lobster boats, and freighters as well as the many islands that dot the bay.

CHOICES: The railroad operates diesel locomotives with authentic open-window coaches and open-sided excursion cars. Tour the museum and see several beautifully restored passenger coaches, including *Rangeley*, the only two-foot gauge private car ever built. Also on display is a railbus used on the Sandy River and Bridgton & Harrison Railroads.

WHEN TO GO: The museum is open year-round, and trains run daily late May through October and on weekends during the rest of the schedule. Various special events, including a Polar Express train, take place throughout the year.

GOOD TO KNOW: Most of the railroad's equipment once operated on two famed Maine two-footers: the Sandy River & Rangeley Lakes and the Bridgton & Harrison. Steam engine No. 7 is currently undergoing restoration and will return to service when work is completed, hopefully in time for the Polar Express trains in December 2011.

WORTH DOING: The Portland waterfront is a busy area for tourists, and there are many other attractions in the area, including much of the original Federal-style architecture found in Maine's second largest city.

DON'T MISS: Ride on the water side of the train for the best views. A walking and bike path follows the line for its entire length, which makes taking action photos easy.

GETTING THERE: Portland International Airport is nearby, and Boston's Logan Airport is about two hours south. Amtrak's *Downeaster* runs between Boston's North Station and Portland. I-95 passes just west of Portland.

DISCOUNT: $1 off each train ticket.

Sandy River & Rangeley Lakes Railroad

LOCATION: 128 Bridge Street, Phillips
PHONE: 207-778-3621
WEBSITE: www.srrl-rr.org

Bob Troup

This growing museum strives to re-create a portion of the legendary two-foot gauge Sandy River & Rangeley Lakes. Volunteers have been laying track on a section of the original roadbed, restoring rolling stock, and moving buildings that once served the railroad to the museum site.

CHOICES: Trains operate on select weekends from June through October. Included with the train ride is a walking tour of the museum and a visit to the replica roundhouse built on the site of the Old Stone Fort, the first roundhouse on the Sandy River. The train is pulled by a replica of locomotive No. 4 or by a gasoline-mechanical locomotive, and visitors ride in a genuine Sandy River coach or a replica caboose.

WHEN TO GO: Trains run five (and sometimes six) times a day on the hour. A ghost train runs in October.

GOOD TO KNOW: At 112 miles, the original Sandy River & Rangeley Lakes was the longest of Maine's five narrow gauge railroads. The railway has more than 25 pieces of equipment.

WORTH DOING: Make time to visit the Phillips Historical Society, which maintains a large collection of Sandy River materials in its museum. Also, the original Phillips depot, seen in many historic photos, is nearby.

DON'T MISS: Be sure to look around the museum yard to view rolling stock awaiting restoration as well as other relics from Franklin County's railroading past.

GETTING THERE: Phillips is in far western Maine near a number of the popular Maine ski resorts and the lakes region. From I-95, take Exit 35 and follow Route 4 about 70 miles to Phillips.

Wiscasset, Waterville & Farmington Railway 🔟

LOCATION: 97 Cross Road, Alna
PHONE: 207-882-4193
WEBSITE: wwfry.org
E-MAIL: info@wwfry.org

Maine

Steve Hussar

The railway is a faithful re-creation of a portion of the original two-foot gauge Wiscasset, Waterville & Farmington Railway, which was abandoned following a wreck in 1933, and it follows the original right-of-way.

CHOICES: Steam- and diesel-powered trains operate between the Sheepscot station and Alna Center. Be sure to ride in Wiscasset & Quebec coach No. 3, a gem built by Jackson & Sharpe in 1894. Then visit the railway's shop, where museum volunteers rebuild and maintain rolling stock using traditional skills and techniques.

WHEN TO GO: The museum is open every Saturday year-round, as well as on Sundays beginning Memorial Day weekend through mid-October. Trains operate Saturdays and Sundays June through September and just on Saturdays the rest of the operating season. September and October are the best months to visit, after the summer crowds have diminished and the insects are dormant.

GOOD TO KNOW: Maine was famous for its two-foot gauge railways, a thrifty New England response to the expense of building and maintaining a railroad. Five two-foot gauge railways once operated in Maine, but all were closed by 1941.

WORTH DOING: The mid-coast region of Maine features plenty of attractions, lodging choices, and restaurants. Be sure to sample the bounty of the sea, especially lobsters, clams, and fish. Room rates are highest in July and August, and reservations are a must. Traffic on Route 1, the main coastal artery, is very heavy and slow moving on summer weekends.

DON'T MISS: Visit the museum during the spring and fall work weekends. At these times, volunteers from all over the country arrive to construct track, extending the railway a thousand feet or more during each session. You can even join in if you like.

GETTING THERE: The closest airports are in Portland and Augusta. The museum itself is on a rural road just off Route 218 about four miles from Wiscasset and Route 1.

MARYLAND

Bowie Railroad Museum ❶

This museum consists of a renovated freight station, switch tower, waiting shed, and caboose. The station and tower contain photos and artifacts. The museum is open Tuesday through Sunday. The Old Town Bowie Welcome Center and Children's Museum is next to the railroad museum.

LOCATION: 8614 Chestnut Avenue, Bowie
PHONE: 301-809-3089
WEBSITE: cityofbowie.org
E-MAIL: pwilliams@cityofbowie.org

Chesapeake Beach Railway Museum ❷

From 1900 until 1935, the Chesapeake Beach Railway carried passengers to the Chesapeake Beach resort in cars such as the *Dolores*, which is on display. Housed in the original station, the museum exhibits photographs and artifacts of the railroad and the resort. It is open daily April through October and on weekends in March and November. Special events also take place.

LOCATION: 4155 Mears Avenue, Chesapeake Beach
PHONE: 410-257-3892
WEBSITE: cbrm.org

Ellicott City Station ❸

Located on the B&O Railroad's historic Old Main Line, Ellicott City Station could be the oldest surviving railroad station in the country. The main depot building was completed in 1831, and the freight house was built in 1855. The museum displays a replica of the first horse-drawn passenger railcar, the *Pioneer*, and a 1927 caboose. Joint admission with the B&O Railroad Museum in Baltimore is available.

LOCATION: 2711 Maryland Avenue, Ellicott City
PHONE: 410-461-1945
WEBSITE: ecborail.org
E-MAIL: form on website

Gaithersburg Community Museum ❹

The museum features permanent and rotating exhibits in a restored 1884 B&O freight house. An outdoor display includes a 1918 Buffalo Creek & Gauley steam locomotive, a C&O bay window caboose, and a troop kitchen car. You can also look through the restored station, which is now a coffee shop, and History Park. It is open Thursday through Saturday.

LOCATION: 9 S. Summit Avenue, Gaithersburg
PHONE: 301-258-6160
WEBSITE: gaithersburgmd.gov/museum

Hagerstown Roundhouse Museum ❺

Located near the roundhouse site in a historic building, the museum presents local rail history through artifacts, photos, and model train layouts. A Baldwin diesel, two Western Maryland cabooses, and a Hagerstown & Frederick trolley are on display. It is open Friday through Sunday.

LOCATION: 300 S. Burhans Boulevard, Hagerstown
PHONE: 301-739-4665
WEBSITE: www.roundhouse.org
E-MAIL: form on website

Baltimore & Ohio Railroad Museum ⑥

LOCATION: 901 W. Pratt Street, Baltimore
PHONE: 410-752-2490
WEBSITE: borail.org
E-MAIL: info@borail.org

Alexander Mitchell IV

Known as the birthplace of American railroading, the B&O Railroad Museum combines a diverse collection of railroad artifacts and rolling stock with a landmark setting and a unique focus upon the Baltimore & Ohio and its subsidiaries and successors.

CHOICES: The museum occupies several vintage buildings, and it houses the largest collection of 19th century locomotives in North America. Its fully covered roundhouse and turntable is a distinctive feature of the skyline. The museum features B&O locomotives dating back to 1836 and operable replicas of the 1831 *Tom Thumb* and the *Lafayette*. Later steamers and diesels are well represented, and numerous passenger cars and freight cars round out the collection. Allow at least a half day for a full tour, including a train ride down the first mile of American intercity railroading.

WHEN TO GO: Between April 2011 and December 2015, the Museum will feature numerous displays and events focused on the 150th anniversary of the American Civil War and its connections to American railroading. The museum is open year-round, with special events offered throughout. Train rides are not offered during February and March.

GOOD TO KNOW: The B&O museum is located in a residential neighborhood just west of downtown and the city's major stadiums. You can walk from downtown's Inner Harbor or Camden Yards district, take a cab or city bus, or ride the Charm City Circulator's Orange Route shuttle directly to the museum.

WORTH DOING: Baltimore has a host of other attractions, including the Baltimore Streetcar Museum, the National Aquarium, the Maryland Zoo, the Walters Art Museum, and Fort McHenry.

DON'T MISS: Combined admission to the nearby Ellicott City Railroad Museum, the oldest railroad station in America, is also available.

GETTING THERE: Baltimore is served by many airlines, Amtrak, and mass transit, and the museum is only a few minutes off I-95 by car.

Baltimore Streetcar Museum ❼

LOCATION: 1901 Falls Road, Baltimore
PHONE: 410-547-0264
WEBSITE: baltimorestreetcar.org
E-MAIL: form on website

Alexander Mitchell IV

Relive a piece of Baltimore's history by hopping on one of the city's original streetcars for a one-mile ride. The trip takes you along the former right-of-way of the Maryland & Pennsylvania in the Jones Falls Valley and passes a former freight house and roundhouse before turning on a loop for the return ride.

CHOICES: In Trolley Theatre, you can view a short presentation about trolleys and streetcars that ran in Baltimore from 1859 to 1963. Guides will also lead you on a tour of the car house, where you can view historic Baltimore streetcars, ranging from a horse car to the last PCC that ran in Baltimore, several buses, and trackless trolleys. The visitors center houses museum displays and a research library. There is a family admission plan as well as individual admissions. Admission includes unlimited rides, the car house tour, and museum access.

WHEN TO GO: The museum is open on Sunday afternoons year-round and additionally on Saturday afternoons June through October. If visiting Baltimore in summer, it can be excessively hot and muggy. Special events take place during the year.

GOOD TO KNOW: Since 1968, the Baltimore Streetcar Museum has operated its distinctive and unique collection of streetcars and other transit equipment, one of the only transit museum collections to focus exclusively on a collection from one city.

WORTH DOING: Baltimore is full of interesting things to see including the picturesque Inner Harbor, National Aquarium, and the USS *Constellation*. The historic Mount Vernon neighborhood, with the Walters Art Museum, Meyerhoff Symphony Hall, eclectic shops and restaurants, is a short rail or bus ride to the south.

DON'T MISS: In the car house, look for Baltimore Transit Company's rare crane car 3715. It is the only known piece of Baltimore Transit's work equipment on rail saved from the '50s. For rail fans, the B&O Railroad museum is 10 minutes away.

GETTING THERE: The museum is two blocks west of Charles Street and Maryland Avenue, major north-south streets. Baltimore has plenty of transportation alternatives. From Amtrak's Penn Station, it is a few minutes' walk. The MTA Light Rail—spiritual successor to the streetcars—also serves Penn Station with connections to downtown and Baltimore Washington International Airport.

National Capital Trolley Museum ❽

LOCATION: 1313 Bonifant Road, Colesville
PHONE: 301-384-6088
WEBSITE: dctrolley.org
E-MAIL: form on website

National Capital Trolley Museum

Inspired by streetcar buildings of the past, the National Capital Trolley Museum has a striking new look. The new visitor center provides an educational and entertaining look at the history of the region's streetcar systems, complete with an authentic trolley ride.

CHOICES: The museum is divided in three halls. In the Main Hall, you'll learn about the history of local streetcar systems, watch several silent films starring streetcars and actor Harold Lloyd, and see a model electric railway. Conduit Hall contains exhibits that explain how streetcars were powered. In Streetcar Hall, you get a close-up look at a variety of trolleys in the museum's collection, some that have not been on recent display.

WHEN TO GO: The museum is open weekends year-round as well as on select Thursdays and Fridays April through November. In summer, the museum offers special programs for children that include activities such as storytelling and crafts.

GOOD TO KNOW: Maintenance and weather determine the length of a trolley ride on a given day. There are three service levels: red, white, and blue. Red provides an 8-minute ride, white is a 15-minute trip, and blue gives you a 20-minute ride. The first streetcar leaves 30 minutes after opening and the last one 30 minutes before closing. Unlimited trolley rides are included with admission. You can call the museum to find out which service level will apply for the day of your visit.

WORTH DOING: Downtown Washington, with its wealth of cultural and historic attractions, is just 14 miles away.

DON'T MISS: Among the museum's streetcar collection, look for Blackpool Transit System No. 606, an unusual open car that ran on Blackpool's promenade in the UK.

GETTING THERE: The museum is located in Northwest Branch Park, about a 20-minute drive from the Capital Beltway. Bonifant Road is 5.5 miles north of I-495. Glenmont is the closest Washington Metrorail subway station. From there, Montgomery County Ride-On Bus No. 26 leaves for the museum at 30-minute intervals on Saturdays and Sundays.

DISCOUNT: 10% off museum shop purchase.

Walkersville Southern Railroad 9

LOCATION: 34 W. Pennsylvania Avenue, Walkersville
PHONE: 877-363-9777 or 301-898-0899
WEBSITE: wsrr.org
E-MAIL: admin@wsrr.org

Alexander Mitchell IV

The Walkersville Southern Railroad takes you on a pleasant eight-mile, 70-minute round trip through woods and farmland, past a restored century-old lime kiln, and crosses the Monocacy River over a rebuilt bridge.

CHOICES: Trains depart from the original Pennsylvania Railroad station pulled by one of the railroad's collection of five industrial switchers, which include a 1939 Davenport gas-mechanical, a rare 1942 EMD Model 40 four-wheel diesel, and a 1942 Plymouth gas-mechanical. Passengers may ride in former Long Island Rail Road coaches, a sheltered open flatcar with benches, a caboose, or a refurbished troop carrier. Parks and picnic stands are located at both ends of the line, and passengers may lay over between runs to eat and play.

WHEN TO GO: In May, June, and September, there are two departures on Saturdays and Sundays. In October, there are three trips on Saturdays and Sundays. In July and August, there are two departures on Saturdays only. Numerous special events run throughout the year, including mystery dinner trains, holiday trains, teddy bear picnics, and Jesse James holdups.

GOOD TO KNOW: The railroad's museum occupies a former ice plant and features rail artifacts from the line and a model railroad.

WORTH DOING: For Civil War buffs, Gettysburg and Harpers Ferry are about an hour away. The railroad also conducts a Civil War reenactment.

DON'T MISS: The railway line between Walkersville and Frederick was built in 1869. Take in the railroad's station, built by the PRR in the late 1800s, and the freight house, which also dates from that period.

GETTING THERE: The railroad is 50 miles from Baltimore or Washington, D.C. From Baltimore, take I-70 west to Exit 53B near Frederick. Follow Route 15 north for six miles and then turn right onto Biggs Ford Road. Travel about two miles and look for a grain elevator, which is adjacent to the station.

Western Maryland Scenic Railroad 🔟

LOCATION: 13 Canal Street, Cumberland
PHONE: 800-872-4650 or 301-759-4400
WEBSITE: wmsr.com
E-MAIL: form on website

Jim Wrinn

Of all the Appalachian freight railroads, the Western Maryland was one of the most beloved because of its excellent steam power, which tackled difficult mountain grades. Today, the trip out of Cumberland on the roadbed of the main line, with a short detour the last few miles onto a branch into Frostburg, is one of the best parts of the Western Maryland.

CHOICES: Traveling through the mountains of western Maryland, this 32-mile round trip take takes you from Cumberland's restored Western Maryland Railway station to an 1891 Cumberland & Pennsylvania depot in Frostburg. You'll ride aboard restored coaches pulled by a 1916 Baldwin steam locomotive or a vintage diesel engine. Club and first-class seating is available on a variety of trains. Club service includes an assigned seat in a dining car or lounge car, a beverage, and food item. First-class seating includes your choice of a lunch. The railroad also offers murder mystery, Christmas, and other special trains.

WHEN TO GO: Trains run May through December. October, during the height of the fall color season, is especially beautiful, and reservations are required because these trains fill up quickly.

GOOD TO KNOW: When the train arrives in Frostburg, you have a 90-minute layover. Be sure to find a good spot to watch the locomotive change directions on the turntable. You will also have time to walk down Main Street for shopping or dining.

WORTH DOING: The Western Maryland Station houses the Chesapeake & Ohio Canal National Historical Park's Cumberland Visitor Center, where you can learn more about the C&O Canal.

DON'T MISS: Stick to the right side of the train. Leaving Cumberland, the train passes through the Narrows, a gap in the mountain that also allows the highway and parallel CSX (the former B&O) an escape to the west. Just beyond is famous Helmstetter's Curve, a sharp turn in the railroad tracks. From here on, views remain mostly on the right side as the train makes its way higher into the mountains.

GETTING THERE: When driving, Cumberland is about 2.5 hours from Baltimore, Washington, or Pittsburgh. From either direction, the Western Maryland Station is easily reached from Exit 43C off I-68 in downtown Cumberland.

MASSACHUSETTS

Chatham Railroad Museum ❶

This restored country depot is situated on its original site. Museum exhibits feature hundreds of railroad artifacts from the Chatham Railroad Company and other railroads, including a restored 1910 New York Central caboose and telegraph instruments.

LOCATION: 153 Depot Road, Chatham
PHONE: 508-945-5199
WEBSITE: town.chatham.ma.us

Edaville USA ❷

This is a family fun park with a two-mile train ride through a 1,300-acre cranberry plantation. There are 11 amusement rides and an indoor play area. Special events include National Cranberry Festival, Christmas Festival of Lights, and many others.

LOCATION: 5 Pine Street, Carver
PHONE: 877-332-8455 or 508-866-8190
WEBSITE: edaville.com
E-MAIL: info@edaville.com

Lowell National Historical Park ❸

The park includes a variety of structures related to industry, 5.6 miles of canals, and restored mill buildings. It displays a Boston & Maine 0-6-0 Manchester locomotive built in 1910, a combine car, and several open-air trolleys. Trolley tours and rides operate March through November. You can also take in the National Streetcar Museum which is across from the park's visitor center.

LOCATION: 246 Market Street, Lowell
PHONE: 978-970-5000
WEBSITE: www.nps.gov/lowe
E-MAIL: form on website

Old Colony & Fall River Railroad Museum ❹

The museum, located in railroad cars that include a renovated Pennsylvania Railroad coach, features artifacts of New England railroads such as Penn Central, Conrail, Amtrak, and the New Haven.

LOCATION: 2 Water Street, Fall River
PHONE: 508-674-9340
WEBSITE: ocandfrrailroadmuseum.com
E-MAIL: info@ocandfrrailroadmuseum.com
DISCOUNT: $2 off an adult coach fare.

Shelburne Falls Trolley Museum ❺

The museum features a 15-minute ride on restored trolley car No. 10, which was built in 1896. For an added fee, and with a little instruction, you can become an instant motorman and run No. 10 yourself. Pump car rides are also available. The museum displays railroad and trolley artifacts, a steam locomotive, a caboose, and other items.

LOCATION: 14 Depot Street, Shelburne Falls
PHONE: 413-625-9443
WEBSITE: sftm.org
E-MAIL: trolley@sftm.org

Berkshire Scenic Railway 6

LOCATION: 10 Willow Creek Road, Lenox
PHONE: 413-637-2210
WEBSITE: berkshirescenicrailroad.org
E-MAIL: form on website

Scott Hartley

The Berkshire Scenic Railway Museum operates excursion trains that follow the scenic Housatonic River over part of the onetime New Haven Railroad's route to Pittsfield. Operations are based out of the railway's beautifully restored New Haven station at Lenox, and trains run south to Stockbridge. The adjacent museum includes many pieces of rolling stock.

CHOICES: Berkshire Scenic operates on Saturdays, Sundays, and federal holidays from Memorial Day to late October. There are two departure times for a 90-minute, 20-mile round trip to Stockbridge. There also is a 45-minute narrated trip to Lee and back, which is well-suited for younger riders. Trains consist of former Delaware, Lackawanna & Western coaches from the 1920s. Operating locomotives include a former New York Central EMD SW8, an ex-Pennsylvania Railroad EMD SW9, a former Maine Central Alco S1, a GE 50-ton switcher, and a borrowed Housatonic Railroad RS3M (a onetime Lackawanna Alco RS3 rebuilt with an EMD engine).

WHEN TO GO: New England's famed fall foliage peaks in this region in early October. During that time, expect full trains, high lodging rates, and crowded roads. It is less congested at other times. Several special events are scheduled during the year.

GOOD TO KNOW: There is abundant lodging in Lenox, Lee, and Pittsfield. The Berkshire Hills are known for skiing, but the area is a year-round tourist destination. Fine dining as well as fast-food chains can be found throughout the region.

WORTH DOING: The museum's 1903 Lenox station contains an impressive collection of local railroad historical artifacts. Housed in an old coach on the museum grounds, the Gilded Age exhibit displays the history of this era in Berkshire County.

DON'T MISS: Nearby attractions include weekend concerts at Tanglewood (the summer home of the Boston Symphony), the Hancock Shaker Village, and the Norman Rockwell Museum.

GETTING THERE: The Berkshire Scenic Railway is located near Routes 7 and 20, five miles north of Massachusetts Turnpike (I-90) Exit 2. In downtown Lenox, take Housatonic Street east for 1.5 miles to Willow Creek Road. Amtrak's *Lake Shore Limited* stops daily at nearby Pittsfield. The nearest commercial air service is at Albany, N.Y., or Hartford, Conn.

Cape Cod Central Railroad 🄬

LOCATION: 252 Main Street, Hyannis
PHONE: 888-797-7245 or 508-771-3800
WEBSITE: capetrain.com
E-MAIL: form on website

Cape Cod Central

The Cape Cod Central Railroad operates diesel-powered scenic excursions and dinner trains, which also include lunch and brunch outings. It runs from Hyannis over 23 miles of the former Old Colony Railroad that became part of the New York, New Haven & Hartford. Along the way, you'll pass cranberry bogs, forests, and marshes. Boarding is also possible at Sandwich.

CHOICES: For evening dining, passengers can select either the Elegant Dinner Train, involving multiple courses served with all the flourishes, or the Family Supper Train, which offers less formal service, a shorter ride, lower fares, a magic show, and special children's meals. The popular Murder Mystery Train, a variation on the Elegant Dinner Train, runs on occasional evenings.

WHEN TO GO: Trains run from late May through October in various combinations and with varying frequencies. Some special event trains run in November and December. Sea breezes mean that Hyannis typically remains temperate throughout the railroad's operating season but visiting outside of summer may minimize crowds.

GOOD TO KNOW: Hyannis is quintessential Cape Cod, with all the sun, sand, salt— and tourists. Whale watching, beaching, fishing, golfing, and biking are among the available outdoor activities. The John F. Kennedy Hyannis Museum is located in town. There are many lodging choices and a wide variety of fine restaurants.

WORTH DOING: The railroad offers a package with Hy-Line Cruises that includes a one-hour boat tour of Hyannis harbor and the Kennedy compound. The boat is a little gem: Maine-style coastal steamer *Prudence* (the real McCoy, though now dieselized, built in 1911).

DON'T MISS: The Elegant Dinner Train offers one decided advantage—in addition to the cuisine—over the other meal trains (and scenic excursions as well). While the other trains are all two hours in length and run briefly along the Cape Cod Canal, only the three-hour Elegant Dinner Train crosses it on a lift bridge into the town of Buzzards Bay. This bridge features outstanding aesthetics and was the longest of its kind when completed in 1935.

GETTING THERE: Hyannis is located on the Atlantic Ocean at the elbow of Cape Cod. Barnstable Municipal Airport hosts commercial flights from Boston and New York.

MICHIGAN

Clinton Northern Railway ❶

Housed in a historic Grand Trunk depot, the museum's artifacts include tools, signs, and station agent items. A 1902 Barney & Smith sleeper car, a 1903 post office-baggage car, and a 1926 Ann Arbor maintenance-of-way crew car are also on display.

LOCATION: 107 E. Railroad Street, St. Johns
PHONE: 989-224-6134 or 502-214-0479
WEBSITE: clintonnorthernrailway.org
E-MAIL: mccampbell60@gmail.com

Coopersville & Marne Railway ❷

Powered by a EMD SW9 diesel locomotive, this railway's 14-mile, 75-minute excursion travels through farmland and over an open-deck girder bridge. At Marne, you can watch the engine uncouple, run along a passing siding, and couple to the other end. Excursions run Wednesdays and Saturdays May through October (on Saturdays in other months), and theme trains run as well.

LOCATION: 311 Danforth Street, Coopersville
PHONE: 616-997-7000
WEBSITE: coopersvilleandmarne.org

Durand Union Station ❸

This 100-year-old depot museum was the second busiest depot in Michigan, and its lower level has been restored to its former glory with terrazzo floors and oak trim. Still functioning as a depot, the building also houses the Michigan Railroad History Museum. The museum contains changing exhibits on state and local railroading.

LOCATION: 200 Railroad Street, Durand
PHONE: 989-288-3561
WEBSITE: durandstation.org
E-MAIL: dusi@durandstation.org
DISCOUNT: Flash your *Trains* discount card and grab a goodie bag on your way out!

Flushing Area Museum ❹

The museum's collection includes permanent displays of railroad artifacts as well as local historical exhibits. It is housed in the Flushing depot, which was built in 1888 and provided passenger service until 1971. The building was restored to its former appearance by the Flushing Area Historical Society.

LOCATION: 431 W. Main Street, Flushing
PHONE: 810-487-0814
WEBSITE: flushinghistorical.org
E-MAIL: fahs@att.net

Houghton County Historical Museum ❺

The museum includes the restored Mineral Range depot, which contains a collection of Copper County railroad artifacts, and other historic buildings. The museum operates the Lake Linden & Torch Lake Railroad. A narrow gauge, 0-4-0 Porter steam locomotive takes you on a half-mile ride. It is open June through September.

LOCATION: 53102 Highway M-26, Lake Linden
PHONE: 906-296-4121
WEBSITE: houghtonhistory.org
E-MAIL: president@houghtonhistory.org
DISCOUNT: 10% off gift shop purchase.

Michigan Transit Museum ❻

The Michigan Transit Museum is housed in a depot restored to its 1900 appearance and includes railroading exhibits from that time. The transit museum displays several locomotives and railcars. Located near the Selfridge Military Air Museum, the transit museum is open weekends year-round.

LOCATION: 200 Grand Avenue, Mount Clemens
PHONE: 586-463-1863
WEBSITE: michigantransitmuseum.org
E-MAIL: info@michigantransitmuseum.org

Old Road Dinner Train ❼

The train provides fine dining and fun entertainment from two locations, Blissfield and Charlotte. The murder mystery dinner trains provide a five-course dinner as you participate in a comical, interactive mystery show. Saturday afternoon excursions out of Blissfield along a segment of the Erie & Kalamazoo Railroad are also offered.

LOCATION: 301 E. Adrian Street, Blissfield
PHONE: 888-467-2451
WEBSITE: murdermysterytrain.com
E-MAIL: form on website

Saginaw Railway Museum ❽

Located in a restored 1907 Pere Marquette Railway depot, this museum displays an RS1 locomotive, several cabooses, a combine coach, and various boxcars. It includes an 1898 Armstrong interlocking tower as well as a variety of smaller artifacts.

LOCATION: 900 Maple Street, Saginaw
PHONE: 989-790-7994
WEBSITE: saginawrailwaymuseum.org
E-MAIL: info@saginawrailwaymuseum.org

SS City of Milwaukee ❾

The SS *City of Milwaukee*, a national historic landmark, is the last surviving traditional Great Lakes railroad car ferry. Built in 1931, the *City of Milwaukee* served the Grand Trunk Western and Ann Arbor railroads. The car deck houses five Ann Arbor boxcars that serve as exhibit spaces and a theater. The Coast Guard cutter *Acacia* is docked on site, and tours of both ships are offered.

LOCATION: 99 Arthur Street, Manistee
PHONE: 231-723-3587
WEBSITE: carferry.com
E-MAIL: form on website

Tri-Cities Historical Museum ❿

The Tri-Cities Historical Museum operates out of two buildings including a former Grand Trunk Western depot. Located on the banks of the Grand River, the depot museum, built in 1871, contains two floors of railroad and other historical artifacts. On display is a Pere Marquette Railway steam locomotive.

LOCATION: 1 North Harbor Drive, Grand Haven
PHONE: 616-842-0700
WEBSITE: tri-citiesmuseum.org
E-MAIL: dswartout@tri-citiesmuseum.org

Greenfield Village at the Henry Ford ⓫

LOCATION: 20900 Oakwood Boulevard, Dearborn
PHONE: 800-835-5237 or 313-271-1620
WEBSITE: thehenryford.org

Jeff Terry

The Henry Ford claims to be America's greatest history attraction, and even though it's in the capital of—and shrine to—the automobile, railroads are well represented here. The centerpiece for this is the Detroit, Toledo & Milwaukee roundhouse, a reconstruction of the original in Marshall, Mich., believed to be one of only seven 19th century roundhouses remaining. A steam railroad encircles the historic 90-acre village.

CHOICES: You can ride the train around the village in open-air cars on a 30-minute narrated trip. Departing from the 1859 Smiths Creek depot, the train also makes stops at strategic locations throughout the village. The roundhouse includes hands-on railroading displays and a 1902 Atlantic engine. A mezzanine provides an excellent vantage point from where you can see work going on. Also, be sure to go inside the Henry Ford museum to view railroad cars and locomotives, including an Allegheny type, one of the largest steam locomotives ever built.

WHEN TO GO: Greenfield Village is open daily mid-April through October. In November, it is open Friday through Sunday, and in December, it is open select evenings for Holiday Nights. It is closed the remainder of the year.

GOOD TO KNOW: Railroad Junction, where the roundhouse and depot are located, is one of seven different historic districts in Greenfield Village. In Henry Ford's Model T District, you can tour a replica of Ford's first factory and ride in a Model T.

WORTH DOING: On December nights, celebrate the holidays in Greenfield Village. The Holiday Nights event features entertainment, carriage and Model T rides, Santa and reindeer, ice skating, and fireworks.

DON'T MISS: Get to the roundhouse early in the day to help the crew turn the steam engine on the turntable. It's so well balanced that two people can do it, but it's more fun when you get to push a giant engine around.

GETTING THERE: Just west of Detroit, the Henry Ford is located in Dearborn on the corner of Village Road and Oakwood Boulevard, just west of the Southfield Freeway and south of Michigan Avenue (Highway 12). There is easy access from I-94 or I-75. You may also ride an Amtrak train that stops at the museum.

Huckleberry Railroad 🔢

LOCATION: 6140 Bray Road, Flint
PHONE: 800-648-7275 or 810-736-7100
WEBSITE: geneseecountyparks.org
E-MAIL: parkswebteam@gcparks.org

Jeff Terry

The Huckleberry Railroad is part of a historical village that is operated by Genesee County Parks in Flint. The narrow gauge railroad is built on an abandoned Pere Marquette Railway right-of-way. An eight-mile, 35-minute ride carries passengers through neighborhoods, by a lake, and into wooded areas.

CHOICES: Ride in one of the railroad's historic coaches or cabooses pulled by a Baldwin 4-6-0 or a Baldwin 2-8-2, two of the seven locomotives owned by the Huckleberry Railroad.

WHEN TO GO: Trains run Memorial Day weekend through Labor Day, with special events held throughout the year, including days out with Thomas the Tank Engine. During the railroad's railfan weekend, usually held in August, you can see all the trains, get good photos, and talk with the train crews.

GOOD TO KNOW: The Huckleberry Railroad was named because it ran so slow that a person could jump off the train, pick some huckleberries, and jump back on the train without breaking a sweat.

WORTH DOING: Take a stroll through Crossroads Village, which has 34 historic structures on 51 acres. Costumed interpreters welcome you to the homes, mills, and shops that date back to the 1800s. Special events are scheduled throughout the summer, and you can take a ride on a paddle-wheel riverboat.

DON'T MISS: Look for Rio Grande 2-8-2 No. 464, one of a rare class of narrow gauge Mikado type steam locomotives on the Colorado railroad. Built in 1903 and restored in 2005, it was nicknamed Mudhen because it waddled like a chicken as it went down the tracks.

GETTING THERE: The railroad is located just north of Flint, about an hour from Detroit. From Detroit, take I-75 to I-475. Follow I-475 north to Saginaw Street (Exit 13). Take Saginaw Street north to Stanley Road, turn east on Stanley Road, and then turn south on Bray Road to the village and railroad.

Little River Railroad 🖪

LOCATION: 29 W. Park Avenue, Coldwater
PHONE: 260-316-0529
WEBSITE: littleriverrailroad.com
E-MAIL: customerservice@littleriverrailroad.com

Jeff Terry

Whoever said bigger is better never visited the Little River Railroad. This railroad is home to one of the smallest standard gauge steam locomotives of its type ever built. No. 110 is a 57-ton Pacific that has all the charm of a ballerina, and the railroad offers 90-minute trips behind it from Coldwater to nearby Quincy.

CHOICES: Ride in a coach or open-air car. During the 30-minute layover in Quincy, be sure to exit the train and watch as the locomotive is switched to the other end of the train. At times, a second locomotive, 0-4-0T No. 1, is in service. The railroad offers a variety of special events throughout the year including a dinner train, pumpkin trains, haunted trains, Christmas trains, and Easter trains.

WHEN TO GO: Trains run weekends Memorial Day through September. On Labor Day weekend, Little River runs both of its engines as well as a motor car.

GOOD TO KNOW: Engine No. 110 started out on the Little River Railroad in east Tennessee. An Indiana family, the Blooms, rescued her and rebuilt it for excursion work in the 1970s, and members of that same family continue this tradition of preservation.

WORTH DOING: The area features many antique shops and preserved buildings. In Coldwater, take in a film at the Capri Drive-in, one of the last of its kind.

DON'T MISS: Take time to look over the exhibits in the Coldwater depot, an 1883 Lake Shore & Michigan Southern depot.

GETTING THERE: Coldwater is in south-central Michigan. Take I-69 to Exit 13 for Coldwater. Follow Highway 12 west, turn left onto Division Street, and then turn right onto Park Avenue to the depot.

Steam Railroading Institute ⑭

LOCATION: 405 S. Washington Street, Owosso
PHONE: 989-725-9464
WEBSITE: michigansteamtrain.com

Jim Wrin

The Steam Railroading Institute is all about preserving steam locomotives, and there is always restoration work going on. The institute displays equipment and offers some all-day train rides.

CHOICES: Both steam- and diesel-powered excursions are offered. The museum's icon, Pere Marquette 2-8-4 No. 1225, is under restoration, and until it returns, Nickel Plate Road 2-8-4 No. 765 is filling in on mainline excursions. The seven-acre site includes a roundhouse, a turntable, and a variety of railcars. It also features an operational miniature train. Look around the visitor center, which is housed in a renovated freight warehouse that was also a creamery. It now contains exhibits, artifacts, and a model train layout.

WHEN TO GO: The rolling stock collection can be seen all year, and special events are scheduled as well. In November and December, the North Pole Express is the big event as a diesel locomotive takes visitors on a 24-mile round trip to the North Pole, where kids can enjoy hot cocoa, activities, and visiting Santa. Reserve early, as this event sells out fast.

GOOD TO KNOW: No. 1225 was the model and sound effects source for the steam train in the poplar movie, *The Polar Express*.

WORTH DOING: If you like to watch things go fast, the Owosso Speedway offers short track racing on Saturday, Saturday, Saturday.

DON'T MISS: The Michigan Railroad History Museum is housed in historic Durand Union Station, 20 minutes away in Durand.

GETTING THERE: Owosso is about 30 miles northeast of Lansing and 30 miles west of Flint. From Flint, take Highway 21 west to Owosso. From Lansing, take I-69 to Highway 52 north to Owosso. In Owosso, the Steam Railroading Institute is on south Washington Street.

MINNESOTA

Depot Museum ❶

Located in the 1907 headquarters of the Duluth & Iron Range Railroad, this museum highlights the timber industry, iron mining, and the railroad. On display is a Mallet steam locomotive and a Baldwin 3-Spot. The Lake County Historical Society operates this museum and three others including an 1896 tugboat. The museums are open daily late May through mid-October.

LOCATION: 520 South Avenue, Two Harbors
PHONE: 218-834-4898
WEBSITE: lakecountyhistoricalsociety.org
E-MAIL: lakehist@lakenet.com

Depot Visitors Center and Railroad Museum ❷

Visitors have several options in exploring this restored 1915 train depot, which is listed on the National Register of Historic Places. You can experience the depot's architecture, waiting rooms, freight room, and exhibits on your own or with a guide. Group tours, with or without lunch, are also available.

LOCATION: 100 Aldrich Avenue SW, Wadena
PHONE: 218-632-5999
WEBSITE: thedepotwadena.org
E-MAIL: thedepotwadena@gmail.com

End-O-Line Railroad Park & Museum ❸

End-O-Line Railroad Park includes a 1901 manually operated turntable, a rebuilt engine house, an original four-room depot, a water tower, an 1899 section foreman's house, a Grand Trunk Western caboose, and two steam locomotives. Open Memorial Day to Labor Day, the site also includes other buildings of historical interest.

LOCATION: 440 N. Mill Street, Currie
PHONE: 507-763-3708
WEBSITE: endoline.com
E-MAIL: endoline@co.murray.mn.us
DISCOUNT: 10% off gift shop purchase.

Iron Horse Central Railroad Museum ❹

Housed in an 1895 St. Paul & Duluth station, the museum displays more than 20 historic railcars. It is open Fridays and Saturdays June through September. The *Bumblebee*, a homebuilt, yellow-and-black motor car, operates in a mile loop around the museum grounds.

LOCATION: 24880 Morgan Avenue, Chisago City
PHONE: 651-257-6225
WEBSITE: ironhorsecentral.com
E-MAIL: thompson@ironhorsecentral.com

Minnehaha Depot ❺

Located in Minnehaha Park, the tiny depot's architecture features delicate gingerbread details. Built in 1875, the building replaced an earlier Milwaukee Road depot on the first line into the Twin Cities from Chicago. Managed by the Minnesota Transportation Museum, the depot is open Sundays Memorial Day weekend through Labor Day.

LOCATION: Highway 55 and Minnehaha Parkway, Minneapolis
PHONE: 651-228-0263
WEBSITE: mtmuseum.org
E-MAIL: contact@mtmuseum.org

Minnesota Discovery Center ❻

The center offers a 2.5-mile trolley ride to a re-created mining community. The 40-minute trip, aboard a 1928 Melbourne trolley, offers views of the Pillsbury mine. Preserving Iron Range history, the center includes a museum and heritage park. It is open year-round, with trolleys operating late May into October. Taconite mine tours are available through the center.

LOCATION: 1005 Discovery Drive, Chisholm
PHONE: 800-372-6437 or 218-254-7959
WEBSITE: mndiscoverycenter.com
E-MAIL: info@mndiscoverycenter.com

Minnesota Streetcar Museum ❼

This museum operates two different streetcar lines from May through November, with a variety of special events. Located southwest of downtown Minneapolis, the Como-Harriet line runs between Lake Harriet and Lake Calhoun. The Excelsior line is about 15 miles west of downtown Minneapolis. The museum exhibits electric streetcars, railcars, and a steamboat.

LOCATION: 2330 W. 42nd Street, Minneapolis
PHONE: 952-922-1096
WEBSITE: trolleyride.org
E-MAIL: mnscmuseum@gmail.com

Jackson Street Roundhouse ❽

LOCATION: 193 E. Pennsylvania Avenue, St. Paul
PHONE: 651-228-0263
WEBSITE: mtmuseum.org
E-MAIL: contact@mtmuseum.org

Steve Glischinski

The former Great Northern Jackson Street Roundhouse was built in 1907 to service passenger locomotives. Closed in 1959, the roundhouse was converted to nonrailroad use and the tracks removed. The Minnesota Transportation Museum purchased it in 1985 and reinstalled the turntable and added new roundhouse doors that were built according to the 1906 blueprints.

CHOICES: Visitors can roam the roundhouse and the outdoor grounds, take a short caboose ride pulled by a switch engine, and participate in interactive exhibits. Tours of the roundhouse where equipment restoration takes place are also available. The collection features three Northern Pacific steam locomotives and Great Northern 400, the first production SD45, owned by the GN Historical Society. A variety of freight and passenger cars are displayed outside, and in a departure from many museums, several boxcars have been neatly repainted in their original color schemes.

WHEN TO GO: The museum is open Wednesdays and Saturdays year-round. Summer or early fall are the best times to visit since it can be chilly inside the roundhouse in the winter and downright cold outside.

GOOD TO KNOW: Walk inside the cab of Dan Patch Lines No. 100, built in 1913 by General Electric, and you've walked into history. One of the first locomotives to use an internal combustion engine, it is the granddaddy of today's diesel locomotives.

WORTH DOING: After taking in the roundhouse, you can visit the St. Paul home of James J. Hill, the Great Northern's founder. Completed in 1891, the 36,000-square-foot mansion was the largest and most expensive home in Minnesota at the time. The Minnesota Historical Society conducts 75-minute guided tours.

DON'T MISS: Take a ride on the miniature *Rock Island Rocket* train, a perfect ⅙ replica of the *Twin Star Rocket*. It was built in 1947 by Larry Sauter, a high school industrial arts teacher, in his spare time. The museum adds a few feet of special narrow gauge track for the train every year, and the kids will love the quick acceleration!

GETTING THERE: The Twin Cities of Minneapolis and St. Paul have Amtrak, airline, and bus service. The roundhouse is located north of the Minnesota State Capitol. Take the Pennsylvania Avenue exit off I-35E and drive west two blocks to the roundhouse.

DISCOUNT: $2 off each adult ticket; up to four adults.

Lake Superior & Mississippi Railroad 🖪

LOCATION: Grand Avenue and Fremont Street, Duluth
PHONE: 218-624-7549
WEBSITE: lsmrr.org
E-MAIL: info@lsmrr.org

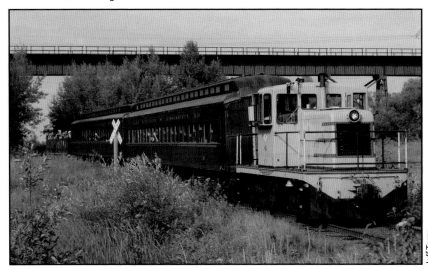

Jeff Terry

Here's a laid-back operation that is a great complement to the marshlands near Duluth. A 90-minute ride on this railroad is a great way to relax and enjoy nature along the St. Louis River estuary, Spirit Lake, and Mud Lake. Keep your eyes on the marshes for egrets!

CHOICES: While taking in the scenery and wildlife when riding in a restored, open-window coach, you can listen to narration of the area's rich history. The coaches, built in 1912, operated between the Iron Range and Duluth. For a truly outdoor experience, ride the Safari Car, a converted flatcar. Power is provided by a General Electric industrial switcher built in 1946.

WHEN TO GO: Excursions operate on Saturdays and Sundays, beginning in June and running until October.

GOOD TO KNOW: The railroad takes its name from the first line built between the Twin Cities and Duluth, and it uses some of that line's original track.

WORTH DOING: Duluth and the Lake Superior area offer much to do. There are historic ships to see (S.S. *William A Irvin*, S.S. *Meteor*), museums to tour, and parks to explore.

DON'T MISS: For a Duluth doubleheader, visit the nearby Lake Superior Railroad Museum, where you can catch a train ride to Two Harbors.

GETTING THERE: Duluth is on Lake Superior, about 150 miles from the Twin Cities. In Duluth, exit I-35 at Cody Street, turn right onto 63rd Avenue, and then turn right onto Grand Avenue to Fremont Street. (Watch for construction on I-35.)

Lake Superior Railroad Museum ⑩

LOCATION: 506 W. Michigan Street, Duluth
PHONE: 218-727-8025 (museum) or 218-722-1273 (train)
WEBSITE: lsrm.org
E-MAIL: form on website

Steve Glischinski

This is a combination of a great railroad museum and a great train ride. The Lake Superior Railroad Museum is located in a historic depot in downtown Duluth. Its extensive rolling stock collection rests in the train shed, and just outside, excursion trains ply the route to Two Harbors, with outstanding views along the way.

CHOICES: The Lake Superior Railroad Museum has a large collection of railroad equipment that changes annually. It includes steam, diesel, and electric locomotives as well as passenger coaches, freight cars, and cabooses. Much of the equipment was used on Minnesota railroads, including the first locomotive operated in the state. The museum also operates the North Shore Scenic Railroad, which conducts two regular excursions. A six-hour round trip takes you through the countryside, over seven bridges, and into Two Harbors. A shorter (90-minute) excursion runs along the shores of Lake Superior to Lester River. Also operating are an elegant dinner train, a pizza train, and a variety of specials.

WHEN TO GO: The museum is open year-round, with extended summer hours. Regular excursions are offered late May through mid-October. Soo Line 4-6-2 steam locomotive No. 2719 operates on select weekends in August and September on trips to Two Harbors.

GOOD TO KNOW: Take a close look at the *William Crooks*, the first locomotive operated in Minnesota. Built in 1861, it is one of a handful of engines remaining from before the Civil War.

WORTH DOING: Admission to the Lake Superior Railroad Museum admits you to three other museums in the building: the Duluth Children's Museum, Duluth Art Institute, and St. Louis County Historical Society.

DON'T MISS: Watch the massive Duluth, Missabe & Iron Range Railroad Yellowstone type locomotive come to life. The clever museum folks have set it up so that every 30 minutes an electric motor sets the drivers in motion, rotating the running gear, and operates lights and sounds.

GETTING THERE: Situated on Lake Superior, Duluth is 150 miles from the Twin Cities. To reach the museum, take Exit 256 off I-35 and follow Michigan Street to the depot.

Milwaukee Road 261

LOCATION: 401 Harrison Street, Minneapolis
PHONE: 651-765-9812
WEBSITE: 261.com

Steve Glischinski

Railroading Heritage of Midwest America and its operating arm, The Friends of the 261, operate main line excursion trips around the Midwest. Until former Milwaukee Road steam locomotive No. 261 returns to service, which could be in fall 2011, diesel-powered excursions are being operated. The group also operates its historic passenger cars on Amtrak trains, most frequently on the *Empire Builder* between the Twin Cities and Chicago. These trips are usually open to the public.

CHOICES: Friends of the 261 offer several options for passengers. All trips include coach, first-class, and premium-class services. Premium-class includes hors d'oeuvres and gourmet meals prepared onboard and a ride in one of two former Milwaukee Road *Hiawatha* cars: Skytop lounge observation *Cedar Rapids* or full-length Super Dome No. 53. First-class includes an upscale meal with hors d'oeuvres and a ride in parlor or lounge cars. Both first- and premium-class include complimentary beverages.

WHEN TO GO: Generally, the Friends operate trips beginning in May and running as late as October. One of the most popular and scenic routes is along the Mississippi River between Minneapolis and Winona, especially in early autumn when the leaves begin to change.

GOOD TO KNOW: For a complete Milwaukee Road experience, stay in one of the two hotels at the former Milwaukee Road Minneapolis passenger depot, built in 1898 and beautifully restored. Rail memorabilia and photographs can be found throughout the building.

WORTH DOING: Trains usually leave from the 261 shop facility in northeast Minneapolis. Head down to the shop in Minneapolis the evening before a trip just to take in the sights and sounds.

DON'T MISS: Get a close look at Skytop lounge observation car *Cedar Rapids*. Built by the Milwaukee Road in 1948, with their large glass area, the Skytops were unlike any other rail passenger car. The *Cedar Rapids* is the only Skytop still in operation.

GETTING THERE: Minneapolis-St. Paul has Amtrak, airline, light rail transit, and bus service. A short walk from the Metro Transit bus stop at Central Avenue and Broadway will get you to the shop, or you can take a taxi. Ample parking is available at the shop on excursion days.

MISSISSIPPI

Canton Train Museum ❶

You can't ride on the *City of New Orleans* anymore, but you can relive the experience in Canton's Illinois Central depot, where passengers could board America's native son and other passenger trains. While in town, you can also visit several movie museums, which are dedicated to films, such as *O Brother, Where Art Thou*, that were filmed in Canton.

LOCATION: 108 Depot Drive, Canton
PHONE: 601-859-4733
WEBSITE: cantontourism.com/trains.html
E-MAIL: trains@canton-mississippi.com

McComb Railroad Museum ❷

Housed in an Illinois Central passenger terminal, the museum contains almost 1,500 artifacts related to railroading in southwest Mississippi. Outside, you can view a restored Illinois Central steam locomotive, aluminum refrigerator car, and caboose. The museum is open Mondays through Fridays.

LOCATION: 108 N. Railroad Boulevard, McComb
PHONE: 601-684-2291
WEBSITE: mcrrmuseum.com
E-MAIL: form on website

MISSOURI

Belton, Grandview & Kansas City Railroad ▮

At this laid-back railroad, you can walk around the yard, look at displayed equipment, and talk to the crew before boarding a five-mile excursion. The 45-minute round trip runs south from Belton. Rides in the caboose with the conductor or in the locomotive with the engineer are also available.

LOCATION: 502 E. Walnut Street, Belton
PHONE: 816-331-0630
WEBSITE: www.beltonrailroad.org
E-MAIL: info@beltonrailroad.org

Chicago & Alton Railroad Depot ❷

Built in 1879, the two-story Chicago & Alton depot features a restored four-room stationmaster's residence on the second floor. The first floor contains a waiting room, baggage room, and stationmaster's room. The depot contains hundreds of C&A artifacts. It is open April through October, and guided tours are available.

LOCATION: 318 W. Pacific Avenue, Independence
PHONE: 816-325-7955
WEBSITE: www.chicagoalton1879depot.com
E-MAIL: info@chicagoalton1879depot.org

KC Rail Experience ❸

Located in historic Union Station, the KC Rail Experience features a vintage railcar, a diesel engine, artifacts, and a locomotive simulator. Enhancing the experience are 20 ghostly figures from the station's past that tell the story of the men and women of the railroads. A model railroad gallery that features model trains of all sizes has been added as a permanent exhibit.

LOCATION: 30 W. Pershing Road, Kansas City
PHONE: 877-724-2489 or 816-460-2000
WEBSITE: unionstation.org
E-MAIL: visitor@unionstation.org

Railroad Historical Museum ❹

Located in Grant Beach Park, this train museum is an actual train. A locomotive, baggage car, commuter car, and caboose contain artifacts from the St. Louis-San Francisco and other railroads. After touring the museum, you can enjoy the park's pool, playground, and picnic area. It is open Saturdays June through September.

LOCATION: 1300 N. Grant Street, Springfield
PHONE: 417-865-6829 or 417-883-5319
WEBSITE: rrhistoricalmuseum.zoomshare.com
E-MAIL: rrhistoricalmuseum@zoomshare.com

St. Louis Iron Mountain & Southern Railway ❺

From May through December, this railway offers a variety of trips including sightseeing excursions, murder mysteries, train robberies, and holiday-themed rides. Trains are pulled by a 1950 EMD E8 diesel engine.

LOCATION: Highway 61 at Highway 25, Jackson
PHONE: 800-455-7245 or 573-243-1688
WEBSITE: slimrr.com
E-MAIL: cherjxmo@aol.com

Branson Scenic Railway 6

LOCATION: 206 E. Main Street, Branson
PHONE: 800-287-2462 or 417-334-6110
WEBSITE: bransontrain.com
E-MAIL: form on website

Patrick Hiatte

Enjoy a 40-mile round trip through the Ozarks on the former Missouri Pacific Railroad White River Line, which was built more than a century ago. View historic towns and townsites as you pass through tunnels and over high bridges along the banks of the White River and its tributaries.

CHOICES: The train may run north or south from Branson, depending on freight traffic on the host Missouri & North Arkansas Railroad. There is open seating on the two vintage dome cars, 60-seat deluxe coach, and the lounge car that comprise the regular train. In addition, a dinner train, serving a candlelit, four-course meal, operates on Saturday evenings April through October. Beginning in late November, the Polar Express begins its holiday run.

WHEN TO GO: The Ozarks are scenic any time of the year, but especially in the fall, when the oaks and other hardwoods turn red, yellow, and orange in a display that rivals any fall foliage in the country. BSR operates four trains a day in October when the colors are at their height, as well as during Branson's peak summer season. At least two trains a day operate from early March through mid-December.

GOOD TO KNOW: Seating is open and boarding is by group based on ticket number—the sooner you buy your ticket, the more likely you are to get a seat in a dome.

WORTH DOING: Branson offers more than 100 shows, including Elvis and Beatles tributes, music and comedy headliners, and dozens of country music shows. For a quiet (and free) getaway, walk the boardwalk along the shore of Lake Taneycomo and enjoy the fire and water fountain show at Branson Landing.

DON'T MISS: At Silver Dollar City theme park, you can ride the RiverBlast, PowderKeg, giant swing, or the Frisco Silver Dollar steam train, named for the Frisco Railway, which had its operating headquarters just up the road in Springfield.

GETTING THERE: Branson is in southwest Missouri about 45 miles south of Springfield on Highway 65. Although most visitors drive to Branson, there's also scheduled air service to the Branson airport. The depot is downtown on Main Street (Highway 76).

Museum of Transportation ❼

LOCATION: 3015 Barrett Station Road, St Louis
PHONE: 314-615-8212
WEBSITE: museumoftransport.org

Museum of Transportation

If you want to be surrounded by trains, this is the place. A visit here brings you in touch with more than 70 locomotives of steam, diesel, and electric power. You'll see scores of railcars and even one of the first railroad tunnels west of the Mississippi. The 150-acre site also houses airplanes, cars, and riverboats.

CHOICES: The museum features miles of switching and exhibition track and includes 10 buildings. Its collection of more than 30 steam locomotives is one of the largest around, and stairs let you climb into the cabs of many of them. Many rare and unusual items grace the site, including the world's largest tank car, an Aerotrain, and even a cast-iron turntable. A miniature train also operates.

WHEN TO GO: The museum is open year-round. It is open daily during its summer schedule, which begins in May and runs through Labor Day. During the rest of the year, the museum is open Tuesday through Sunday.

GOOD TO KNOW: Check out Electro-Motive Corp. FT demonstrator No. 103. It was the first mainline diesel locomotive built for freight service in North America back in 1939. Its national tour proved the worth of diesel power and launched a full change of power from steam to diesel.

WORTH DOING: Of course, if you haven't already done so, enjoy the view from the top of Gateway Arch. You can also take a riverboat cruise, play some ragtime at Scott Joplin's home, enjoy the Missouri Botanical Garden, or view the mosaics at Cathedral Basilica.

DON'T MISS: Climb into the cab of the Union Pacific Big Boy No. 4006 and see what it felt like to be the engineer on one of the world's largest steam locomotives. And climb aboard Santa Fe No. 5011 and ring the engine's bell.

GETTING THERE: The museum is about 12 miles west of downtown St. Louis. When driving from I-270, either north or south, exit at Dougherty Ferry Road (Exit 8), go west about one mile to Barrett Station Road, and turn left. The museum is on the right.

DISCOUNT: Buy one adult admission, get one free in August.

MONTANA

Alder Gulch Short Line [1]

This narrow gauge railroad connects the former gold mining towns of Virginia City and Nevada City. The line winds along Alder Creek, where you can view the remains of gold mining operations, dredge tailings, and a variety of wildlife. Be sure to explore the historic buildings and displays in Nevada City. A gas-powered train operates while steam engine No. 12 is out of service.

LOCATION: Wallace Street, Virginia City
PHONE: 406-843-5247
WEBSITE: virginiacitymt.com
DISCOUNT: 10% gift store discount; 10% off each train ticket, up to four tickets.

Charlie Russell Chew-Choo Dinner Train [2]

This dinner train takes you on a 3.5-hour excursion over the old Chicago, Milwaukee, St. Paul & Pacific Railroad line from Kingston Junction to Denton. The ride crosses three historic trestles, passes through a 2,000-foot tunnel, and travels through the land that inspired artist Charles Russell. Along the way, you'll enjoy a catered prime rib dinner. Just keep your eyes open for masked bandits! North Pole runs take place in December.

LOCATION: 408 NE Main Street, Lewistown
PHONE: 866-912-3980 or 406-555-5436
WEBSITE: montanacharlierussellchewchoo.com
E-MAIL: lewchamb@midrivers.com

Historical Museum at Fort Missoula ❸

Located in Fort Missoula, the Historical Museum includes 13 structures that depict the area's history. One is the Drummond depot, which was constructed by the Chicago, Milwaukee, St. Paul & Pacific Railroad in 1910. Fort Missoula is on the National Register of Historic Places.

LOCATION: South Avenue, Missoula
PHONE: 406-728-3476
WEBSITE: fortmissoulamuseum.org
E-MAIL: ftmslamuseum@montana.com
DISCOUNT: Buy one admission, get one free.

Upper Musselshell Museum ❹

If you like the Milwaukee Road, you'll like Harlowton, which is located in central Montana. The museum contains a large collection of books and more than 450 models related to the Milwaukee Road. Also in town is a restored depot, ES-3 electric locomotive No. E57B, and several other pieces of equipment. The museum, housed in two buildings, contains a stagecoach, replica dinosaur skeleton, and other artifacts.

LOCATION: 11 S. Central Avenue, Harlowton
PHONE: 406-632-5519
WEBSITE: harlowtonmuseum.org
E-MAIL: museum@mtintouch.net

NEBRASKA

Cody Park Railroad Museum ❶

The Cody Park Railroad Museum displays one of the two remaining Challenger class locomotives. Also displayed are a UP diesel engine, baggage car, mail car, and caboose. The restored Hershey, Neb., depot contains Union Pacific items, telegraph equipment, and other exhibits. It is open May through September.

LOCATION: 1400 N. Jeffers Street, North Platte
WEBSITE: visitnorthplatte.com/CodyParkRailroadMuseum.html

Durham Museum ❷

Built in 1931, Omaha's Union Station is a beautiful example of Art Deco style. This historic railroad station now houses permanent and traveling historical exhibits. Rail displays include an 1890s steam locomotive, a streetcar, a caboose, and several passenger cars. Be sure to have a malt, ice cream soda, or phosphate at the restored soda fountain as travelers did in 1931.

LOCATION: 801 S. 10th Street, Omaha
PHONE: 402-444-5071
WEBSITE: durhammuseum.org
E-MAIL: info@durhammuseum.org

Fremont & Elkhorn Valley Railroad ❸

This excursion train runs over a route laid out in 1869. On the 16-mile round trip from Fremont to Nickerson, a diesel locomotive pulls vintage railcars across historic territory. Excursions run on weekends May through October. The Fremont Dinner Train also operates year-round over the railroad's track offering murder mysteries, five-course dinners, and special events.

LOCATION: 1835 N. Somers Avenue, Fremont
PHONE: 402-727-0615
WEBSITE: fremontrailroad.com
E-MAIL: fevr@fremontrailroad.com

Nebraska

Rock Island Depot Railroad Museum ❹

The museum is located in one of the state's only remaining Rock Island depots. Built in 1914, the brick building also housed the railroad's Western Division Headquarters. The collection features Rock Island artifacts and a restored baggage room, lobby, and ticket office. The site also includes restored gardens.

LOCATION: 910 Bacon Road, Fairbury
PHONE: 402-729-5131
WEBSITE: fairbury.com
E-MAIL: fairburyridepot@windstream.net

Stuhr Museum of the Prairie Pioneer ❺

This interactive museum takes you back to an 1890s railroad town with more than 60 restored buildings. During the summer, townspeople dressed in period clothing demonstrate daily life on the Plains. A 1901 steam locomotive, a 1912 caboose, an 1871 coach, and other railcars are on display.

LOCATION: 3133 W. Highway 34, Grand Island
PHONE: 308-385-5316
WEBSITE: stuhrmuseum.org
E-MAIL: info@sturhmuseum.org

Trails & Rails Museum ❻

The Rails portion of the museum includes an 1898 Union Pacific depot. The depot houses transportation exhibits, and its waiting room and ticket office have been restored. On display are a 2-8-0 Baldwin steam engine, a UP flatcar, a caboose, and other equipment. Open year-round, the museum features other historic buildings including the distinctive Freighters Hotel.

LOCATION: 710 W. 11th Street, Kearney
PHONE: 308-234-3041
WEBSITE: bchs.us
E-MAIL: bchs.us@hotmail.com

Golden Spike Tower ❼

LOCATION: 1249 N. Homestead Road, North Platte
PHONE: 308-532-9920
WEBSITE: goldenspiketower.com
E-MAIL: form on website

Golden Spike Tower

The Golden Spike Tower is an eight-story tower with a commanding view of the world's largest railroad yard: Union Pacific's Bailey. This freight yard is the heart of the nation's largest railroad. A train arrives every 14 minutes on average, and in the two hump yards, 20 trains are separated, classified, and reassembled by destination every day.

CHOICES: The open-air seventh floor gives visitors an unimpeded vantage point to watch operations, which photographers will love. Inside the climate-controlled eighth floor, a guide explains what's happening on the rails below.

WHEN TO GO: Any time of the year is a good time to view the train activity from the Golden Spike Tower. North Platte offers Rail Fest each September, and during that time, visitors can take motor coach tours of Bailey Yard, plus view UP train displays. It also features an art show, entertainment, and children's activities. Also in the fall, you can work through a local corn maze in the shape of a locomotive that features a short track (easier path) and the long haul (more challenging).

GOOD TO KNOW: The tower's operator is currently renovating a dining car that when completed will offer visitors a glimpse of historic rail travel. From the visitor center, you'll see flags flying from every state that the UP operates in.

WORTH DOING: Spend an hour alongside UP's triple-track main line east of town and experience trains virtually nonstop. It's the busiest freight main line in America, and as soon as the tail end of one train disappears, you're likely to see another headlight approaching.

DON'T MISS: Watch the train crews shoving cars over Bailey's twin humps. It's all done by remote control.

GETTING THERE: Exit I-80 at Highway 83 (Exit 177) and head north into town. Turn left onto Philip Avenue and drive for three miles. Turn right at Lakeview Boulevard and then left onto A Street for one mile. Turn right onto Homestead Road and the tower will be straight ahead.

DISCOUNT: 10% off gift shop purchase.

NEVADA

Nevada Northern Railway ⬛

LOCATION: 1100 Avenue A, East Ely
PHONE: 866-407-8326 or 775-289-2085
WEBSITE: nevadanorthernrailway.net
E-MAIL: info@nnry.com

Jim Wrinn

The Nevada Northern is often hailed as the best-preserved standard gauge railroad in the country. The operating railway museum is headquartered on a 56-acre complex with 66 historic buildings, set amid the vastness of the Great Basin. The Nevada Northern was completed in 1906 to haul copper from area mines and smelters to the outside world. Most cars and locomotives have been on the railroad since the first day of their service lives, and they're maintained in the company's own shops.

CHOICES: The Nevada Northern offers something for everyone, railfan or not. It operates on two routes. The Keystone route goes through an old tunnel on the way to Ruth, and the train can be diesel- or steam-powered. Steam engines usually run weekends between April and October. The McGill Junction route takes you through desert country to Adverse. The railroad operates a variety of special and seasonal trains, including barbecue trains, chocolate trains, wine trains, and a Halloween ghost train that features stories from the region's colorful past.

WHEN TO GO: The railroad operates from mid-April through December. Summer is busy, with trains running daily, except on some Tuesdays. Temperatures are usually in the 80s.

GOOD TO KNOW: An annual highlight for photographers is the Winter Steam Spectacular that is held in January or February. Cold, dry desert air often makes for spectacular photos.

WORTH DOING: Visit Great Basin National Park, which is 60 miles from Ely. In this diverse environment, you'll see 13,000-foot mountains, 5,000-year-old bristlecone pines, and Lehman Caves.

DON'T MISS: At the railway, you can see steam engines, wooden passenger cars, a steam-powered rotary plow, and a steam-powered wrecking crane. Structures include the original depot, engine house, freight shed, coaling tower, and water tower. Diesels include everything from an SD9 to a Baldwin VO1000 and a trio of Alco RS-model road switchers.

GETTING THERE: Ely is in east-central Nevada at the junction of Highways 6, 50, and 93.

DISCOUNT: Buy one adult ticket, get one free.

Nevada Southern Railway ②

LOCATION: 600 Yucca Street, Boulder City
PHONE: 702-486-5933
WEBSITE: nevadasouthern.com

Nevada Southern Railway

The railway offers a train ride with a historical twist. This was part of the construction railroad from Las Vegas to Hoover Dam, with tracks having been laid in 1931. It's a nice ride in the desert and a break from the hustle of Las Vegas.

CHOICES: Located within former Union Pacific rail yards, the site includes a platform built to resemble a past structure. Along the 45-minute round trip, you get an up-close look at desert plant life, especially when riding in the train's open-air car. The other cars are air-conditioned, restored Pullman coaches dating back to 1911. A generator car behind the locomotive supplies power to the coaches. Operated by the Nevada State Railroad Museum, the railway's outdoor interpretative area displays a variety of equipment, including steam locomotive No. 264 and its unique Vanderbilt tender.

WHEN TO GO: The railway operates on weekends. Summer in Nevada can be hot, with temperatures hitting triple digits. Halloween, Santa, train robbery, and other special trains run.

GOOD TO KNOW: You'll save money in Boulder City. It's the only community in Nevada where gambling is not legal.

WORTH DOING: Take a trip to nearby Boulder Dam and tour this technological wonder. Boating on Lake Mead is a popular activity any time of the year.

DON'T MISS: Ride a train pulled by a historic diesel. One of the locomotives used, UP No. 844, is one of the last GP30 diesel locomotives—an early 1960s diesel that replaced the first generation of diesel locomotives that had themselves replaced steam power.

GETTING THERE: Boulder City is a 30-minute drive from Las Vegas and McCarran International Airport. It is an easy drive from Las Vegas along Highway 93 into Boulder City. Once there, turn left on Yucca Street to the museum.

Nevada State Railroad Museum ➌

LOCATION: 2180 S. Carson Street, Carson City
PHONE: 775-687-6953
WEBSITE: nevadaculture.org
E-MAIL: form on website

Jim Wrinn

Few states can claim as rich a railroading heritage as Nevada, and this museum does an admirable job of interpreting it. The first transcontinental railroad, the state's many mining railroads, and the historic Virginia & Truckee—which ran right past the museum property—are all represented here. The museum boasts a particularly fine collection of 19th century rolling stock, much of which originally came from the V&T and was used in dozens of Hollywood films and television shows.

CHOICES: Star of the museum's collection is *Inyo*, a wood-burning 4-4-0 built for the V&T in 1875, and the museum still steams it over the July 4th holiday. When *Inyo* isn't operating, it's on display along with other beautifully restored pre-1915 freight and passenger equipment including an ex-V&T McKeen motor car.

WHEN TO GO: The museum is open Fridays through Mondays. Steam trains or motor cars operate most weekends from May until October, with added Thanksgiving and Christmas runs. Mid-summer highs are usually in the 80s, with little chance of precipitation.

GOOD TO KNOW: Carson City's downtown area is very walkable. The state capitol grounds and surrounding neighborhoods of historic homes are particularly pleasant. A wide variety of hotels, motels, and restaurants can be found nearby.

WORTH DOING: For those whose interests run toward scholarly pursuits, the museum has impressive static displays exploring such topics as the Central Pacific Railroad in Nevada railroading and the evolution of V&T motive power. Lectures by leading rail historians are offered, and the museum also hosts an annual symposium on Nevada railroad history.

DON'T MISS: Examine and ride aboard the restored McKeen self-propelled rail car No. 22, built for the Virginia & Truckee. The amazing boat-like car even has portholes!

GETTING THERE: The museum is on Highway 395 (Carson Street) on the south side of Carson City. Carson City is within a day's drive of most major cities on the West Coast. Amtrak's *California Zephyr* stops at Reno, about 35 miles away, and several major airlines also serve Reno.

Virginia & Truckee Railroad

LOCATION: 370 F Street, Virginia City
PHONE: 775-847-0380
WEBSITE: www.virginiatruckee.com
E-MAIL: info@virginiatruckee.com

Jim Wrinn

The famous Comstock Lode yielded more than $400 million of silver and gold during a roughly 30-year period beginning in 1859—and it led to the creation of both Virginia City and the Virginia & Truckee Railroad. The city saw up to 45 arrivals and departures a day. Today's V&T operates a 35-minute, five-mile round trip from Virginia City to Gold Hill.

CHOICES: You can ride the historic route from Virginia City to Gold Hill and back, with spectacular views of rugged mountain scenery and mine ruins. This is a short trip. For those with the desire for a trip over a longer route, choose the Sisters in History run over the newly rebuilt track from just outside Carson City into Virginia City. The railroad powers its trains with either a 1916 Baldwin 2-8-0 steam locomotive from the Longview, Portland & Northern or a General Electric 80-ton diesel. Passenger cars include a restored 1914 Pullman coach and a 1907 private car.

WHEN TO GO: V&T operates daily from late May to the end of October, when it runs its haunted Halloween train that is not only fun but offers spectacular stargazing on V&T's mountain right-of-way, far from city lights. Temperatures are comfortable throughout the operating season, with average highs topping out in the low 80s during July and August.

GOOD TO KNOW: Virginia City boasts a variety of restaurants, hotels, and B&Bs that recall the town's frontier heritage, and many are within walking distance of the V&T station.

WORTH DOING: The historic Virginia City walking tour provides a good sense of the Comstock mining boom. It includes historic mansions, churches, the Piper Opera House, and the *Territorial Enterprise* newspaper, where young Mark Twain worked as a reporter.

DON'T MISS: The Nevada State Railroad Museum in nearby Carson City displays more than 30 pieces of equipment that operated on the V&T.

GETTING THERE: Virginia City is on Highway 341, 25 miles south of Reno and 15 miles north of Carson City.

DISCOUNT: $1 off regular fare.

NEW HAMPSHIRE

Ashland Railroad Station Museum ❶

The museum was built by the Boston, Concord & Montreal Railroad as a station around 1869. It is one of the state's best preserved examples of a 19th century passenger station. The museum contains rail artifacts and photo displays. Occasionally, an excursion train stops at the museum. It is open Saturdays during July and August.

LOCATION: 69 Depot Street, Ashland
PHONE: 603-968-7716
WEBSITE: www.oldashlandnh.org

Café Lafayette Dinner Train ❷

Ride aboard a restaurant with a view of mountains and forests. This two-hour, 20-mile round trip follows the Pemigewasset River over a 100-year-old spur of the Boston & Maine Railroad. Enjoy a five-course dinner in several restored Pullman cars, including the *Granite Eagle*, a dome car that rode on the *City of New Orleans*.

LOCATION: Route 112, North Woodstock
PHONE: 800-699-3501 or 603-745-3500
WEBSITE: nhdinnertrain.com

Gorham Historical Society Museum ❸

The 1907 former Grand Trunk Railroad station houses a museum that exhibits rail and local historical items. It displays a 1911 Baldwin steam locomotive, a 1949 F7 diesel locomotive, and several boxcars. Operated by the Gorham Historical Society, the museum is open Memorial Day weekend through mid-October.

LOCATION: 25 Railroad Street, Gorham
PHONE: 603-466-5338
WEBSITE: gorhamnewhampshire.com/railroadmuseum.html
E-MAIL: gorhamhistoricalsociety@gmail.com

Potter Place Railroad Station ❹

The wooden Potter Place station, which was built in 1874, features striking Victorian Stick-style architectural elements. Listed on the National Register of Historic Places, the station includes a preserved station master's office and exhibits on local history. This historical site also includes a Central Vermont caboose and freight house, both from the early 1900s, as well as a general store and schoolhouse.

LOCATION: 105 Depot Street, Andover
WEBSITE: andoverhistory.org
E-MAIL: pres@andoverhistory.org

Sandown Depot Museum ❺

The museum is located in the restored Sandown railroad depot that was built in 1873. It contains a stationmaster's room with a working telegraph key and a waiting room with a pot-bellied stove. The museum also features two Flanger cars. It is open weekends May through October.

LOCATION: 1 Depot Road, Sandown
PHONE: 603-887-6100
WEBSITE: sandown.us/historical_society/museum_main.htm

Silver Lake Railroad ❻

Situated just south of North Conway, the Silver Lake Railway offers a 45-minute round trip through a scenic chain of ponds. From the open-air cars, passengers can see a variety of scenery, from mountains to swamps. The railroad's museum displays a range of vintage equipment and buildings, including an ice cream parlor in a diner. It is open weekends July through September.

LOCATION: Route 113, Madison
WEBSITE: silverlakerailroad.com
E-MAIL: form on website

Conway Scenic Railroad 🔟

LOCATION: 38 Norcross Circle, North Conway
PHONE: 800-232-5251 or 603-356-5251
WEBSITE: conwayscenic.com
E-MAIL: info@conwayscenic.com

Conway Scenic, Travis Bragg

Here is a New England excursion train ride bursting with great scenery and Yankee character. The setting is in the Mount Washington Valley in the charming village of North Conway. With three different trips to choose from, this railroad offers a bounty of great journeys.

CHOICES: Two Valley Train excursions are offered: a 55-minute, 11-mile round trip to Conway and a longer 21-mile round trip to Bartlett. The Notch Train carries passengers from North Conway into the rugged Crawford Notch, as the first trains did more than 130 years ago. Passengers may choose from coach, first-class, or dining car service. Valley Train passengers can dine aboard the *Chocorua*, and those on the Notch Train, on the *Hattie Evans*, which had been used on the Norfolk & Western's *Powhatan Arrow* and *Pocahontas*. Steam engines operate excursions and special trains on a limited basis.

WHEN TO GO: Valley Trains operate excursions April through December and the Notch Train runs June through October. What can be better than a autumn train ride in New England? Special trains operate throughout the year. For a change of scenery, try riding a snow train in late December.

GOOD TO KNOW: Stick to the right side of the Notch Train as it ascends Crawford Notch and crosses the Frankenstein Trestle (named for artist Godfrey Frankenstein, not because it's a monster trestle) and Willey Brook Bridge for excellent views of bluffs, ravines, and streams. The later in fall you travel, the fewer colors you'll see, but the better the vistas are from the train.

WORTH DOING: The surrounding Mount Washington Valley and White Mountain National Forest offer four seasons of recreational activities, attractions, and spectacular scenery.

DON'T MISS: Well, you can't miss the Victorian station in North Conway. Take some time to appreciate this ornate structure that's been at work as a railroad depot since 1874.

GETTING THERE: The Conway Scenic Railroad is less than a three-hour drive from Boston. From Boston, take 1-95 to Route 16, which runs to North Conway.

DISCOUNT: Buy full-price adult coach fare, get second at half price; subject to availability.

Hobo & Winnipesaukee Scenic Railroads ▣

LOCATION: 64 Railroad Street, Lincoln (Hobo)
LOCATION: 154 Main Street, Meredith (Winnipesaukee)
PHONE: 603-745-2135 (Hobo) or 603-279-5253 (Winnipesaukee)
WEBSITE: www.hoborr.com
E-MAIL: form on website

Hobo Railroad, George Kenson

Boston & Maine's 72-mile White Mountain Branch from the state capital of Concord north to Lincoln long served paper mills and other forestry companies, but the railroad abandoned this route as those businesses shut down. Fortunately, the entire line has survived, and two tourist train operations on the northern 54 miles keep portions busy for visitors throughout the year.

CHOICES: The Hobo Railroad offers 15-mile round trips on the north end of the branch to the many tourists who visit the White Mountain region. Trains out of Lincoln follow the scenic Pemigewasset River south, crossing numerous trestles, and passing such locations as Grandma's Crossing and Swimming Hole Bridge, before changing directions at the Jack O'Lantern Resort near Thornton. Farther south, on the shores of its namesake lake, the Winnipesaukee Scenic Railroad offers trains out of Meredith and Weirs Beach to and from Lakeport, always in view of New Hampshire's largest lake. Trains include open-window coaches as well as first-class parlor accommodations. The railroads also run caboose trains and hold a track car weekend.

WHEN TO GO: Both railroads operate weekends from May through mid-June, and daily through the summer. The daily operations continue through the fall foliage season on the Hobo, while the Winnipesaukee reverts to a weekend schedule. Santa Claus specials run on December weekends.

GOOD TO KNOW: Lake Winnipesaukee is a major summer vacation destination, and the White Mountains also attract large crowds through summer and for fall foliage. Advance bookings for lodging are advised during these busy periods.

WORTH DOING: To see more of Lake Winnipesaukee, daytime and dinner cruises are available from Weirs Beach. You can explore the quaint shops, antique stores, and historic buildings of Meredith. There is much to do in the White Mountains, from hiking and kayaking to viewing covered bridges, waterfalls, and wildlife.

DON'T MISS: Try a hobo picnic lunch, complete with a souvenir bindle stick.

GETTING THERE: For the Hobo, take I-93 to Exit 32. For the Winnipesaukee, take I-93 to Exit 23. The drive through the center of New Hampshire is beautiful year-round.

DISCOUNT: $1 off ticket on regular excursions Jul.-Aug.; not valid with other discounts.

Mount Washington Cog Railway ⑨

LOCATION: Base Road, Bretton Woods
PHONE: 800-922-8825 or 603-278-5404
WEBSITE: www.thecog.com
E-MAIL: info@thecog.com

Karl Zimmermann

England may have invented the railroad, but the United States invented the mountain-climbing cog railroad. The first such successful cog—a standard railroad with flanged wheels but with the addition of a gear engaging a toothed "rack" rail in the center of the tracks—was the Mount Washington Cog Railway, which opened in 1869 and has been in operation ever since. The trip takes you to the top of 6,288-foot Mount Washington, infamous for its bad weather but famous for its great views.

CHOICES: Sit back and enjoy the views during the trip to the summit and back. On good days, you can see four states, Canada, and the Atlantic Ocean. The trains operate on a steep track that resembles a ladder plunked down on the mountainside. The faster diesel-powered run up the mountain now allows visitors a full hour at the summit.

WHEN TO GO: Excursion trains operate spring through fall, and reservations are recommended. In fall, the White Mountains are always spectacular. In May, trains operate only on weekends. From the beginning of June through the end of November, service is daily.

GOOD TO KNOW: Though most trips are now powered by the railroad's biodiesel-powered engines, one trip a day is typically operated in the traditional manner, with a coal-burning steam locomotive.

WORTH DOING: Explore the mountains. Mount Washington State Park is at the summit and contains hiking trails, an observatory, a visitor center, and the stone Tip Top House, a hotel built in 1853 and restored as a museum. It is surrounded by the White Mountain National Forest, which is filled with a variety of recreational activities.

DON'T MISS: View the railway's original cog engine, *Old Peppersass*, which is on display at Marshfield, the base station. The railway's museum is also located there.

GETTING THERE: The Cog Railway is a pleasant drive from Boston, Hartford, New York, or Montreal. It is 90 miles from Portland off Route 302. In Bretton Woods, follow Base Road for six miles to the railway.

White Mountain Central Railroad 🔟

LOCATION: Route 3, Lincoln
PHONE: 603-745-8913
WEBSITE: www.whitemountaincentralrr.com
E-MAIL: info@clarkstradingpost.com

Priscilla Carton

The White Mountain Central Railroad is part of the popular family-owned Clark's Trading Post amusement park deep in New Hampshire's White Mountains. The railroad offers 30-minute excursions across the Pemigewasset River over a 1904 Howe truss railroad covered bridge that was moved from the Barre & Chelsea Railroad in Vermont.

CHOICES: Once a center for the logging and paper industries, the region now caters to tourists. Five decades ago, the Clark family added a 1.25-mile railroad to their small amusement park and acquired an impressive collection of geared steam locomotives. The park includes a variety of museums, displays, and attractions. Admission includes the train ride as well as other activities.

WHEN TO GO: Operations are daily beginning in mid-June through the end of August and on weekends in early June, September, and October. The best fall foliage usually occurs in early October, which is also the peak tourist season. Special excursions and displays occur on Railroad Days, which is scheduled on a September weekend.

GOOD TO KNOW: Lodging, including motels and B&Bs, and restaurants can be found in Lincoln and the surrounding communities. Rates will be the highest during fall, so reservations should be made far in advance for this season.

WORTH DOING: The White Mountain National Forest is worth visiting any time of year for camping, hiking, history, and scenic drives.

DON'T MISS: The star attractions of the park's locomotive collection are a wood-burning International Shoe two-truck Heisler and Beebe River Railroad two-truck Climax, joined by a East Branch & Lincoln two-truck Shay, and only known Reo railbus.

GETTING THERE: If driving on I-93, take Exit 33, and go south one mile on Route 3. In fall, driving along the Kangamangus Highway from Conway offers exceptional views.

NEW JERSEY

Maywood Station Museum ❶

This station has been restored, inside and out, to preserve its Victorian style. The station museum features local railroad artifacts and photos. Also on display are a restored caboose that contains additional exhibits and a New York, Susquehanna & Western Alco S2 diesel locomotive. It is open on a limited schedule.

LOCATION: 269 Maywood Avenue, Maywood
WEBSITE: maywoodstation.com
E-MAIL: info@maywoodstation.com
DISCOUNT: 10% off gift shop purchase.

Black River & Western Railroad 2

LOCATION: 105 John Ringo Road, Ringoes
WEBSITE: brrht.org
E-MAIL: info@brrht.org

Karl Zimmermann

The Black River & Western, which also hauls freight, operates hour-long passenger excursions over a short segment of the former Pennsylvania Railroad's Flemington Branch between Flemington and Ringoes.

CHOICES: While recent trains have been diesel-powered, look for steam engine No. 60's return to service. In addition to standard weekend excursions, various family-friendly special trains and events are offered throughout the year. These include an Easter Bunny Express, murder mystery trains, trains to a corn maze and pumpkin patch, Santa Express, North Pole Express, and others. You can board the trains for round trips from either station.

WHEN TO GO: The Black River & Western operates on weekends from May through August, and in October for the the fall foliage season, which is an ideal time to take this idyllic ride.

GOOD TO KNOW: Flemington is a mixture of quaint and commercial, with 60 percent of its buildings on the National Register of Historic Places. There are also plenty of shops and a handful of B&Bs.

WORTH DOING: Northlandz, an extraordinary model railroad rich in spectacle, is located in Flemington. With eight actual miles of track, dozens of trains moving at once, and 35-foot-tall model mountains, it's acres of whimsical fun. It also features a collection of 200 dolls.

DON'T MISS: Just across the Delaware River in Pennsylvania is the New Hope & Ivyland Railroad, which makes it easy to ride two excursion trains in the same day. Almost as close is the Delaware River Railroad in Phillipsburg, N.J.

GETTING THERE: Flemington is roughly 35 miles from Philadelphia and 50 miles from New York City. Ringoes is about 15 miles farther from each city. Both Ringoes and Flemington are located just off Route 202. The Flemington station is on Stangl Road.

New Jersey

Delaware River Railroad ▪3

LOCATION: 100 Elizabeth Street, Phillipsburg
PHONE: 877-872-7433
WEBSITE: 877trainride.com
E-MAIL: ccotty@fastwww.com

Dave Crosby

Ride along the scenic Delaware River in western New Jersey from Phillipsburg to Carpentersville aboard one of the only steam trains in the state. The railroad continues to rehabilitate additional trackage and excursions are expected to reach as far south as Riegelsville.

CHOICES: The Delaware River Railroad operates several themed trains in addition to the standard excursions along the Delaware River. Activities include Great Pumpkin, Corn Maze, and Mine Train specials, which are fun for the whole family as are the seasonal holiday rides, while the Warren County Wine Train offers more adult fare on its trip to two local wineries.

WHEN TO GO: Beginning in May, regular excursions operate on Saturdays and Sundays May through October. Autumn provides particularly breathtaking views of the changing leaves along the Delaware River.

GOOD TO KNOW: Although it resembles an early American locomotive, engine No. 142 was constructed in 1988 by the TangShan Locomotive Works in the People's Republic of China.

WORTH DOING: Across the river, nearby Easton, Pa., features a historic downtown with activities the whole family can enjoy such as visiting the Crayola Museum and the National Canal Museum.

DON'T MISS: Having been served by five different railroads, Phillipsburg is rich in railroad history. Be sure to visit the nearby Phillipsburg Union Station, a museum containing artifacts, maps, and photos of New Jersey railroad history. A short distance away, the Phillipsburg Railroad Historians offer a miniature train ride.

GETTING THERE: Situated on the Delaware River, Phillipsburg is located along the New Jersey-Pennsylvania border. It is easily reached by automobile via Route 22 or I-78. The station is just off Main Street in Phillipsburg.

New Jersey Museum of Transportation ❹

LOCATION: 4265 Route 524, Farmingdale
PHONE: 732-938-5524
WEBSITE: njmt.org

Jim Wrinn

The museum is home to many rare pieces of equipment, and it offers a short ride on a narrow gauge train on the grounds of Allaire State Park.

CHOICES: Besides looking at the equipment on display, you have the opportunity to tour the museum's shops and see the progress on the various restoration projects. The train travels through the scenic state park, which is home to the Manasquan River.

WHEN TO GO: The vintage locomotives run weekends April through June and September through December. In summer, diesel locomotives run daily. During the Railroader's Weekend Celebration in mid-September, all the equipment in running shape operates. The Christmas Express, which started more than 30 years ago, begins running in late November and continues into December.

GOOD TO KNOW: Formed by one of the oldest all-volunteer railroad preservation groups, the museum began as the Pine Creek Railroad in 1952, using rail salvaged from sand pits.

WORTH DOING: In the park, you can explore Allaire Village, a historic 19th century ironmaking town. The park also contains hiking and biking trails.

DON'T MISS: Look for the Ely-Thomas Lumber Company Shay locomotive. While not operable at present, it is one of the smallest Shays left in existence.

GETTING THERE: The museum is located in Allaire State Park, not far from the ocean. It is easily accessible from the Garden State Parkway or I-195 off Exit 31B. Signs show the way to the park.

Whippany Railway Museum ➎

LOCATION: 1 Railroad Plaza, Whippany
PHONE: 973-887-8177
WEBSITE: whippanyrailwaymuseum.net
E-MAIL: wrym-web@comcast.net

Steve Hepler

The Whippany Railway Museum, which is housed in a restored 1904 freight house, displays a large selection of historic locomotives and rolling stock. Much of the collection focuses on New Jersey railroading.

CHOICES: The Whippany Railway Museum also operates several themed and special-event excursions throughout the year including caboose rides and Easter, pumpkin, and Santa Claus trains. The museum's collection features a 100-year-old Baldwin 2-8-0 steam locomotive, a CNJ observation car, a D&H caboose, a railbus, and several vintage diesels including an RS-1 and two GE 70-tonners. Among the structures on the grounds are a Morristown & Erie Railroad passenger station made of fieldstone and a wooden water tank. Interior exhibits are changed each year to highlight a different railroad.

WHEN TO GO: The Whippany Railway Museum is open Sundays April through October. Special excursions run on select dates throughout the year.

GOOD TO KNOW: The museum grounds are adjacent to the Morristown & Erie Railroad, an active freight hauler. The museum was originally founded as the Morris County Central Railroad Museum in 1967 to complement the Morris County Central's steam excursion line. Several pieces of former Morris County Central have been acquired by the museum.

WORTH DOING: The town of Whippany plays host to a number of outdoor recreational activities such as the Patriots Path hiking and biking trail.

DON'T MISS: Ride the 1927 Jersey Coast club car which has been magnificently restored and features a *Blue Comet* paint scheme. Also view steam locomotive No. 4039, which is listed on the National Register of Historic Places.

GETTING THERE: Whippany is in northeast New Jersey, about 20 miles from Newark. It easily reached via I-80, I-78, or I-287. The museum is located at the intersection of Routes 10 and 511 (Whippany Road) in Whippany.

NEW MEXICO

Belen Harvey House Museum ❶

Adjacent to the BNSF Division yard, the museum contains exhibits on Harvey Houses and the Santa Fe Railroad. Listed on the National Register of Historic Places, the Southwestern-style structure is one of state's few surviving Fred Harvey eating establishments. The museum is open Tuesday through Sunday.

LOCATION: 104 N. First Street, Belen
PHONE: 505-861-0581
WEBSITE: belenharveyhouse.com

Las Cruces Railroad Museum ❷

The museum is housed in a 1910 AT&SF depot with a Mission Revival look. Its photographs, artifacts, and displays highlight the depot itself, railroad workers, and communication. It also features a model railroad train room. The museum offers a variety of lectures and programs, including Railroad Days in May. It is open Thursday through Saturday.

LOCATION: 351 N. Mesilla Street, Las Cruces
PHONE: 575-647-4480
WEBSITE: las-cruces.org
E-MAIL: gcourts@las-cruces.org

Cumbres & Toltec Scenic Railroad ▣

LOCATION: 500 Terrace Avenue, Chama
PHONE: 888-286-2737 or 575-756-2151
WEBSITE: cumbrestoltec.com
E-MAIL: info@cumbrestoltec.com

Jim Wrinn

If you have ever craved going back in time to the 1920s to see what railroading was like, here's your chance. The Cumbres & Toltec operates 64 miles of track through the San Juan Mountains. Steam locomotives still labor up steep grades, cross 100-foot-tall trestles, and hug narrow shelves above yawning gorges. For more than 125 years, excursion passengers have ridden over Cumbres Pass, and the line crosses the border between Colorado and New Mexico 11 times.

CHOICES: The railroad offers a choice of excursions, and you can leave from either Chama or Antonito, Colo. From either station, there is a round trip to Osier, Colo., where a hot meal is provided. To see the scenic area in two different ways, you can ride the train one way and return by motor coach. The ride from Chama to Antonito shows you steam locomotives at work as the 2-8-2 Mikado type engines original to this line dig in and go upgrade for several miles. Ride an open-window coach or a first-class car, and as your train moves along, be sure and walk back to the open gondola car. It's a great view and a lot of fun.

WHEN TO GO: Excursion trains operate daily from the end of May until mid-October. Wild West trains and other special events take place during the season.

GOOD TO KNOW: The railroad hopes to have the Loboto trestle just outside Chama, which was damaged by fire in July 2010, repaired in time for the 2011 season. Until repairs are completed, the railroad will make trips out of Chama but bus passengers to Cumbres Pass for the journey to Osier or Antonito.

WORTH DOING: The nearby Rio Grande National Forest contains the headwaters of the Rio Grande River and features the moonlike landscape of the Wheeler Geologic Area and a variety of other natural wonders.

DON'T MISS: Walk the Chama shop complex and yard and return to the 1920s. You'll see the coaling tower, water tank, back shop, and all sorts of clutter that is natural to a railroad yard.

GETTING THERE: The railroad is located between Santa Fe and Colorado Springs. To reach Chama from Santa Fe, take Highway 285 to Highway 84. Highway 285 also takes you to Antonito.

Santa Fe Southern Railway [4]

LOCATION: 410 S. Guadalupe Street, Santa Fe
PHONE: 888-989-8600 or 505-989-8600
WEBSITE: sfsr.com
E-MAIL: depot@sfsr.com

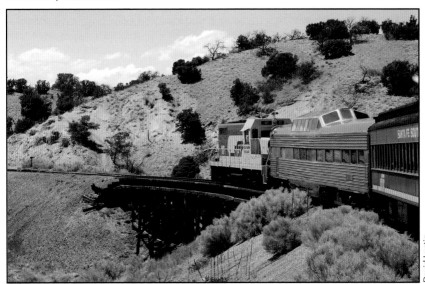

David Lustig

One of the most famous railroad names of all is the Atchison, Topeka & Santa Fe Railway, usually known simply as the Santa Fe. This railway offers the chance to ride through the desert from Santa Fe along a historic spur to the junction city of Lamy.

CHOICES: Even if it wasn't a beautiful trip through the desert, the Santa Fe Southern offers something special: a chance to ride a working freight train. The railroad's scenic day train is a four-hour round trip aboard a real working mixed train. Along with vintage coaches, the train will most likely pull boxcars between Santa Fe and Lamy. You have the choice of riding in coach or silver class. Silver-class cars are vintage AT&SF *Super Chief* cars.

WHEN TO GO: The excursion trains operate year-round. There are numerous special events scheduled throughout the year, especially around holidays, as well as barbecue dinners and evening desert runs.

GOOD TO KNOW: If you would like to see one of the last surviving Harvey Houses, you can visit La Fonda Hotel located in Santa Fe's historic plaza.

WORTH DOING: The Lamy depot, built in 1880, has been renovated to match the style of the depot in Santa Fe.

DON'T MISS: Santa Fe is well known for its Southwest culture and art galleries, which number more than 200. Be sure and visit the Georgia O'Keefe Museum.

GETTING THERE: Santa Fe is 60 miles northeast of Albuquerque on I-25 and Highway 285. In Santa Fe, the station is on Guadalupe Street between Cerrillos Road and Agua Fria Street.

NEW YORK

Alco-Brooks Railroad Display ❶

Located at the Chautauqua County Fairgrounds, this display features an Alco-Brooks 0-6-0 locomotive built in 1916, a Delaware & Hudson wood-sided boxcar, a wooden New York Central caboose, and other railroad artifacts.

LOCATION: 1089 Central Avenue, Dunkirk
PHONE: 716-366-3797
WEBSITE: wnyrails.org/cities/dunkirk/display.htm
E-MAIL: wnyrails@wnyrails.org

Central Square Station Museum ❷

The museum has various pieces of rail equipment on outdoor display including two 0-4-0 steam locomotives, a 1929 Brill car, a circus car, a streetcar, and a GE diesel switcher. Indoor exhibits are housed in an early 20th century depot. It is open Sundays May through October.

LOCATION: 132 Railroad Street, Central Square
PHONE: 315-676-7582
WEBSITE: www.cnynrhs.org/CentralSq.html
E-MAIL: csquare@cnynrhs.org

Cooperstown & Charlotte Valley Railroad ❸

On a 16-mile round trip between Milford and Cooperstown, the railroad takes you through a variety of landscapes found in the Upper Susquehanna River Valley. You cross the river twice over two steel-truss bridges. In the restored 1869 Milford depot, you can view an array of railroad displays.

LOCATION: 136 East Main Street, Milford
PHONE: 607-432-2429 or 607-286-7805
WEBSITE: lrhs.com
E-MAIL: wendy@lrhs.com

Empire State Railway Museum ❹

Through photos, films, and artifacts, the museum highlights the history of railroads that served the Catskills. The museum, located in a restored 1899 Ulster & Delaware Railroad station, is also restoring several railway cars and a 1910 2-8-0 locomotive. It is open weekends and holidays from Memorial Day through October.

LOCATION: 70 Lower High Street, Phoenicia
PHONE: 845-688-7501
WEBSITE: esrm.com

Finger Lakes Scenic Railway ❺

The Finger Lakes Railway runs passenger excursions (and freight trains) over 130 miles of track. The railroad offers a multitude of themed train rides leaving from a variety of boarding locations. Family friendly outings focus on events such as Halloween and Christmas. Excursions run May through December.

LOCATION: Railroad Place and Wadsworth Street, Geneva
PHONE: 315-209-1029
WEBSITE: fingerlakesscenicrailway.com
E-MAIL: form on website

Hyde Park Railroad Station ❻

Built in 1914, the Hyde Park Railroad Station is listed on the National Register of Historic Places. You can tour the restored station, which was designed by the same architects who designed Grand Central Station, and view displays on the area's railroading history. It is open weekends from mid-June to mid-September, on Monday evenings, and for special events.

LOCATION: 34 River Road, Hyde Park
PHONE: 845-229-2338
WEBSITE: hydeparkstation.com
E-MAIL: webmaster@hydeparkstation.com
DISCOUNT: 10% off any purchase.

Martisco Station Museum ❼

This restored 1870 New York Central station contains two floors of local railroad artifacts. On the first floor of this Victorian-style brick structure, you'll enter a replica of a small-town railroad station. Items are displayed outside as well. It is open Sunday afternoons late May until October.

LOCATION: 5085 Martisco Road, Marcellus
PHONE: 315-673-1749
WEBSITE: cnynrhs.org/Martisco.html
E-MAIL: martisco@cnynrhs.org

New York Museum of Transportation ❽

The museum exhibits various trolley cars, a steam locomotive, a caboose, and rail artifacts as well as highway and horse-drawn vehicles. It features trolley rides and a short track-car ride that takes you to the nearby Rochester & Genesee Valley Railroad Museum. The museum is open Sundays year-round, and for some special events, diesel trains operate.

LOCATION: 6393 E. River Road, West Henrietta
PHONE: 585-533-1113
WEBSITE: nymtmuseum.org
E-MAIL: info@nymtmuseum.org

New York Transit Museum ❾

Located in a 1936 subway station, the New York Transit Museum features restored subway cars and other exhibits related to urban transit. Exhibits highlight elevated rail lines and the construction of New York City's first subway line. The museum also offers special subway tours and events during the year.

LOCATION: Boerum Place at Schermerhorn Street, Brooklyn
PHONE: 718-694-1600
WEBSITE: mta.info/mta/museum

North Creek Railway Depot Museum ➓

Step into the North Creek Depot Museum and you'll relive a piece of presidential history. The depot was where Theodore Roosevelt learned he had become president at the death of President McKinley. The museum also tells the story of the Adirondack Railroad and the central Adirondack Mountains. The Upper Hudson River Railroad boards from the building's platform.

LOCATION: 5 Railroad Place, North Creek
PHONE: 518-251-5842
WEBSITE: northcreekdepotmuseum.com
E-MAIL: director@northcreekdepotmuseum.com

Railroad Museum of Long Island ➓

The Railroad Museum of Long Island has two locations: Greenport and Riverhead. Greenport, situated in a Victorian-style Long Island Rail Road freight station, exhibits photos and artifacts of Long Island rail history. It displays an 1898 snowplow and a 1927 wooden caboose. An operating tower and turntable are also on site. At Riverhead, the museum restores its rolling stock and displays several steam locomotives and various railcars. A miniature train ride also operates around the site. The Riverhead visitor center is located at 416 Griffing Avenue. At times, you can take the LIRR and tour both sites in one day.

LOCATION: 440 Fourth Street, Greenport
PHONE: 631-477-0439 (Greenport) or 631-727-7920 (Riverhead)
WEBSITE: www.rmli.us
E-MAIL: info@rmli.us

Railroad Museum of the Niagara Frontier ➓

Housed in the restored Erie Railroad freight depot, which was built in 1922, the museum contains a collection of artifacts that recognizes the region's railroading heritage. Also on display are several industrial locomotives, an Erie caboose, and a New York Central caboose.

LOCATION: 111 Oliver Street, North Tonawanda
PHONE: 716-694-9588
WEBSITE: railroadniagara.com
E-MAIL: rrmuseum@nfcnrhs.com

Rochester & Genesee Valley Railroad Museum ⓭

The Rochester & Genesee Valley Railroad Museum is housed in a restored 1918 Erie Railroad depot. Inside, you'll see the original ticket agent's office, waiting room, and artifacts. You can also inspect various early diesel and steam locomotives, freight cars, and passenger cars. It is open Sundays mid-May through October. Start your visit with a track-car ride from the nearby New York Museum of Transportation.

LOCATION: 282 Rush-Scottsville Road, Rush
PHONE: 585-533-1431
WEBSITE: rgvrrm.org
E-MAIL: form on website

Roscoe O&W Railway Museum ⓮

This museum complex features a station building, a restored Ontario & Western caboose, a Beaverkill trout car, and watchman shanties. The museum specializes in O&W memorabilia and artifacts but also contains other railroad and local historical items.

LOCATION: 7 Railroad Avenue, Roscoe
PHONE: 607-498-4346
WEBSITE: www.nyow.org/museum.html
E-MAIL: wilsip@frontiernet.net

Salamanca Rail Museum ⓯

This Buffalo, Rochester & Pittsburgh depot has been fully restored right down to the telegraph key in the ticket office, and it includes a ladies retiring room and a baggage room. Artifacts and photos show the history of railroads in western New York and Pennsylvania. A boxcar, a crew camp car, and two cabooses are on display.

LOCATION: 170 Main Street, Salamanca
PHONE: 716-945-3133
WEBSITE: mysite.verizon.net/bizxyrad/salamancarailmuseumassociation
E-MAIL: salarail@verizon.net
DISCOUNT: 10% off gift shop purchase.

Trolley Museum of New York ⓰

The museum operates a trolley ride from Kingston to the banks of the Hudson River, where you can enjoy a picnic lunch. With a stop at the museum, you can learn about trolleys and see them being restored. The museum's collection dates back to 1897 with its Oslo, Norway, car that was built in Germany.

LOCATION: 89 E. Strand Street, Kingston
PHONE: 845-331-3399
WEBSITE: tmny.org
E-MAIL: admin@tmny.org

Adirondack Scenic Railroad 🔟

LOCATION: 321 Main Street, Utica
PHONE: 800-819-2291 or 315-724-0700
WEBSITE: adirondackrr.com
E-MAIL: train@adirondackrr.com

Karl Zimmermann

The Adirondack Scenic Railroad currently operates excursions over two sections of line—52 miles of the former New York Central's Adirondack Division from Utica to Thendara (plus an additional six miles on to Carter Station) and 10 miles between Lake Placid and Saranac Lake.

CHOICES: For serious riders, the railroad offers all-day excursions from Utica to Thendara Thursdays and Sundays in summer and Wednesdays through Sundays in fall. There is time for visiting the resort town of Old Forge and taking a two-hour cruise on the Fulton Chain of Lakes. Shorter round trips (of 20 miles, either south to Otter Lake or north to Carter Station) are offered from Thendara. Similar trips operate between Saranac Lake and Lake Placid at the other end of the railroad. You can ride in coaches or in open-air cars to soak in the scenery.

WHEN TO GO: The brilliant foliage of fall makes that season perhaps the choicest time to ride. In late November through mid-December, the railroad offers Polar Express trains in emulation of the Chris Van Allsburg children's book.

GOOD TO KNOW: The Adirondack Scenic Railroad offers a complete smorgasbord of special trains and events throughout the year including dinner, wine-tasting, Halloween, and Doo Wop '50s trains.

WORTH DOING: Thendara (adjacent to Old Forge), Saranac Lake, and Lake Placid are all deep in the Adirondacks, replete with natural beauty. The region's history is interestingly presented at the Adirondack Museum in Blue Mountain Lake. The six-million-acre Adirondack Park offers 2,000 miles of hiking trails and hundreds of miles of canoe routes.

DON'T MISS: The Adirondack Scenic Railroad shares Utica's grand 1914 Union Station with Amtrak, making it among the few excursion railroads with rail connections. Take time to look through this historic station. An easy walk away is the Hotel Utica, which predates the station by two years. Its restored lobby is also worth a look.

GETTING THERE: Served by multiple Amtrak trains each day, Utica also has excellent highway access, being located right on the New York State Thruway (I-90). The nearest major airport is in Syracuse, 56 miles away. Lake Placid is 30 miles from the Adirondack Northway (I-87). Adirondack Regional Airport is in Clear Lake, 15 miles away.

New York

Arcade & Attica Railroad ⏸18

LOCATION: 278 Main Street, Arcade
PHONE: 585-492-3100
WEBSITE: arcadeandatticarr.com
E-MAIL: form on website

Dave Crosby

When steam engine No. 18 blows its whistle, you get a real blast from the past. The Arcade & Attica Railroad offers the last remaining steam locomotive excursion in New York. This 90-minute scenic ride rolls through countryside that has changed little since the line was formed in the early 1880s.

CHOICES: On the 14-mile round trip, you can ride aboard steel heavyweight coaches that were built around 1915 or an open-air gondola observation car (just watch out for soot). The train may also be pulled by a General Electric 44-ton center cab diesel, either No. 111 or No. 112. No. 111 was originally purchased by the railroad in 1947. In the Arcade station, you can view historic photographs, artifacts, and operating model railroad layouts. A 1920s boxcar and caboose are also on display.

WHEN TO GO: Regular excursions run on weekends from Memorial Day through September. During July and August, additional rides take place on Wednesdays and Fridays, and there is a special extended schedule in October for viewing fall foliage aboard a steam train. Murder mystery, Halloween, Christmas, and other special trains also run during the season.

GOOD TO KNOW: Tourist steam excursions began in 1962 with the purchase of No. 18, a 1920 2-8-0 American Locomotive. This locomotive typically operates on noon departures only.

WORTH DOING: A special Civil War reenactment takes place in August that includes a battle with Union and Confederate troops fighting on and off the train. A free shuttle bus takes you to a park where the troops are encamped, so you can see how soldiers and civilians lived in the 1860s.

DON'T MISS: On the 15-minute stopover at Curriers depot, watch No. 18 run around for the return trip to Arcade. You can even take pictures and talk to the crew. Then, for a unique experience, hop in the gondola, which is now coupled to the front of the engine, for the ride back.

GETTING THERE: Arcade is located about an hour's drive south of Buffalo. The museum is located three miles east of Route 16 on Main Street at Railroad Avenue.

178

Catskill Mountain Railroad 🔟

LOCATION: 5408 Route 28, Mount Tremper
PHONE: 845-688-7400
WEBSITE: catskillmtrailroad.com
E-MAIL: info@catskillmtrailroad.com

Karl Zimmermann

The Catskill Mountain Railroad operates at two locations, both segments of the former Ulster & Delaware Railroad, which later became New York Central's Catskill Mountain Branch. The longer section runs from Phoenicia to Cold Brook, a distance of six miles. The railroad recently opened a shorter stretch, about a mile and a half, in Kingston.

CHOICES: Of the two operations, the more extensive and scenic is the one from Phoenicia, which runs along Esopus Creek. You can ride in either an open car or a restored 1917 Delaware, Lackawanna & Western coach pulled by an ex-Long Island Rail Road Alco S1 built in 1946. Trains may be boarded at Mount Tremper or Phoenicia for the full round-trip. The Kingston City Shuttle, powered by an Alco RS1 built in 1950 for the Illinois Terminal, boards at the Westbrook station.

WHEN TO GO: The fall foliage season is the prime time to ride along the Esopus, although trains operate through the summer as well—and that too is a lovely time to visit the Catskill Mountains. The Esopus trains run only on weekends, which includes Fridays in peak season. The *Twilight Limited* runs on several summer evenings from Mount Tremper for a look at the night sky. The Kingston Shuttle runs special event trains on Saturdays from July 4 through Labor Day as well as haunted Halloween and winter holiday trains.

GOOD TO KNOW: Long-range plans call for linking the two segments by opening the 22 miles along the Ashokan Reservoir.

WORTH DOING: When the Catskill Mountain Railroad first opened, its primary function was to haul whitewater inner tubers, rafters, and kayakers upstream along Esopus Creek. These sports remain popular, and the trout fishing is good as well.

DON'T MISS: The restored Phoenicia depot, which opened in 1900, is home to the Empire State Railway Museum, and just a short drive from Phoenicia, the Delaware & Ulster Railroad offers excursions from Arkville.

GETTING THERE: Both sections of the railroad are easily accessible from Exit 19 of the New York State Thruway (I-87). The Kingston Shuttle is virtually right there. For Mount Tremper, follow Route 28 west for roughly 20 miles.

Delaware & Ulster Railroad [20]

LOCATION: 43510 Route 28, Arkville
PHONE: 800-225-4132 or 845-586-3877
WEBSITE: durr.org
E-MAIL: form on website

Karl Zimmermann

The Delaware & Ulster Railroad's 11-mile excursions, a round trip of just under two hours, run from Arkville north to Roxbury, much of it along the scenic East Branch of the Delaware River, across rolling fields and through small towns in the heart of the Catskill Mountains.

CHOICES: In addition to the scenic excursions aboard open cars or ex-Pennsylvania Railroad coaches, the D&U also operates a luncheon train, the *Rip Van Winkle Flyer*. While the *Flyer* doesn't have a set schedule, operating only if a group has made a booking, the public is welcome on these occasions whenever there's available space, which there most often is. Motive power for the excursion and luncheon trains is generally an Alco RS36 resplendent in its original Delaware & Hudson livery.

WHEN TO GO: The Delaware & Ulster operates on Saturdays and Sundays from Memorial Day through the end of October, with Thursday and Friday trains added in July and August. On the railroad route through the Catskill Mountains, there's no more spectacular time for a visit than during the fall foliage season.

GOOD TO KNOW: The *Rip Van Winkle Flyer* is a handsome, five-car Budd-built streamliner, featuring an ex-New York Central parlor-observation car and a dome diner that began life as a Missouri Pacific dome coach.

WORTH DOING: The Catskill Scenic Trail lies along 26 miles of the former Catskill Mountain Branch line. It passes through seven towns and connects with hundreds of miles of other trails. The four-season trail is used by hikers, bicyclists, cross country skiers, and horseback riders.

DON'T MISS: In addition to the depot museums in Roxbury and Phoenicia, the Arkville station offers a small display of photographs and artifacts highlighting the history of the Ulster & Delaware. Allow time for a visit before boarding the train.

GETTING THERE: Arkville is a 43-mile drive on Route 28 from Exit 19 on the New York State Thruway (I-87). Route 28 passes right by the depot.

DISCOUNT: $1 off adult, senior, and children tickets.

Medina Railroad Museum ㉑

LOCATION: 530 West Avenue, Medina
PHONE: 585-798-6106
WEBSITE: railroadmuseum.net
E-MAIL: office@railroadmuseum.net

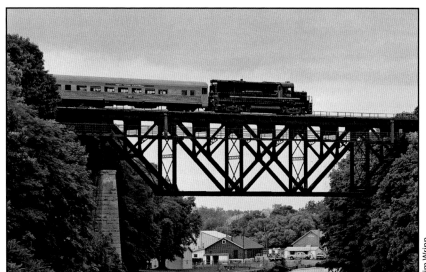

Jim Wrinn

The area east of Buffalo provides a pleasant distraction with small towns, farms, and a relaxed existence. Here, you'll find a museum located inside one of the largest, surviving wooden freight houses around. You will also have the opportunity to ride a streamlined passenger train.

CHOICES: The old New York Central freight house is huge—301 feet long and 34 feet wide—and contains memorabilia, models, and artifacts. Enter the Union Station archway, and you'll see displays dedicated to the trains such as the *Empire State Express* and *20th Century Limited*, and railroads, including the Pennsylvania Railroad, that helped develop the area. On a former New York Central main line, you can ride in 1947 Budd coaches pulled by a historic Alco Century diesel locomotive. The two-hour, 34-mile round trip parallels and then crosses the Erie Canal. The trains are run as special excursions. One special is an all-day winery train.

WHEN TO GO: The museum is open year-round Tuesday through Sunday. Fall foliage trips during October and Santa trains during December are very popular train rides.

GOOD TO KNOW: Ask about the bridge at Lockport, which, according to legend, was built upside down so as to limit the size of barge traffic on the competing Erie Canal.

WORTH DOING: For a unique experience, take a one-of-a-kind ride in a mule-drawn packet boat on the Erie Canal.

DON'T MISS: In the museum, watch a large HO scale model railroad in action. The prototypical railroad layout measures 14 feet by 204 feet. Also, take a close look at the lobby, which is refinished as the freight depot office.

GETTING THERE: Medina is situated between Buffalo and Rochester, not far from Lake Ontario. From Buffalo, take I-90 east to Route 77. Continue north on Route 77/63 to downtown Medina. There, turn left onto North Avenue and then turn right onto West Avenue.

NORTH CAROLINA

Charlotte Trolley Powerhouse Museum ❶

The museum features exhibits devoted to streetcars, including Car 85, which is one of Charlotte's original electric trolley cars. The museum also hosts arts and other special events. Charlotte Trolley is looking to run its vintage trolleys in a new location.

LOCATION: 1507 Camden Road, Charlotte
PHONE: 704-375-0850
WEBSITE: www.charlottetrolley.org
E-MAIL: form on website

Wilmington Railroad Museum ❷

The museum is housed in an 1880s railroad freight warehouse, where you can view Atlantic Coast Line artifacts and a re-creation of a country station. Outside, you can inspect a 1910 Baldwin steam locomotive, a hobo display in a boxcar, and an Atlantic Coast Line caboose. The museum is open year-round.

LOCATION: 505 Nutt Street, Wilmington
PHONE: 910-763-2634
WEBSITE: wrrm.org
E-MAIL: wrrmnc@bellsouth.net

Great Smoky Mountains Railroad ▣

LOCATION: 226 Everett Street, Bryson City
PHONE: 800-872-4681 or 828-586-8811
WEBSITE: gsmr.com
E-MAIL: info@gsmr.com

Jim Wrinn

Few mountain railroads in the southeastern United States traverse such splendid scenery as this line does. Created from a portion of Southern Railway's Murphy Branch, the GSMR hugs the Tuckaseegee and Nantahala Rivers, climbs a mountain at Red Marble Gap, and rolls out over a 700-foot-long trestle at Fontana Lake.

CHOICES: GSMR offers a variety of accommodations on two different train rides. The train features open-air cars, traditional coaches, and air-conditioned lounge cars. One excursion travels to Nantahala Gorge on a 44-mile round trip and includes a layover at the Nantahala Outdoor Center. The other is a 32-mile round trip along the Tuckasegee River to Dillsboro. Seating options include coach, crown class, and first-class. A variety of special-event dinner trains, from murder mysteries to wine tasting, runs throughout the year.

WHEN TO GO: The railroad runs year-round. Spring and fall offer mild weather best suited to open cars and being able to see beyond the trees and into the forest. Summer can be humid, and the tremendous foliage of the Southeast can restrict the views.

GOOD TO KNOW: The railroad offers numerous special events, including some ideal for kids (Thomas the Tank Engine and the Polar Express) and others for the enthusiast, such as the Railfest weekend each September.

WORTH DOING: In the area, you can visit several theme parks, discover Cherokee culture, and explore Great Smoky Mountains National Park from the North Carolina side.

DON'T MISS: Try an adventurous combination package in which you ride the train from Bryson City into the Nantahala Gorge and then raft the river for three hours.

GETTING THERE: The railroad is about three hours from Atlanta and one hour from Asheville. Major highways to the area include I-40, Route 19/23, and Route 441. The stations in both Bryson City and Dillsboro are downtown.

DISCOUNT: $3 off adult ticket, up to four; new reservations only, excludes special events.

New Hope Valley Railway

LOCATION: 5121 Daisy Street, Bonsal
PHONE: 919-362-5416
WEBSITE: nhvry.org
E-MAIL: info@nhvry.org

Patrick Treadaway Jr.

Operating from the North Carolina Railroad Museum, the New Hope Valley Railway provides an hour-long trip through the scenic pine forests situated south of Raleigh and Durham in central North Carolina.

CHOICES: The railway offers both steam and diesel round trips between Bonsal and New Hill. You can ride in an open-air car, but try a ride in a real caboose. It doesn't get any better than that! The museum features an outdoor exhibit of railroad equipment as well as displays of local rail artifacts. It includes a variety of industrial and short line diesel locomotives.

WHEN TO GO: The railway operates on select Saturdays and Sundays each month from May through November, with holiday trains scheduled in December. For a taste of regional entertainment, go during a special event that features music. The North Carolina Railroad Museum is open Saturdays and Sundays.

GOOD TO KNOW: The railroad offers the chance to operate a diesel electric or 0-4-0T steam locomotive, which is an oil-burning switcher that began operation in 1941, by advance reservations.

WORTH DOING: The American Tobacco Trail runs near the railway. The trail is built over part of an old rail line that carried tobacco. You can hike, bike, and ride horses along the trail. Special events take place in the trail's New Hill parking lot.

DON'T MISS: Kids will especially enjoy the G scale garden railroad that operates on the grounds.

GETTING THERE: Located between Bonsal and New Hill, the railroad is a 30-minute drive from Raleigh along Route 1. Take Exit 89, turn right on New Hill Holleman Road, and then turn left onto old Route 1 for 2.5 miles. The museum is on the right on Daisy Street, and parking for the train rides is on the left on Bonsal Road.

North Carolina Transportation Museum ⑤

LOCATION: 411 S. Salisbury Avenue, Spencer
PHONE: 704-636-2889
WEBSITE: nctrans.org
E-MAIL: nctrans@nctrans.org

North Carolina Transportation Museum

The state's transportation museum is housed in shop buildings from Southern Railway's largest steam locomotive repair shop that date from before 1900 to 1924. But this is no static museum. Trains run most of the year on 2.5 miles of track, giving visitors the chance to experience a 25-minute train ride that covers most of the 57-acre site.

CHOICES: Among the giant structures you'll see are the nation's largest preserved roundhouse, the 37-stall Bob Julian Roundhouse, which houses railroad displays, a restoration shop, active locomotives, and rolling stock. You will also see the back shop, a 600-foot-long, 80-foot-tall building once used to overhaul steam locomotives. The narrated train rides take place daily during summer, and you can ride in the locomotive cab for an extra fare. You'll get a unique view and a personalized tour. You might even get to blow the horn.

WHEN TO GO: Any time of the year is enjoyable, but take plenty of water along if you go during the sweltering summer. Rail Days, the annual railroad festival when all the trains run, is usually held in June. Fall is long and mild. From November until May, the museum is closed on Mondays.

GOOD TO KNOW: The visitor center served as a train depot in Barber. The building was cut into three sections and moved to the site in 1980. The flue shop, used to repair the flues (pipes) in steam locomotive boilers, houses a collection of antique automobiles.

WORTH DOING: There are plenty of pork barbecue places in the region if you want to sample real Piedmont food.

DON'T MISS: Take a five-minute ride on the turntable. The 100-foot-long lazy Susan is used to turn locomotives at the roundhouse, and it helps define the term "in the round."

GETTING THERE: About an hour's drive from Charlotte or Winston-Salem, the museum is a few minutes off I-85. Take Exit 79 and then follow the signs to the museum in Spencer.

185

Tweetsie Railroad

LOCATION: 300 Tweetsie Railroad Lane, Blowing Rock
PHONE: 800-526-5740 or 828-264-9061
WEBSITE: tweetsie.com
E-MAIL: form on website

Jim Wrinn

One of the original Wild West theme parks of the 1950s when TV cowboys were popular, Tweetsie has roots in one of the most famous Southeastern narrow gauge railroads, the East Tennessee & Western North Carolina. The three-mile train ride gives the historic, coal-fired engines a chance to work and show that they are still the real thing.

CHOICES: The train is pulled by steam locomotive No. 12. The native engine worked for the East Tennessee & Western North Carolina and is listed on the National Register of Historic Places. Ride in a coach close to the engine, so you can hear it work up grade and listen to the whistle echo about the mountains.

WHEN TO GO: The park is open May through October. From Memorial Day weekend through August, it is open daily. An annual railfan weekend is held in September, and a ghost train runs in October.

GOOD TO KNOW: The East Tennessee & Western North Carolina ran from Elizabeth City, Tenn., to Boone, N.C., for many years. Its whistle sounded a "tweet," and from that, locals nicknamed the railroad *Tweetsie*.

WORTH DOING: Visit the Blowing Rock and learn its legend. Hike or drive through the scenic Blue Ridge Mountains. At Grandfather Mountain, you can cross the Mile High Swinging Bridge, a 228-foot long suspension bridge that spans an 80-foot chasm.

DON'T MISS: Bring the entire family along—there's lots to see and do for kids in the park. Admission to the railroad includes amusement rides, live shows, and other attractions.

GETTING THERE: The railroad is west of Winston-Salem in the Blue Ridge Mountains near the Tennessee border. It is located off Route 321 between Boone and Blowing Rock.

NORTH DAKOTA

Bonanzaville USA ❶

The museum features more than 40 historic buildings and 400,000 artifacts that depict life when bonanza homes dotted the Plains. Rail structures include a vintage Northern Pacific train depot, a water tower, and a train shed. The train shed displays an 1883 NP 4-4-0 steam locomotive, a caboose, and a 1930s Pullman car.

LOCATION: 1351 W. Main Avenue, West Fargo
PHONE: 701-282-2822
WEBSITE: bonanzaville.com
E-MAIL: form on website

Fort Lincoln Trolley ❷

A restored trolley car takes you on a nine-mile excursion along the Heart River. The restored American Car streetcar, which was built in the 1890s, takes you from Mandan to Fort Abraham Lincoln State Park and back. The park features several reconstructed buildings that would have been found in the original fort. Mandan is also home to the North Dakota State Railroad Museum.

LOCATION: 2000 Third Street SE, Mandan
PHONE: 701-663-9018
WEBSITE: realnd.com/fortlincolntrolleyindex.htm
DISCOUNT: $2 off a round-trip fare.

Old Soo Depot Transportation Museum ❸

This museum focuses on the transportation history of the American West and includes materials on trains, planes, and automobiles. Located in a completely restored 1912 Soo Line depot, it also offers an excellent location for train-watching. The museum is open Monday through Friday.

LOCATION: 15 N. Main Street, Minot
PHONE: 701-852-2234
WEBSITE: minotchamber.org
E-MAIL: soodepot@srt.com

Railroad Museum of Minot ❹

The Railroad Museum of Minot contains artifacts relating to the Great Northern Railway and other railroads of the area. A Great Northern Railway caboose and a snowplow car are also on display. The museum is open 10-2 on Saturdays.

LOCATION: 19 First Street NE, Minot
PHONE: 701-852-7091
WEBSITE: railroadmuseumofminot.com
E-MAIL: info@railroadmuseumofminot.com

OHIO

AC&J Scenic Line 1

The railway offers a one-hour round trip that takes you over the last remaining portion of the New York Central's Ashtabula-to-Pittsburgh passenger line. On the 12-mile excursion, you'll travel on 1920s passenger cars pulled by a first-generation diesel through scenic forests and farmland and cross two bridges. A variety of special events are scheduled throughout the year.

LOCATION: 161 E. Jefferson Street, Jefferson
PHONE: 440-576-6346
WEBSITE: familytrainrides.com
E-MAIL: info@acjrscenic.net

Byesville Scenic Railway 2

Located in the heart of southeastern Ohio Coal Country, the Byesville Scenic Railway offers 10-mile round trips aboard vintage open-window coaches. A captivating narration details the life of the coal miners who worked the mines. Wine-tasting, fall foliage, and other special excursions run throughout the season.

LOCATION: Second Street and Seneca Street, Byesville
PHONE: 740-685-0614
WEBSITE: www.bsrw.org
E-MAIL: info@visitguernseycounty.com
DISCOUNT: $1 off all regular excursion tickets.

Cincinnati Dinner Train 3

Operating every Saturday throughout the year, the dinner train travels east from Madisonville to downtown Cincinnati, along the riverfront, and back. You'll enjoy the scenery and a four-course meal during a leisurely three-hour excursion aboard two restored 1940s dining cars, one from the New York Central.

LOCATION: 4725 Madison Road, Cincinnati
PHONE: 513-791-7245
WEBSITE: www.cincinnatirailway.com/dinnertrain
E-MAIL: info@cincinnatirailway.com

Conneaut Railroad Museum ❹

Located in a former New York Central depot, which was built in 1900, this museum displays railroad memorabilia, photos, and artifacts such as lanterns and timetables. Be sure to climb aboard and inspect the cab of Nickel Plate Berkshire No. 755 displayed outside.

LOCATION: 363 Depot Street, Conneaut
PHONE: 440-599-7878

Jefferson Depot Village ❺

The Jefferson Depot is more than a depot. It is a small village. In addition to the restored 1872 Lake Shore & Michigan Southern Railroad station, the site features a 1918 caboose and several 19th century buildings including a one-room schoolhouse, a post office, and a church. From June through October, guided tours are offered on Sundays. The AC&J Scenic Line is right next door.

LOCATION: 147 E. Jefferson Street, Jefferson
PHONE: 440-576-0496
WEBSITE: jeffersonohio.us/depot.htm
E-MAIL: duttonjg@hotmail.com
DISCOUNT: $1 off each adult ticket for Jefferson Depot Village tour.

Lebanon Mason Monroe Railroad 🆖

The LM&M runs one-hour excursions through southwestern Ohio from May through October. You can ride in vintage coaches or an open-air gondola. The railroad also offers a mystery dinner train and variety of special events that children will enjoy such as a ride to a pumpkin patch and a visit with Santa.

LOCATION: 127 S. Mechanic Street, Lebanon
PHONE: 513-933-8022
WEBSITE: lebanonrr.com
E-MAIL: info@lebanonrr.com

Lorain & West Virginia Railway 🆖

Excursion rides take you on a 12-mile round trip over a restored portion of the L&WV. Trains run weekends in October with additional Halloween excursions on which passengers can walk a haunted hobo path. During the Lorain County Fair in August, the train operates daily from the fairgrounds. Cab rides are available in the railway's E8 locomotive.

LOCATION: 46485 Route 18, Wellington
PHONE: 440-647-6660
WEBSITE: lakeshorerailway.org

Marion Union Station ❽

The station contains a museum, and a fully restored Erie Railroad tower is also on site. Located between two diamond crossings, the station is a great place to watch trains from. More than 100 go by daily. The museum is open Tuesdays and Thursdays.

LOCATION: 532 W. Center Street, Marion
PHONE: 740-383-3768
WEBSITE: mariononline.com

Mount Vernon B&O Railroad Depot ❾

The B&O depot celebrated its 100th birthday with a complete renovation. Built in 1907, the Romanesque-styled building features masonry construction, arches, and a red quarry tile roof. Designed by Henry Richardson, the former freight and passenger station underwent a four-year restoration, which was completed in 2007. The beautifully restored interior contains exhibits on the B&O railroad.

LOCATION: 507 W. High Street, Mount Vernon
WEBSITE: mountvernondepot.org
E-MAIL: cory.samuell@gmail.com

Orrville Railroad Heritage Society ❿

The society offers a variety of excursions, including trips on the Wheeling & Lake Erie Railway, fall rides, and holiday trains. Railroad Days in August and other special events take place at the restored Orrville depot.

LOCATION: 145 Depot Street, Orrville
PHONE: 330-683-2426
WEBSITE: orrvillerailroad.com
E-MAIL: questions@orrvillerailroad.com

Toledo, Lake Erie & Western Railway ⓫

Board the *Bluebird* passenger train at a historic depot and take a 60-minute ride over part of the Cloverleaf Division of the Nickel Plate Railroad. Along the way, you'll see an 1817 log cabin and other structures amid scenic views. Trains run Wednesdays and Thursdays during summer and on weekends May through October. Special events are also scheduled during the year.

LOCATION: 49 N. Sixth Street, Waterville
PHONE: 866-638-7246 or 419-878-2177
WEBSITE: tlew.org

Cuyahoga Valley Scenic Railroad 🖪

LOCATION: 1630 Mill Street West, Peninsula
PHONE: 800-468-4070 or 330-657-2000
WEBSITE: cvsr.com
E-MAIL: form on website

Mark Perri

The Cuyahoga Valley Scenic Railroad operates over 47 miles of ex-B&O trackage through northeastern Ohio, from Independence (near Cleveland) through Peninsula and Akron to Canton. Much of the railroad is in the picturesque Cuyahoga Valley National Park, along the Cuyahoga River, and the route of the abandoned Ohio & Erie Canal.

CHOICES: The CVSR runs an extensive schedule of regular trains from various boarding stations. In addition, special events run February through November. They include wine trains, Young at Heart excursions, and a premier Polar Express train.

WHEN TO GO: The summer months offer the most extensive schedule of regular trains. Mid-October offers extra trains for viewing the beautiful fall foliage. Trains are less crowded yet still offer spectacular scenery in April and September.

GOOD TO KNOW: The Cuyahoga Valley National Park features the Towpath Trail, which was built along much of the Ohio and Erie Canal Towpath. It is excellent for hiking and biking, and the railroad has an extensive schedule of heavily discounted Bike Aboard fares that cater to bicyclists. Many intermediate flag stops have been added to enable bikers to ride the trail one way and the train the other.

WORTH DOING: Explore many of the restored historical buildings in the national park, including the Canal Visitor Center (accessible by train) that details the canal's history and includes an operating canal lock.

DON'T MISS: The east side of the train generally includes the best views of the Cuyahoga River, which parallels the railroad, especially on the north end from Peninsula up to Independence. Many photo opportunities abound, and the park has re-created the feel of the early 1900s by building many of the railroad's depots and shelters in a style modeled after the railroad's original structures.

GETTING THERE: By air, Cleveland is closest, but Akron-Canton is a convenient and often a more economical option. Amtrak's *Lakeshore Limited* and *Capitol Limited* stop in Cleveland. If driving, the Ohio Turnpike crosses the CVSR near Peninsula, and I-77 generally parallels the railroad from Cleveland to Canton.

Dennison Railroad Depot Museum ⑬

LOCATION: 400 Center Street, Dennison
PHONE: 877-278-8020 or 740-922-6776
WEBSITE: dennisondepot.org
E-MAIL: director@dennisondepot.org

Mark Perri

This meticulously restored ex-Pennsylvania Railroad depot, built in 1873, houses a comprehensive collection of exhibits highlighting the depot's significance as a World War II serviceman's canteen.

CHOICES: Dennison Railroad Depot Museum offers both guided and self-guided tours. Take time to explore a recent addition, which is made up of five remodeled coaches including a rare hospital car. A variety of interactive exhibits, many designed for children, allow visitors to climb in a caboose, sleep in a Pullman bunk, and send a message by telegraph. The museum also contains local history exhibits, houses a research library, and features a collection of railcars.

WHEN TO GO: The museum is open year-round but is closed on Mondays. It hosts numerous special events including an annual three-day Soldiers Homecoming Festival, complete with reenactors, that celebrates the museum's wartime heritage.

GOOD TO KNOW: If you are hungry, a full-service restaurant, Trax Diner, is located in the depot and offers excellent lunches and dinners. Across the street, Dennison Yard, a local bar and grill, features a wonderful home-cooked Italian menu. There is also a picnic area on the museum's platform.

WORTH DOING: Dennison is close to Ohio's Amish Country in the east-central part of the state. The Pro Football Hall of Fame is 45 minutes north in Canton.

DON'T MISS: If you would like to see a hand-carved wooden locomotive, Warther Carvings Museum, 15 minutes away near Dover, features an extensive collection of carved railroad pieces in walnut, ebony, and ivory.

GETTING THERE: The nearest cities having air service are Columbus, Akron, and Pittsburgh. By car, Dennison is easily reached from I-77 via Route 250 (from the north) or Route 36 (from the south). Once in Dennison, take Second Street past the tracks and then turn left on Center Street.

DISCOUNT: Buy one admission, get one of equal or lesser value free.

Hocking Valley Scenic Railway 🔳

LOCATION: 33 E. Canal Street, Nelsonville
PHONE: 800-967-7834 or 740-753-9531
WEBSITE: hvsry.org
E-MAIL: hvsrwy@gmail.com

Mark Perri

The Hocking Valley Scenic Railway offers diesel-powered excursions with vintage open-window coaches between Nelsonville and Logan, over part of the original Hocking Valley Railway's Athens branch. The train takes you through Wayne National Forest, in the foothills of the Appalachians, and along the Hocking River.

CHOICES: The railroad's basic excursions are a 14-mile trip to Haydenville and a 22-mile trip to Logan. The trips are narrated, and you can ride in a 1920s coach, 1930s heavyweight passenger car, or open-air car. Along the way, besides enjoying the scenery, you'll see a canal lock, take in historical landmarks, and stop at Robbins Crossing, an 1850s-era log village.

WHEN TO GO: Excursions begin weekends in May and continue through October. To view the stunning fall foliage in the national forest, Thursday and Friday trains are added in October. Holiday and theme trips are scheduled during the year and include Easter, Halloween, and Christmas trains.

GOOD TO KNOW: Once a year, the HVR runs a special caboose train that railfans and photographers will especially enjoy.

WORTH DOING: There is something to do for everyone in Wayne National Forest. It has more than 300 miles of trails for hiking and riding bikes, horses, and ATVs. In Nelsonville, you can explore the Public Square, which contains Stuart's Opera House, the Dew House, and other historic buildings.

DON'T MISS: On your visit to Robbins Crossing, you'll see a group of original log cabins arranged into a historical village. The include a schoolhouse, blacksmith shop, general store, and several homes.

GETTING THERE: Nelsonville is approximately 56 miles from Columbus and about 200 from Cleveland. From Columbus, take Route 33 to Nelsonville. In downtown Nelsonville, take Hocking Parkway south to the depot. Costumed inhabitants offer commentary and demonstrate crafts.

Mad River & NKP Railroad Museum ⑮

Ohio

LOCATION: 253 Southwest Street, Bellevue
PHONE: 419-483-2222
WEBSITE: madrivermuseum.org
E-MAIL: madriver@onebellevue.com

Mark Perri

The Mad River & NKP Railroad Museum opened on our nation's bicentennial in 1976 as a lasting tribute to the transportation industry. The museum has a widely varied collection of railroad locomotives, coaches, freight cars, equipment, and structures. While the museum focuses on the Nickel Plate Road and its successors, many other unique pieces of equipment, such as CB&Q Silver Dome No. 4714 (the first dome car built in the United States) are presented.

CHOICES: The museum is comprised of static exhibits. However, many pieces, especially the passenger equipment, have interiors that are open for inspection. In addition, some cars are outfitted with museum displays.

WHEN TO GO: Since the museum operates a seasonal schedule, summertime from Memorial Day to Labor Day is best. In addition, the museum is open on weekends in May, September, and October.

GOOD TO KNOW: Bellevue is a thriving, quaint rural Ohio town, with ample amenities for food and lodging, and many other options for tourists such as antique shops and flea markets. Henry Flagler, who built the Florida East Coast Railroad, once lived on the property where the museum is now located.

WORTH DOING: Bellevue is a 30-minute drive from Sandusky and the Cedar Point amusement park, which is known for its roller coasters and its steam-powered, narrow gauge railroad.

DON'T MISS: Many opportunities exist for watching and photographing trains from public property around town. It is a major hub for the Norfolk Southern and home of one of the largest classification yards in the eastern United States. Mainline tracks bisect the museum and also host regional Wheeling & Lake Erie Railway trains.

GETTING THERE: The nearest major airports are Toledo, Cleveland, and Detroit. Amtrak's *Lakeshore Limited* and *Capitol Limited* stop in Toledo. For those driving, Bellevue is 20 minutes from the Ohio Turnpike off Exit 110.

DISCOUNT: $1 off each adult ticket.

OKLAHOMA

Farmrail 1

Farmrail's *Quartz Mountain Flyer* takes passengers on refurbished, air-conditioned coaches through the scenic Wichita Mountains of southwestern Oklahoma on two-hour narrated round trips. The train operates a limited number of themed trips during the year.

LOCATION: 1601 W. Gary Boulevard, Clinton
PHONE: 580-323-1234 or 580-846-9078
WEBSITE: farmrail.com

Frisco Depot Museum 2

Once a main hub for the Frisco, the depot in Hugo is now a museum. Listed on the National Register of Historic Places, the museum features preserved Harvey Girl rooms, railroad artifacts, and displays on local history. It also features a restored and operational Harvey House restaurant. Outside the museum, the depot park contains a narrow gauge steam locomotive and picnic areas.

LOCATION: 309 N. B Street, Hugo
PHONE: 580-326-6630
WEBSITE: www.friscodepot.org
E-MAIL: friscodepot@live.com

Heritage Express Trolley 3

This 25-minute trolley ride is the only rail-based trolley in operation in Oklahoma. It runs from Heritage Park to downtown. Heritage Park is also home of the Canadian County Museum, which is based in a historical Rock Island train depot.

LOCATION: 300 S. Grand Avenue, El Reno
PHONE: 888-535-7366
WEBSITE: elreno.org/tour/attractions.asp
E-MAIL: info@elreno.org

Oklahoma Railway Museum 4

The Oklahoma Railway Museum possesses an interesting collection of equipment that includes a Santa Fe diner, a Porter 0-6-0, and a Santa Fe FP45 with a warbonnet paint scheme. it also operates a variety of train rides and special events. It is open Thursday through Saturday, with train rides taking place April to October.

LOCATION: 3400 NE Grand Boulevard, Oklahoma City
PHONE: 405-424-8222
WEBSITE: oklahomarailwaymuseum.org
E-MAIL: drake@oklahomarailwaymuseum.org

Railroad Museum of Oklahoma ➎

Located in a former Santa Fe freight house, this museum houses a large collection of railroad artifacts and memorabilia. In the yard, you can climb aboard a 1925 Baldwin 4-8-2 steam locomotive, wander through cabooses from nine different railroads, and view an assortment of freight cars. The museum also sponsors several all-caboose excursions.

LOCATION: 702 N. Washington Street, Enid
PHONE: 580-233-3051
WEBSITE: railroadmuseumofoklahoma.org

Santa Fe Depot Museum ➏

This 1905 Santa Fe depot has been restored and now contains a collection of railroad photos and other local historical artifacts. On display are 1907 Baldwin steam locomotive Santa Fe No. 1951, a coal tender, and a caboose. The museum is open Monday through Saturday, and it features a convenient picnic area. A toy and action figure museum is also located in Pauls Valley.

LOCATION: 204 S. Santa Fe Street, Pauls Valley
PHONE: 405-238-2244
WEBSITE: paulsvalley.com

Waynoka Air-Rail Museum ➐

The Waynoka Station complex includes a restored 1910 Santa Fe depot and Harvey House, 1918 section foreman's house, water tower, and diesel locomotive. The museum contains displays on Fred Harvey, the Santa Fe Railroad, Waynoka transportation history, and other subjects.

LOCATION: 1386 S. Cleveland Street, Waynoka
PHONE: 580-824-1886
WEBSITE: waynoka.org
E-MAIL: waynokahs@hotmail.com

Yukon's Best Railroad Museum ➑

Located in the hometown of Garth Brooks, the museum, made up of a Rock Island boxcar and a Union Pacific caboose, contains artifacts of the Rock Island and other railroads.

LOCATION: Third Street and Main Street, Yukon
PHONE: 405-354-5079

OREGON

Ashland Historic Railroad Museum ❶

The museum preserves Ashland's railroad history through exhibits, photos, talks, and films. It also conducts walking tours of the city's railroad district. It is open Tuesday through Saturday year-round.

LOCATION: 258 A Street, Ashland
PHONE: 541-261-6605
WEBSITE: ashlandrrmuseum.org

Canby Depot Museum ❷

The Canby Depot Museum is housed in what could be the oldest railroad station in Oregon, which has been around since at least 1873. The museum's displays provide a look at 19th century life of this historic community and include a Union Pacific caboose and other rail items. It is open Thursday through Sunday.

LOCATION: 888 NE Fourth Avenue, Canby
PHONE: 503-266-6712
WEBSITE: canbyhistoricalsociety.org
E-MAIL: form on website

Willamette Shore Trolley ❸

You can ride an antique trolley along a scenic six-mile rail line between Lake Oswego and Portland. Traveling along the Willamette River, you'll go through parks, past mansions, over bridges, and through a tunnel. It is open May through October. The trolley is operated by the Oregon Electric Railway Historical Society. The society also operates the Oregon Electric Railway Museum located in Brooks, which is 30 miles south of Lake Oswego. The museum offers trolley rides, and its collection includes streetcars, interurbans, and several double-deck trams.

LOCATION: 311 N. State Street, Lake Oswego
PHONE: 503-697-7436
WEBSITE: oerhs.org
E-MAIL: webmaster@oregonelectricrailway.org

Eagle Cap Excursion Train ▪4

LOCATION: 300 N. Eighth Street, Elgin
PHONE: 800-323-7330 or 541-963-9000
WEBSITE: eaglecaptrain.com
E-MAIL: travel@alegretravel.com

Martin Hansen

The Eagle Cap excursion train offers 3.5-hour excursions along the 63-mile Joseph Branch in northeastern Oregon that was first constructed in 1890. Much of the excursion line passes through spectacular rugged and remote areas, inaccessible to cars, following the Grande Ronde River downstream and then the wild and scenic Wallowa River.

CHOICES: The railroad provides diesel-powered excursion trains with beautifully restored coaches, including concession cars on each trip. The cars are climate-controlled and have restrooms. Additional trips along the same route in RDC self-powered cars are also offered. Certain excursions feature train robberies.

WHEN TO GO: Train rides are available Saturdays May through October. Fall foliage trips in the heavily wooded forests are offered in October.

GOOD TO KNOW: In 1912, Rocky Mountain elk were transported from Wyoming to Wallowa County via the railroad to reestablish the area's depleted elk herds. These animals are responsible for many of the elk you will see trackside during your excursion.

WORTH DOING: The towns of Elgin, Enterprise, and Joseph all contain historic buildings and quaint shops worth visiting during a trip to northeastern Oregon, following the same route early settlers took along the Oregon Trail.

DON'T MISS: Look for future caboose rides. An antique wooden caboose is currently being restored and will be put in service when complete.

GETTING THERE: Exit I-84 at LaGrande and follow Highway 82 to Elgin. In the center of Elgin, continue past the opera house and city hall to the boarding area.

Oregon

Mount Hood Railroad 5

LOCATION: 110 Railroad Avenue, Hood River
PHONE: 800-872-4661 or 541-386-3556
WEBSITE: mthoodrr.com
E-MAIL: form on website

Mount Hood Railroad

The Columbia River Gorge is filled with magnificent scenery, and the area around Mount Hood especially so because of its abundant orchards and vineyards. The Mount Hood Railroad offers a 44-mile round trip to Parkdale that features spectacular views of its namesake mountain. The train ends at a park, where passengers can relax and picnic before the return trip.

CHOICES: The four-hour excursion departs in the morning and follows the valley between the Columbia River and Mount Hood, providing views of Mount Adams as well. For half the journey, narration provides information about local history. Two-hour excursions to Odell run on weekend afternoons June through September. In addition, the railroad schedules train robberies, murder mysteries, Sunday brunch trains, and dinner trains every month. Other special events, such as the Polar Express, take place during the season.

WHEN TO GO: Trains run April through December, operating Tuesday through Sunday during summer (July and August) and other peak times. Otherwise, trains run four or five days depending on the time of year.

GOOD TO KNOW: The railroad still carries a limited amount of freight, so don't be surprised if you see a boxcar somewhere along the line. Not far out of the Mount Hood depot, the train traverses a switchback, where it zigzags up the side of the mountain to gain elevation quickly. The rear of the train becomes the front for the rest of the trip into Parkdale.

WORTH DOING: There is much to do in the area. Sample apples and pears from orchards, visit a local winery, or watch wind surfers try to master the winds from the Columbia River Gorge. You can also take a drive on the Mount Hood Loop, which gives you a view of many scenic waterfalls.

DON'T MISS: On excursions, for an added fee, you can enjoy the same view of the scenery as the engineer by sitting in the double-decker dome car.

GETTING THERE: The Mount Hood Railroad is located 60 miles east of Portland off I-84. In Hood River, take Exit 63 to reach the depot. If driving from the south, Highway 35 also goes to Hood River.

Oregon Coast Scenic Railroad 6

LOCATION: 403 American Way, Garibaldi
PHONE: 503-842-7972
WEBSITE: ocsr.net
E-MAIL: info@ocsr.net

Jim Wrinn

Experience the Pacific Ocean on a 10-mile, 90-minute excursion along the shores of Tillamook Bay. The train is pulled by a 1910 Heisler locomotive and runs between Garibaldi and Rockaway Beach.

CHOICES: On your trip along the coast, you can ride in a flatcar, the newly restored Southern Pacific 1924 coach named the *Wilson River*, or for an extra fee, in the steam locomotive's cab. Wherever you sit, find a seat on the left side of the train. It's on the ocean side, and the views are spectacular. Dinner trains operate throughout the year, a special fireworks train runs in July, and the Candy Cane Express runs in December.

WHEN TO GO: Regular excursions operate on weekends from Memorial Day through September.

GOOD TO KNOW: The OCSR's steam engines are oil fired and run on recycled motor oil.

WORTH DOING: Oregon's dairy industry is based in Tillamook, and it produces some of the best cheese and ice cream in North America. Be sure to stop at the Tillamook Cheese factory in nearby Tillamook. In addition, the area features an aviation museum housed in a World War II blimp hanger. You can also view numerous lighthouses along the Pacific shore.

DON'T MISS: There is a layover between each run that provides the opportunity to explore Garibaldi or Rockaway Beach, get a bite to eat, or just enjoy the oceanside.

GETTING THERE: The railroad is located along the Oregon coast, 10 miles north of Tillamook, in Garibaldi just off Highway 101. From Portland, take Highway 26 west to Highway 6 at Banks and follow Highway 6 over the forested Coast Range Mountains to Tillamook. At Tillamook, take Highway 101 north to Garibaldi. In Garibaldi, turn left on Third Street to Lumberman's Park, where the train boards.

Sumpter Valley Railway ▣

LOCATION: Highway 7, Sumpter
PHONE: 866-894-2268 or 541-894-2268
WEBSITE: www.svry.com
E-MAIL: sumptervalleyinfo@yahoo.com

Martin Hansen

A five-mile portion of one of the most charming narrow gauge lines of the Pacific Northwest has been re-created amid forests and the spoils of a former gold-mining dredge operation. It is a good approximation of a remote steam line in eastern Oregon, where snowcaps rise in the distance even in June.

CHOICES: The railway runs between McEwen and Sumpter. Both round-trip and one-way excursions are available at either station. The railroad is operating the W.H. Eccles Lumber Co. two-truck Heisler while SV 2-8-2 No. 19 is under repair. This geared locomotive is one of a handful of wood-burning locomotives in service today in North America. Train robberies take place throughout the season.

WHEN TO GO: The railway is open on weekends and holidays from Memorial Day through September. A special fall foliage photography train runs in October, and Christmas trains run in December.

GOOD TO KNOW: The Sumpter depot is a replica of the original depot. Located on the Elkhorn Scenic Byway, Sumpter is surrounded by the Elkhorn Mountains. The area is filled with history, and nearby Baker City boasts at least 60 restored buildings.

WORTH DOING: Near the Sumpter station, in the Sumpter Valley Dredge State Heritage Area, visit the historic gold dredge that churned up all the rocks the railroad runs through—it's as big as a house and a monster of a machine well worth touring.

DON'T MISS: Cab rides aboard the steam locomotive are available.

GETTING THERE: The railway is about 330 miles from Portland in northeast Oregon. From Portland, take I-84 to Baker City and then take Highway 7 south 22 miles to McEwen.

DISCOUNT: 10% off a regular schedule ticket; one per customer.

PENNSYLVANIA

Allegheny Portage Railroad ❶

This national historic site preserves the remains of the Allegheny Portage Railroad that operated from 1834 to 1854. You can explore the 900-foot Staple Bend Tunnel, the first railroad tunnel built in the United States, visit the engine house, or take a hike. For bikers, a 2.5-mile trail takes you to the Staple Bend Tunnel. The site conducts a large number of special events.

LOCATION: 110 Federal Park Road, Gallitzin
PHONE: 814-886-6150
WEBSITE: www.nps.gov/alpo

Electric City Trolley Museum ❷

Located on the grounds of the Steamtown National Historic Site, the museum is housed in a restored mill building. In addition to displaying vintage regional trolleys, the museum features a unique under-the-skin look at a restored trolley and other interactive exhibits. Ten-mile trolley excursions travel through a 4,747-foot interurban tunnel.

LOCATION: 300 Cliff Street, Scranton
PHONE: 570-963-6590
WEBSITE: ectma.org
E-MAIL: webmaster@ectma.org

Fayette Central Railroad ❸

The railroad operates weekend excursions from Uniontown to Dunbar or Fairchance with Budd Rail Diesel Car No. 9913 or behind a diesel locomotive. For a view of the Youghiogheny River, try the Dunbar excursion. The Fairchance run provides a view of the Appalachians. On hot summer Saturdays, you can ride to Shady Grove and cool off in the pool.

LOCATION: 39 N. Gallatin Avenue, Uniontown
PHONE: 877-321-3277
WEBSITE: fayettecentralrailroad.com
E-MAIL: fcrr@live.com

Franklin Institute Science Museum ❹

The museum features the Train Factory, a permanent, interactive exhibit showcasing Baldwin's experimental locomotive No. 60000, which has been at the museum since 1933, and two other locomotives. You'll explore past and present railroad technology as you journey through the exhibit and even take No. 60000 for a test run. The museum is open year-round.

LOCATION: 222 N. 20th Street, Philadelphia
PHONE: 215-448-1200
WEBSITE: www.fi.edu
E-MAIL: guestservices@fi.edu

Friends of the East Broad Top Museum ❺

Located at the former southern operating terminus of the East Broad Top Railroad, the museum includes two historic buildings, an EBT station and a post office, both constructed around 1915. Exhibits illustrate the history of the railroad and the people who constructed, maintained, and operated it. The museum is open on weekends, June through October.

LOCATION: 550 Main Street, Robertsdale
PHONE: 814-635-2388
WEBSITE: febt.org

Greenville Railroad Park and Museum ❻

This railroad museum displays Union Railroad 0-10-2 No. 604. Built in 1936, it is the largest steam switcher built. Several other cars are also on display. The museum includes a reconstructed dispatcher's office and stationmaster's quarters. It is open weekends during May, September, and October. During summer months, the museum is open Tuesday through Sunday.

LOCATION: 314 Main Street, Greenville
PHONE: 724-588-4009
WEBSITE: greenvilletrainmuseum.org
E-MAIL: greenvillerailroadpark@gmail.com

Harris Switch Tower Museum ❼

Visitors to the switch tower can operate an actual interlocking machine and model board that controls virtual trains from the 1940s. Throw any of the 113 levers on the interlocking machine, which controlled track switches and signals, and watch the model board light up to show what would happen. The tower is next to operating tracks, so railfans can watch Norfolk Southern and Amtrak trains go by. It is open Saturdays late May through October.

LOCATION: Seventh Street and Walnut Street, Harrisburg
PHONE: 717-232-6221
WEBSITE: nrhs-hbg.pennsyrr.com
E-MAIL: harristower@verizon.net

Kiski Junction Railroad ❽

This freight-hauling railroad also hauls passengers. From June to October, it offers train rides along the scenic Kiski River to Bagdad and back. On Tuesdays and Fridays, the train may stop to service a steel mill, but on Saturdays, the rides are just for fun. You can ride aboard a caboose, coach, or open-air car.

LOCATION: 130 Railroad Street, Schenley
PHONE: 724-295-5577
WEBSITE: kiskijunction.com
E-MAIL: info@kiskijunction.com

Ligonier Valley Rail Road Museum ❾

The Ligonier Valley Rail Road Museum is housed in the restored Darlington station, and its exhibits show the history of the Ligonier Valley Rail Road. Museum volunteers are also in the process of restoring a 1905 wooden Pennsylvania Railroad caboose that is on site.

LOCATION: 3032 Idlewild Hill Lane, Ligonier
PHONE: 724-238-7819 or 724-238-7859
WEBSITE: lvrra.org
E-MAIL: info@lvrra.org

Museum of Erie GE History ❿

The museum displays models, pictures, and memorabilia related to the production locomotives at the General Electric plant in Erie. The collection includes materials from 1906, when the plant was being planned, to the present. It is open most Saturdays during the year.

LOCATION: 2901 E. Lake Road, Erie
PHONE: 814-875-2494
WEBSITE: www.getransportationsystems.net/about-us

Pennsylvania Trolley Museum ⑪

A visit to the museum includes a guided tour of the carbarn and unlimited four-mile trolley rides. In the carbarn, you can see some trolleys and restoration projects. For an added fee, you can tour the trolley display building that houses 30 additional trolleys. Special events are scheduled throughout the year.

LOCATION: 1 Museum Road, Washington
PHONE: 724-228-9256
WEBSITE: www.pa-trolley.org
E-MAIL: ptm@pa-trolley.org

Pioneer Tunnel Coal Mine & Steam Train ⑫

Take a scenic ride along Mahanoy Mountain as you hear stories about mining, bootlegging, and the Centralia Mine fire. A 1927 narrow gauge 0-4-0 steam locomotive takes you around the mountain. You can also tour a real anthracite coal mine in open mine cars. It is open April through October.

LOCATION: 19th Street and Oak Street, Ashland
PHONE: 570-875-3850
WEBSITE: www.pioneertunnel.com

Portage Station Museum ⑬

The museum is located in a restored Pennsylvania Railroad train station, originally built in 1926. The stationmaster's office contains artifacts from the Pennsylvania Railroad, and on the second floor, there is a display of Allegheny Portage Railroad items. The building is listed on the National Register of Historic Places.

LOCATION: 400 Lee Street, Portage
PHONE: 814-736-9223
WEBSITE: portagepa.us
E-MAIL: mlcgeo@verizon.net

Reading Railroad Heritage Museum ⑭

You can't take a ride on the Reading Railroad, but you can discover its heritage in this museum. You can tour the museum's large outdoor collection of vintage Reading railroad cars and locomotives. Inside, you can view a 1930s station agent's office, photographs, and artifacts.

LOCATION: 500 S. Third Street, Hamburg
PHONE: 610-562-5513
WEBSITE: readingrailroad.org
E-MAIL: info@readingrailroad.org

Rockhill Trolley Museum ⑮

Located adjacent to East Broad Top Railroad, the museum offers a three-mile ride aboard a vintage electric trolley car to Blacklog Narrows. You can tour the museum's collection, which includes an operating open trolley, high-speed interurban cars, and maintenance-of-way cars, and watch restoration projects in progress. It is open weekends June through October with special events in November and December.

LOCATION: 430 Meadow Street, Rockhill Furnace
PHONE: 814-447-9576
WEBSITE: rockhilltrolley.org
E-MAIL: info@rockhilltrolley.org
DISCOUNT: Buy one ticket, get one free.

Stourbridge Line Rail Excursions ⑯

Located in the Pocono Mountains, the railway runs along the scenic Lackawaxen River, closely following the original route of the Delaware & Hudson Canal. Leaving from Honesdale, a restored BL2 diesel locomotive pulls vintage cars on two-hour excursions to Hawley or four-hour excursions to Lackawaxen. Train robberies, fall foliage trains, and other specials also run.

LOCATION: 32 Commercial Street, Honesdale
PHONE: 570-253-1960 or 570-251-7770
WEBSITE: thestourbridgeline.com or waynecountycc.com
E-MAIL: train@waynecountycc.com

Tunnels Park & Museum ⑰

From the nearby Jackson Street Bridge, you get a great view of the twin tunnels, which are 3,605 feet long. The site also features a museum and a restored 1942 Pennsylvania Railroad caboose. The museum includes railroad artifacts and photos. It is open Tuesday through Sunday.

LOCATION: 411 Convent Street, Gallitzin
PHONE: 814-886-8871
WEBSITE: gallitzin.info
E-MAIL: info@gallitzin.info

West Chester Railroad ⑱

The railroad offers a variety of special excursions during the year. The 16-mile round trip runs from West Chester to Glen Mills, following scenic Chester Creek. Events include pizza trains, summer picnics, and fall foliage runs. For history buffs, Valley Forge National Historical Park is less than 20 miles away.

LOCATION: 250 E. Market Street, West Chester
PHONE: 610-430-2233
WEBSITE: westchesterrr.com
E-MAIL: info@westchesterrr.com

East Broad Top Railroad 🔟

LOCATION: Route 994, Rockhill Furnace
PHONE: 814-447-3011
WEBSITE: ebtrr.com
E-MAIL: office@ebtrr.com

Jim Wrinn

A National Historic Landmark, the East Broad Top Railroad celebrated 50 years as a tourist railroad in 2010. The line runs through a scenic valley that has changed little since the line closed in 1956.

CHOICES: The railroad still uses one of six original Baldwin steam locomotives and wooden coaches acquired in the 1920s over a line laid out in 1874. In addition to the wooden coaches, the train features an open car, a caboose, and the wonderful observation car *Orbisonia*, which requires an extra fare. Tours of the shops and roundhouse, where the railroad once built its own freight cars and maintained its locomotives, are also offered.

WHEN TO GO: The EBT is open Saturdays and Sundays from mid-May through October. During July, August, and October, trains also run Thursdays and Fridays. Santa trains operate beginning in November and into December.

GOOD TO KNOW: Across the street from the station, you can take a two-mile round trip speeder ride.

WORTH DOING: Be sure to visit the adjacent Rockhill Trolley Museum, whose trolley cars traverse the former Shade Gap Branch. Other attractions within an hour's drive include Horseshoe Curve and the Railroaders Memorial Museum in Altoona, as well as Raystown Lake, a 29,000-acre recreational area.

DON'T MISS: Since a highway parallels the railroad, you can follow a train for action photos across the field or from an overhead bridge. Stick around after a day's runs to watch the hostlers clean the fire and prepare the engine for its overnight rest.

GETTING THERE: The East Broad Top is off the beaten track, about 10 miles south of Route 22 on Route 522, and about 16 miles north of I-76's Exit 189. The nearest commercial airport is in Altoona, about 50 miles distant. Amtrak's *Pennsylvanian* stops in Altoona and Lewistown.

Horseshoe Curve National Historic Landmark ⑳

LOCATION: 1300 Ninth Avenue, Altoona
PHONE: 888-425-8666 or 814-946-0834
WEBSITE: www.railroadcity.com
E-MAIL: form on website

Jim Wrinn

Horseshoe Curve is an engineering marvel completed in 1854 as part of the Pennsylvania Railroad's main line over the Allegheny Mountains. By curving the track across the face of a mountain, builders were able to gain elevation without making the grade too steep for trains to climb. Today, the curve is as vital as ever, serving as a key link in the Norfolk Southern system, with more than 50 trains passing over its three tracks each day.

CHOICES: Attractions at Horseshoe Curve consist of a visitor center at ground level and the trackside park, which is accessible by a 194-step walkway or by a funicular railway. First-timers will want to tour the visitor center, ride the funicular up to track level, and then take the stairway back down. The best show at the curve is the passage of a heavy westbound train, laboring up the grade with helper engines on the front and/ or rear. Try to stay long enough to catch this spectacle.

WHEN TO GO: The visitor center and funicular are open April through November. In October, the fall colors can be brilliant. Freight traffic tends to build toward the end of each week, so there may be more trains to see on Thursday, Friday, and Saturday.

GOOD TO KNOW: The site is managed by the superb Altoona Railroaders Memorial Museum in downtown Altoona. Combined admission tickets are available.

WORTH DOING: Continue west on Kittanning Point Road to Gallitzin and visit the small park at the west portal of one of the tunnels the railroad uses to pierce the spine of the Alleghenies. Cresson, a little further west is also a good place to watch trains. Both towns have trackside, railfan-oriented lodging.

DON'T MISS: The longer you stay at Horseshoe Curve, the greater the chances of seeing two or even three trains rounding the curve simultaneously, a thrilling occurrence.

GETTING THERE: Horseshoe Curve is located five miles west of Altoona. Altoona is on I-99, 33 miles north of I-70/76. Amtrak's New York-Philadelphia-Pittsburgh *Pennsylvanian* stops at Altoona daily.

Pennsylvania

Lake Shore Railway Museum ㉑

LOCATION: 31 Wall Street, North East
PHONE: 814-725-1911
WEBSITE: www.grape-track.org

Jim Wrinn

A restored 1899 New York Central passenger station, built by the Lake Shore & Michigan Southern, houses extensive rail displays. Displayed on the grounds are 24 pieces of rolling stock and an 1869 station.

CHOICES: The restored New York Central passenger station houses numerous artifacts, and rolling stock is also displayed outdoors. A passenger and freight station built in 1869 by the LS&MS also sits on the grounds. View fireless 0-6-0 No. 6, one of 29 such locomotives built between 1934 and 1941 by the Heisler Locomotive Works. Demonstrations of the locomotive occur on selected weekends.

WHEN TO GO: The museum building is open weekends from Memorial Day through Labor Day, while the grounds are open every day. Enjoy Christmas at the Station in December with lunch in the diner, speeder rides, and caboose rides.

GOOD TO KNOW: The museum hosts occasional Dinner-in-the-Diner events.

WORTH DOING: Time your visit with the cherry festival in July or the wine festival in September. There are five wineries in or near North East. You can also drive along Lake Erie and stop at one of the local beaches.

DON'T MISS: CSX's Chicago-New York main line and Norfolk Southern's line to Buffalo run beside the museum. You can watch 60-80 trains each day from the platform, including Amtrak's *Lake Shore Limited* passenger train.

GETTING THERE: The museum is located about 15 miles east of Erie, Pa., near the New York state border. From Erie, take Route 20 to North East, where it becomes Main Street. Turn right on Clinton, right on Mill Street, and then left on Wall.

DISCOUNT: $1 off each adult ticket, up to four adults.

Lehigh Gorge Scenic Railway 22

LOCATION: 2 Susquehanna Street, Jim Thorpe
PHONE: 570-325-8485
WEBSITE: www.lgsry.com
E-MAIL: info@lgsry.com

Jim Wrinn

This 16-mile round trip into the Lehigh Gorge is among the most beautiful in Pennsylvania, a state blessed with numerous great tourist railroads and museums because of its abundant railroad development. Trains run on the tracks of the Reading & Northern regional railroad, paralleling a bike path into an isolated, narrow chasm.

CHOICES: The one-hour, narrated excursion follows the winding Lehigh River, curve after curve, and crosses it in several places, until it reaches Old Penn Haven. Leaving from the renovated, distinct Central Railroad of New Jersey depot, you can ride behind a diesel locomotive in a vintage 1920s coach, an open-air car, or a caboose, from which you can stand on the rear platform.

WHEN TO GO: The railway operates on Saturdays and Sundays mid-May through mid-December. The mountains present a new look for each season, but fall offers beautiful foliage and an extended schedule in October.

GOOD TO KNOW: In 1953, the towns of Mauch Chunk and East Mauch Chunk merged into one town with the name of Jim Thorpe when that famous athlete was buried there. Looking for a place that would help develop a memorial for her husband, who had no previous ties to the area, Thorpe's widow found assistance from the two towns.

WORTH DOING: Explore the town of Jim Thorpe, a charming village of shops, stores, and B&Bs, many featuring Victorian architecture. The town was once known as the Switzerland of America for its steep hillsides, narrow streets, and terraced gardens.

DON'T MISS: The railroad, from time to time, fires up and uses 4-6-2 No. 425, a steam locomotive built for passenger service on the Gulf, Mobile & Northern in 1928.

GETTING THERE: Located in the heart of the Poconos, Jim Thorpe is approximately 90 miles from Philadelphia. From there, take I-476 to Exit 74. Then take Route 209 south into Jim Thorpe, where it becomes Susquehanna Street, and follow it to the railway.

Middletown & Hummelstown Railroad 23

LOCATION: 136 Brown Street, Middletown
PHONE: 717-944-4435
WEBSITE: www.mhrailroad.com
E-MAIL: form on website

Jim Wrinn

If you're looking for that relaxed train ride in central Pennsylvania, here's your ride. The M&H provides a trip along the Swatara Creek, past the ruins of a canal, and ends with a dramatic bridge crossing of a creek and a stop at another tourist attraction, Indian Echo Caves. A nice package in an 11-mile round trip.

CHOICES: The M&H offers plenty of different trips, from scenic outings to murder mystery barbecues. You have a choice of departure locations, as trains operate from both the 1891 freight station in Middletown and the Indian Echo Caverns platform. However, the special event trains operate only out of Middletown. Aboard the train's Delaware, Lackawanna & Western coaches, you'll hear informative narration about the area, and be prepared to sing some railroading songs. You can even reserve a hobo sack lunch, complete with bandana and pole. Caboose and trolley rides are also available.

WHEN TO GO: Excursions begin Memorial Day weekend and end in October. There are numerous special events, including a Civil War reenactment, during the year.

GOOD TO KNOW: Formerly part of the Reading Railroad, the M&H also provides freight service. At the Middletown yard, the railroad displays a collection of rolling stock.

WORTH DOING: Top off your relaxing train ride with a stop in Middletown at the Cone-A-Cabana for ice cream. In Hershey, you can hop on more than 60 rides, including roller coasters and water rides, at Hersheypark amusement park.

DON'T MISS: The railroad offers a combination ticket with Indian Echo Caves for an interesting rail-cavern outing.

GETTING THERE: Middletown is situated between Harrisburg and Hershey, both 10 miles away, and 100 miles from Philadelphia. From Philadelphia, take I-76 to Route 283. Exit at Middletown and from Main Street, turn left on Pine Street, and then left on Brown Street to get to the station.

New Hope & Ivyland Railroad 24

LOCATION: 32 W. Bridge Street, New Hope
PHONE: 215-862-2332
WEBSITE: newhoperailroad.com
E-MAIL: info@newhoperailroad.com

Jim Wrinn

The New Hope & Ivyland Railroad provides a scenic, 45-minute trip through the rolling hills and valleys of Bucks County, leaving from the quaint resort village of New Hope on the Delaware River.

CHOICES: There are lots of trains to ride, from scenic excursions to murder mysteries and dinner trains, as well as story and sing-along rides for children. You can board regular excursion trains at either New Hope or Lahaska. The 1920s vintage passenger coaches are pulled by a steam engine like Old Number 40, a 1925 Baldwin-type 2-8-0, or a diesel locomotive. Try out open-air car No. 1525 and enjoy the breeze—and unobstructed views. The former Reading car was built in 1925.

WHEN TO GO: The New Hope & Ivyland operates year-round. From January through March, excursions run on Saturdays and Sundays. In April, May, and November, Friday runs are added to the weekend schedule. And beginning Memorial Day weekend, excursions operate daily through the end of October. Special trains operate throughout the year, and December is filled with holiday trains. The annual railfan weekend in September, when all of the trains run, is a great time to visit.

GOOD TO KNOW: The restored Victorian station at New Hope has been in operation since 1891. An original "witch's hat" station, it once housed the railroad's telegraph operator.

WORTH DOING: History buffs can visit Valley Forge National Historical Park, which is about 40 miles from New Hope.

DON'T MISS: You can get off at either station and take a later train back to the originating station. At Lahaska, you can enjoy a family picnic, and in New Hope, you can take a mule-drawn boat ride in the Delaware Division of the Pennsylvania Canal or stroll along the Delaware River.

GETTING THERE: New Hope is 45 miles northeast of Philadelphia. From Philadelphia, take the Pennsylvania Turnpike east to the Willow Grove exit. Then take Route 611 to Route 202. Turn north on Route 202 and go 10 miles to Route 179, which leads you into New Hope. In town, take a left onto Bridge Street to the station. Lahaska is five miles southwest of New Hope, and the station is on Street Road one mile east of Route 202.

Oil Creek & Titusville Railroad 🎟25

LOCATION: 409 S. Perry Street, Titusville
PHONE: 814-676-1733
WEBSITE: octrr.org
E-MAIL: ocandt@usachoice.net

Oil Creek & Titusville Railroad

The Oil Creek & Titusville Railroad follows Oil Creek through the nation's first oil patch, where oil was discovered by Col. Edwin L. Drake in 1859. Along the way, the train passes a number of ghost towns that sprang up during the oil boom and just as quickly disappeared when the rush faded.

CHOICES: Much of the route along the three-hour excursion runs through Oil Creek State Park, a popular venue for camping, fishing, and canoeing. Along the way, tour guides tell stories about Oil Country. You don't have to return right away. You may visit Drake Well Park, ride one way and bike the other, or canoe down Oil Creek and then ride the train back.

WHEN TO GO: The Oil Creek & Titusville operates from June through October. Schedules vary with the season, with trains running Wednesday through Sunday during the peak fall color season in October. The fall foliage season is spectacular in the area and is a favored time to visit.

GOOD TO KNOW: At various times throughout the year, special murder mystery dinner trains, Peter Cottontail trains, and Santa trains operate. A highlight is Speeder Day, when visitors have an opportunity to ride small railway maintenance cars along part of the line.

WORTH DOING: Stopping at Drake Well Park gives you a chance to see a replica of the very first oil well in the United States, from which oil still flows today. The park also displays a large collection of machinery and equipment used to produce oil, including interactive displays.

DON'T MISS: The OC&TR operates the only Railway Post Office in regular service in the United States. Postcards mailed on the train will receive the official "Oil Creek & Titusville R.P.O." cancellation, which is valued by collectors.

GETTING THERE: Titusville is in the forested mountains of northwestern Pennsylvania. From I-80, take Exit 29 and then Route 8 north through Oil City to Titusville. From Erie and I-90, take Route 97 south to its junction with Route 8 and then follow Route 8 to Titusville.

Railroad Museum of Pennsylvania ㉖

LOCATION: 300 Gap Road, Strasburg
PHONE: 717-687-8628
WEBSITE: rrmuseumpa.org
E-MAIL: info@rrmuseumpa.org

Jeff Terry

The Railroad Museum of Pennsylvania boasts one of the top rolling stock collections in the United States. The highlight is a dozen steam locomotives preserved by the Pennsylvania Railroad in the 1950s; very few PRR engines exist elsewhere. The collection also includes about 100 other locomotives and cars from the PRR and other railroads serving the state, many displayed in a 100,000-square-foot exhibition hall.

CHOICES: Go up, down, and out: an elevated walkway gives a fine view of the Rolling Stock Hall, a pit between the rails allows inspection of the underside of one of the locomotives, and tours of the rolling stock yard are sometimes available. Be sure to see PRR 4-4-2 No. 7002, a beautiful example of a high-wheeled passenger speedster from the early 20th century; PRR GG1 No. 4935, the best-preserved example of the most famous class of electric locomotives; and PRR E7 No. 5901, the only surviving example of General Motors' top-selling passenger diesel.

WHEN TO GO: The museum is open every day except for certain major holidays and most Mondays November through March. A variety of special events are scheduled throughout the year.

GOOD TO KNOW: Look for upcoming new exhibits, such as a 1915 railroading street scene, and other changes at the museum. If you would like to see trains on a smaller scale, the National Toy Train Museum is also located in Strasburg.

WORTH DOING: Spend part of the day at the museum and then take a ride on a steam train on the Strasburg Rail Road, located right across the road. Combined admissions are available.

DON'T MISS: Grab the controls of a diesel locomotive with the museum's cab simulator and feel the thrill of operating a locomotive on a trip from Lancaster to Harrisburg.

GETTING THERE: The museum is on Route 741 (Gap Road) one mile east of Strasburg, which is about 15 minutes from Lancaster, one hour from Harrisburg or Reading, and 90 minutes from Philadelphia. Most folks take Route 30 to Route 896 south to Route 741.

DISCOUNT: $1 off regular adult admission.

Railroaders Memorial Museum ㉗

LOCATION: 1300 Ninth Avenue, Altoona
PHONE: 888-425-8666 or 814-946-0834
WEBSITE: railroadcity.com
E-MAIL: form on website

Railroaders Memorial Museum

Of all the places in the United States deserving a first-rate railroad museum, Altoona is certainly at the top of the list. The museum here is among the best when it comes to providing an interactive experience and telling the story of this shop town that in the 1920s employed more than 15,000 Pennsylvania Railroad workers. Today, Altoona is still a shop city for Norfolk Southern, and the museum tells the story of how it became so important and the people who made it so.

CHOICES: Be sure to step into the bar exhibit and hear all about the lives of railroaders as they sit and sip a cold one. Also look at the exhibit on the PPR's testing and research lab. Some of their efforts were astounding.

WHEN TO GO: The museum is open daily May through October and Friday through Monday in November and December.

GOOD TO KNOW: The museum is housed in the Pennsylvania Railroad's former master mechanic's building, which was built in 1882. The museum broke ground on a roundhouse facility in 2010.

WORTH DOING: The Allegheny Portage Railroad National Historic Site and Staple Bend Tunnel are both within 25 miles of Altoona.

DON'T MISS: Take a day and spend half of it in the museum and the other half watching trains at Horseshoe Curve. Combined admission tickets are available.

GETTING THERE: Altoona is about 95 miles east of Pittsburgh. From Pittsburgh, take Route 22 to I-99 north. Take Exit 33, 17th Street, and a right turn on Ninth Avenue takes you to the museum.

Steamtown National Historic Site ㉘

LOCATION: Lackawanna Avenue and Cliff Avenue, Scranton
PHONE: 888-693-9391 or 570-340-5200
WEBSITE: www.nps.gov/stea

Jeff Terry

The former Delaware Lackawanna & Western railroad shop complex is home to one of the East's most complete railroad history exhibits. Housed in several buildings on the site of the Lackawanna's roundhouse, Steamtown provides a shrine to steam-era railroading in the northeastern United States. It also offers both short and long train rides. The real treat is a walk through the active portion of the roundhouse, where steam locomotives are still maintained.

CHOICES: The site includes both a steam history museum as well as a technology museum. The orientation movie, hands-on exhibits about workers as well as hardware, and equipment displays are excellent. Demonstrations of the turntable and shop tours are also conducted. For a brief visit, you can walk through the exhibits and take the *Scranton Limited*, a half-hour ride on vintage commuter coaches. If you have time, schedule your visit when you can spend a day with the exhibits and then ride a longer steam excursion train to Moscow, a two-hour trip that includes a climb up the Poconos, or through the countryside to Tobyhanna. This is one of the few places where a large, mainline steam locomotive can operate at track speed on a mountain railroad.

WHEN TO GO: Steamtown is open year-round. Summer can be sultry, but spring and fall are pleasant. Winter sees less activity. Steamtown's excursion trains run on select days between June and October. The *Scranton Limited* usually runs Wednesday through Sunday mid-April until December.

GOOD TO KNOW: The Union Pacific Big Boy, one of 25 of its type built in the early 1940s, is one of the largest steam locomotives ever built. Operated in Wyoming and Utah, this is the only one of its type on exhibit in the eastern United States. It is so big, you could hold a dinner party in the firebox.

WORTH DOING: Nearby, you can view the Scranton Iron Furnaces or tour a coal mine.

DON'T MISS: The 45-minute shop tour, offered regularly, provides a good behind-the-scenes look at heavy-duty restoration work underway on several locomotives.

GETTING THERE: From I-81, take Exit 185. Stay in the left lanes to downtown Scranton and turn left at first traffic light. Follow Lackawanna Avenue to Cliff Avenue, where the park entrance is located.

Strasburg Rail Road 29

LOCATION: 301 Gap Road, Strasburg
PHONE: 717-687-7522
WEBSITE: strasburgrailroad.com
E-MAIL: srrtrain@strasburgrailroad.com

Strasburg Rail Road

The nine-mile, 45-minute round trip from Strasburg to Paradise through Amish farmland aboard authentic 19th century wooden coaches being pulled by a steam locomotive recalls travel before automobiles. Narration provides an entertaining and educational ride.

CHOICES: Different types of service are available on regular excursions, and you can ride in a coach, open-air, dining, or first-class car. Locomotives pull trains tender-first east out of the station and pilot-first west. Sit on the right-hand side of the train out of Strasburg for the best view of the engine changing ends at Paradise. Get off the train at Groffs Grove for a picnic or to just watch the action, which in the busy season includes a meet between two trains every half hour. Lunch, dinner, wine-and-cheese, and other special trains are offered as well. Tours of the shop and engine house are available.

WHEN TO GO: Steam trains run every day nearly all year, and in summer, two trains run simultaneously. A rare, wooden self-propelled doodlebug from a long-abandoned Lancaster County short line runs several days in March and in November. Strasburg's Thomas the Tank Engine events draw immense crowds.

GOOD TO KNOW: For an interesting overnight experience, you can stay in one of 38 cabooses at the nearby Red Caboose Motel.

WORTH DOING: Located in the heart of Pennsylvania Dutch Country, a drive through the area lets you explore scenic farmlands with covered bridges and experience Amish culture. Buggy rides are offered by various enterprises. You can get lost for hours in the Cherry Crest Adventure Farm's five-acre corn maze and other activities.

DON'T MISS: View the Railroad Museum of Pennsylvania's world-class collection, which is right across the road (a combo pass is available), or take in the Toy Train Museum.

GETTING THERE: The railroad is on Gap Road (Route 741) one mile east of Strasburg.

Tioga Central Railroad

LOCATION: Route 287 and Muck Road, Wellsboro
PHONE: 570-724-0990
WEBSITE: www.tiogacentral.com
E-MAIL: form on website

Sam Botts

Here's a short railroad that still carries freight on its 34-mile route but also knows how to have some fun. The ride takes you along Crooked Creek, through forests, and to Lake Hammond, a large reservoir. It's a good trip at a brisk pace behind rare Alco diesels.

CHOICES: The Tioga Central, in addition to operating its regular, 24-mile, 90-minute excursions, offers a variety of special trains, including a Friday night ice cream train, dinner and brunch trains, and a Happy Hour Express. Ride the train's open-air car and keep a lookout for wildlife such as osprey, blue herons, deer, and even bald eagles.

WHEN TO GO: The railroad offers regular excursions Thursdays through Sundays from Memorial Day weekend to December. In fall, to take advantage of the spectacular foliage, added excursions operate.

GOOD TO KNOW: The railroad owes its good views of Lake Hammond, which it parallels for much of its journey, to a dam project that almost resulted in the railroad's abandonment. Fortunately, the railroad was relocated to the side of the reservoir.

WORTH DOING: Explore the nearby Pine Creek Gorge however you like. You can take a hike, ride a bike, or raft a river. Called the Grand Canyon of Pennsylvania, the 1,000-foot-deep gorge winds its way through acres of scenic landscape. Various parks provide breathtaking views of the canyon from hiking trails. You can also bike the Pine Creek Trail, a former rail line, through the canyon. Rafting is best in spring.

DON'T MISS: At the station, take a look at the railroad's oldest piece of rolling stock. Now an office, Car 54 was originally a double-ended, open-platform paymaster car built in 1894 for the Grand Trunk Western.

GETTING THERE: Wellsboro is in north-central Pennsylvania, 50 miles north of Williamsport. Trains leave from Wellsboro Junction, which is about three miles north of Wellsboro on Route 287.

Wanamaker, Kempton & Southern Railroad 31

LOCATION: 42 Community Center Drive, Kempton
PHONE: 610-756-6469
WEBSITE: kemptontrain.com
E-MAIL: info@kemptontrain.com

Wayne Laepple

While short on mileage, Wanamaker Kempton & Southern is long on atmosphere. For nearly 50 years, this little line has preserved the atmosphere of a Reading branch line railroad, operating authentically painted and lettered equipment.

CHOICES: Diesel locomotives power trains on the 40-minute round trip, with hourly departures each day. In addition to regular trains, there are special events, including Easter Bunny, Harvest Moon, Halloween, and Santa specials, as well as murder mystery trains and a Kids Fun Weekend.

WHEN TO GO: WK&S operates weekends July through November and Sundays only in May and June. Passing prosperous farms and crossing Ontelaunee Creek, the excursion takes riders through beautiful scenery at any time of year. The fall colors in late September and early October on the surrounding mountains are breathtaking.

GOOD TO KNOW: WK&S is much less formal than some tourist railroads and features a picnic grove accessible only by train. Two steam locomotives are on hand and under restoration for eventual service.

WORTH DOING: A visit to WK&S can easily be combined with a trip to other rail attractions such as Steamtown National Historic Site and Pioneer Tunnel Coal Mine. Also nearby are the Mid-Atlantic Air Museum, Crystal Cave, Hawk Mountain Raptor Sanctuary, and Roadside America, where you can see 200 years of American life in a fantastic miniature display.

DON'T MISS: Ride the left side of the train for the best views of Ontelaunee Creek and vistas of the nearby mountains, orchards, and farms. Be sure to leave the train at Wanamaker for a quick look at the charming station and a nearby general store.

GETTING THERE: WK&S is located in east-central Pennsylvania, five miles north of I-78, just off Route 737 in Kempton. Follow signs to the station, which is a short distance north of the town.

DISCOUNT: $1 off each ticket in a group; excludes special events.

RHODE ISLAND

Newport Dinner Train 1

Aboard the Newport Dinner Train, you can enjoy lunch or dinner in elegantly restored 1940s Budd dining cars. The 22-mile round trip takes you along scenic Narragansett Bay. The menu offers several entree choices including the train's specialty, baby back ribs. The Islander Touring Train offers 90-minute scenic train excursions aboard self-propelled commuter cars. Special packages are offered, some featuring boat cruises of Newport Harbor.

LOCATION: 19 America's Cup Avenue, Newport
PHONE: 800-398-7427 or 401-841-8700
WEBSITE: newportdinnertrain.com
E-MAIL: info@newportdinnertrain.com

Old Colony & Newport Railway 2

Enjoy a unique 80-minute train ride along the shores of Narragansett Bay, where you will travel through a naval base and see two decommissioned aircraft carriers. The ride also offers views of various craft plying the bay, rocky beaches, and wildlife. First-class service is available aboard an 1884 parlor car, and coach passengers ride in a 1904 open-platform coach. The railway operates Sundays year-round.

LOCATION: 19 America's Cup Avenue, Newport
PHONE: 401-624-6951
WEBSITE: www.ocnrr.com
E-MAIL: info@ocnrr.com

SOUTH CAROLINA

Railroad Historical Center ❶

A walk-through display of rolling stock includes a 1906 2-8-2 steam engine, Pullman cars, and Piedmont & Northern cars. It is operated in partnership with The Museum in Greenwood, located four blocks north, which features a wide range of historical exhibits and educational programs. The Railroad Historical Center is open Saturdays April through October.

LOCATION: 908 S. Main Street, Greenwood
PHONE: 864-229-7093
WEBSITE: emeraldtriangle.sc/museum
E-MAIL: themuseum@greenwood.net

South Carolina Railroad Museum ❷

LOCATION: 110 Industrial Park Road, Winnsboro
PHONE: 803-635-4242 or 803-635-9893
WEBSITE: scrm.org
E-MAIL: info@scrm.org

Bill White

A slice of Southeastern shortline history awaits visitors to the South Carolina Railroad Museum. Located on the former Rockton & Rion Railway, a granite quarry short line, this museum brings the experience of a casual Southeastern short line to life through a 10-mile, one-hour ride, interesting exhibits, and rolling stock displays.

CHOICES: The Rockton, Rion & Western Railroad runs west past antebellum plantation remains and through pine forests on the trip to Rion. You can enjoy the ride in a coach, open-air car, or caboose. The museum's collection showcases South Carolina's railroad heritage and includes exhibits of track tools, artifacts, and photographs. Rolling stock features passenger cars, freight cars, cabooses, and other equipment from the Lancaster and Chester, Norfolk Southern, CSX, and other railroads.

WHEN TO GO: The museum is open on Saturdays June through August, with regular train rides scheduled on those days, and several Saturdays in fall. It also hosts a variety of special events throughout the year, including Santa trains.

GOOD TO KNOW: The railroad is more than a hundred years old and is listed on the National Register of Historic Places. The museum's 100-ton General Motors diesel saw action during the Korean War.

WORTH DOING: Wet a line in one of the state's top fishing lakes. Lake Wateree has more than 13,700 acres and contains bream, catfish, crappie, and bass. Dammed in 1919, it is also one of the oldest manmade lakes in the state. Lake Wateree State Recreation Area also includes a nature trail for a short hike.

DON'T MISS: Take a look at steam locomotive 4-6-0 No. 44 from the Hampton & Branchville, which is in process of being restored. It is one of the few steam locomotives on display in South Carolina.

GETTING THERE: About 30 miles from Columbia, Winnsboro is between Columbia and Rock Hill, just off I-77. Take Exit 34 and follow Route 34 about five miles and turn left at the steam locomotive that marks the museum's entrance.

SOUTH DAKOTA

Prairie Village ❶

Prairie Village is a collection of restored buildings, rail equipment, and farm machinery that preserves the past. Rail structures include several historical depots, a roundhouse, and an operating turntable. On Sundays, you can take a two-mile train ride around the village. Several steam and diesel locomotives, various cabooses, and a unique chapel car are featured. Railroad Days takes place in July.

LOCATION: Highway 34, Madison
PHONE: 800-693-3644 or 605-256-3644
WEBSITE: prairievillage.org
E-MAIL: info@prairievillage.org

Black Hills Central Railroad 2

LOCATION: 222 Railroad Avenue, Hill City
PHONE: 605-574-2222
WEBSITE: www.1880train.com
E-MAIL: office@1880train.com

Steve Glischinski

This railroad gives you a chance to ride on a real mountain railroad with its steep grades, mines, and scenic hills. Situated close to Mount Rushmore, the Black Hills Central, also known as the 1880s Train, carries riders between Keystone and Hill City.

CHOICES: The two-hour, 20-mile round trip is a beautiful journey through the historic, rugged landscape of the Black Hills. You can ride in a coach or pile into the drover's car, believed to be one of only two left from the Chicago & North Western Railroad and the only one in use. Cattlemen lived in these cars while following their herds, which were loaded onto stock cars, to market. Fitting for the area, Wild West shootouts take place during several special events.

WHEN TO GO: With a few exceptions, trains operate several times daily between May and into October, departing from both Keystone and Hill City. Some last-train departures from Keystone are one-way trips only.

GOOD TO KNOW: Keystone is rich in tourist offerings including restaurants, shows, and shops. Hill City has amenities but without the tourist hubbub.

WORTH DOING: The Black Hills area is filled with must-see activities, including a trip to Mount Rushmore. You can experience the rugged beauty of the Badlands, see bison in Custer State Park, and visit the Wild West town of Deadwood.

DON'T MISS: Try to ride behind steam locomotive No. 110, the nation's only operating Mallet locomotive. What makes this engine special is that it has two sets of cylinders and drivers, and the exhaust steam from the back set of cylinders moves the front set of drivers. It is like having two smaller engines under one boiler. The locomotive is impressive as it tackles grades as steep as 5 percent for almost a mile but never breaks a sweat.

GETTING THERE: Whether traveling east or west, I-90 gets you to the train. To reach Keystone from Rapid City, take Highway 16 to Highway 244. To reach Hill City from Deadwood, take Highway 385.

TENNESSEE

Casey Jones Railroad Museum ❶

At Casey Jones Village, you can learn about the life and legend of this famous engineer by touring his family home and a replica of No. 382, Casey's engine. A re-created 1890s train station also contains related displays and artifacts as well as those of Jackson's railroad history. Be sure to go into the village's old-fashioned ice cream parlor and treat yourself to a fountain favorite.

LOCATION: 30 Casey Jones Lane, Jackson
PHONE: 877-700-7942 or 731-668-1222
WEBSITE: caseyjones.com
E-MAIL: caseyjonesmuseum@gmail.com

Cookeville Depot Museum ❷

The railroad museum is housed in a Tennessee Central Railway depot. Built in 1909, the building is listed on the National Register of Historic Places. Inside, there are changing displays of railway artifacts and photos highlighting local railroad history. A renovated caboose contains additional exhibits, and a Tennessee Central locomotive, tender, and caboose are on display. It is open year-round Tuesday through Saturday.

LOCATION: 116 W. Broad Street, Cookeville
PHONE: 931-528-8570
WEBSITE: www.cookeville-tn.org/ls
E-MAIL: depot@cookeville-tn.com

Cowan Railroad Museum ❸

Located in this century-old depot are displays, photographs, and artifacts relating to Cowan and the railroads around the city. Led by a 1920 Porter locomotive, a complete train is displayed next to the museum. Also on display are a GE diesel switcher and several motor cars. Located near the CSX main line, trainspotting opportunities exist at the museum.

LOCATION: 108 Front Street, Cowan
PHONE: 931-967-3078 or 931-967-1560
WEBSITE: cowanrailroadmuseum.org
E-MAIL: secretary@cowanrailroadmuseum.org

Little River Railroad Museum ④

The museum holds a number of tools, artifacts, and photographs dedicated to the Little River Railroad and the lumber company it served. It displays a restored 1909 Shay locomotive, several pieces of rolling stock, logging equipment, and a water tower. It is open April through October.

LOCATION: 7747 E. Lamar Alexander Parkway, Townsend
PHONE: 865-428-0099
WEBSITE: littleriverrailroad.org
E-MAIL: president@littleriverrailroad.org
DISCOUNT: 10% off gift shop purchase.

Lynnville Railroad Museum ⑤

The museum features a 1927 2-6-2 Baldwin steam locomotive and a replica depot tha contains a two-ton scale model of a locomotive and rail artifacts. The museum is open daily, and in October, you can ride the Terror Train.

LOCATION: 162 Mill Street, Lynnville
PHONE: 931-527-3158
WEBSITE: lynnvillerailroadmuseum.com
E-MAIL: tim@lynnvillerailroadmuseum.com

Nashville, Chattanooga & St. Louis Depot and Railroad Museum ⑥

The museum houses a collection of artifacts, photographs, and memorabilia associated with railroad and local history. The grounds feature a dining car and two cabooses. Built in 1907, the depot is listed on the National Register of Historic Places. It is open year-round, Monday through Saturday.

LOCATION: 582 S. Royal Street, Jackson
PHONE: 731-425-8223
WEBSITE: www.cityofjackson.net
E-MAIL: thedepot@cityofjackson.net

Southern Appalachia Railway Museum ❼

LOCATION: Highway 58, Oak Ridge
PHONE: 865-241-2140
WEBSITE: techscribes.com/sarm

Barton Jennings

For many years, the government did not acknowledge the existence of the huge nuclear research lab at Oak Ridge or the railroad that served it. Now that the lab is closed, the railroad to "Secret City" is now a tourist attraction, giving visitors some insight into this unusual bit of railroading as well as a nice ride through the east Tennessee hills.

CHOICES: Pulled by 1950s Alco diesels, the 14-mile, 60-minute round trip takes you through the former secret atomic facility. Once outside the Secret City, the train enters the countryside, where it crosses Poplar Creek and passes Watts Bar Lake before returning. Two-hour dinner trains are scheduled from February to September.

WHEN TO GO: Excursions run several Saturdays a month from April through September. A full slate of fall foliage trains run throughout October. Halloween, Thanksgiving, and Santa trains also run.

GOOD TO KNOW: Non-U.S. citizens must show a passport and visa before riding the train. When the train leaves, it passes through an enclosure used to check railcars for hobos, and it still provides a way to screen the train from unwanted spies. The boarding station is a former guardhouse.

WORTH DOING: To learn more about the secrets of atomic power, you can visit the American Museum of Science & Energy in Oak Ridge or take a self-guided auto tour of some Manhattan Project sites in the area.

DON'T MISS: Arrive 30 minutes early and you may be able to get a caboose seat when they are available.

GETTING THERE: Oak Ridge is about 30 miles west of Knoxville, and the Heritage Center is situated between Oak Ridge and I-40 on Route 58. To get there from Knoxville, take I-40 west to Exit 356. Turn right and travel north on Route 58 approximately five miles to the Heritage Center. Turn left into the main entrance and take the first left inside the plant.

Tennessee Central Railway Museum ⑧

LOCATION: 220 Willow Street, Nashville
PHONE: 615-244-9001
WEBSITE: tcry.org

Ralcon Wagner

The museum offers day trips on a streamlined passenger train through scenic middle Tennessee over the tracks of the Nashville & Eastern Railroad to various destinations. Duration of excursions range from two to seven hours.

CHOICES: Leaving from the Nashville station, excursions travel to Watertown, Baxter, Lebanon, Cookeville, and Monterey. Passengers have a choice of coach, first-class, or dome seating. All excursion seats are reserved and offer large windows with great views, but dome seating is limited and sells out early on most trips. Many trips include a special event such as a train robbery, Civil War reenactment, onboard murder mystery, or seasonal theme including Easter Bunny, fall foliage, and North Pole trains.

WHEN TO GO: The museum is open Monday through Saturdays year-round. Excursions run on select Saturdays throughout the year. The majority of the longer, 180-mile round-trip excursions to Cookeville take place in the fall when the foliage is most brilliant. During early September, kids of all ages can ride with Thomas the Tank.

GOOD TO KNOW: The museum is housed in the former Tennessee Central Railway's master mechanic's office, and it includes a large collection of Tennessee Central Railway artifacts. It also features a collection of locomotives and railcars.

WORTH DOING: Only minutes away are numerous downtown attractions that will appeal to the entire family. These include the Country Music Hall of Fame and Museum, Bicentennial Capitol Mall State Park, Historic Ryman Auditorium, Tennessee State Capitol building, and Riverfront Park.

DON'T MISS: Tour Nashville's historic 111-year old restored Union Station, which is now an upscale hotel. Ride Nashville's Music City Star commuter train from Riverfront Station.

GETTING THERE: The museum is located a mile east of downtown Nashville. From I-40, take Exit 212 and turn north. Go a block to Hermitage Avenue (Highway 70) and turn left. Turn right at Fairfield Avenue which becomes Willow Street. Follow signs to museum, located at bottom of the hill on the left.

Tennessee Valley Railroad ▣

LOCATION: 4119 Cromwell Road, Chattanooga
PHONE: 423-894-8028
WEBSITE: tvrail.com
E-MAIL: form on website

TVR, Steve Freer

If you were to take a major steam railroad from the 1920s, shrink it and preserve it, you'd have the Tennessee Valley Railroad. It offers a steam-powered train ride that leaves from a magnificent station, crosses trestles over streams and another active railroad line, and passes through a tunnel before it reaches the terminal at the opposite end of the run.

CHOICES: The railroad offers a variety of excursions. You can take the *Missionary Ridge Local* on a six-mile round trip between Grand Junction and East Chattanooga, traveling through a unique horseshoe tunnel as you do. On the *Chickamauga Turn*, a six-hour ride takes you to Chickamauga and back. Departing out of Etowah, the railroad, with the Tennessee Overhill Association, also offers a trip through the Hiwassee River Gorge that rides to the top of the Great Hiwassee Loop. The railroad's Dixie Land excursions feature various special trains, the most popular being the Autumn Leaf runs.

WHEN TO GO: Excursions run almost every day February through December, with dinner trains and other specials scheduled throughout the year. Anytime the steam train is running is a good time to go.

GOOD TO KNOW: If you want an all-railroad experience, stay at the Chattanooga Choo Choo, a Holiday Inn in the former terminal station. You can eat at the station complex in one of several venues, including a real railroad dining car, and sleep on a train car.

WORTH DOING: In Chattanooga, activities include visiting the Tennessee Aquarium and taking a riverboat cruise on the Tennessee River. History buffs can explore both the Lookout Mountain and Chickamauga battlefields.

DON'T MISS: At East Chattanooga, a guided tour of the shop and turntable is included with the *Missionary Ridge Local*. The shop features one of the few complete wheel shops in the country, and on any given visit, there's no telling what set of wheels from what engine is there for repairs.

GETTING THERE: The railroad is in the northeast section of Chattanooga. To get there, take Route 153 to Exit 3. At the end of the exit ramp, turn left over Route 153 and turn right onto Cromwell Road.

Three Rivers Rambler

LOCATION: Volunteer Landing on Neyland Drive, Knoxville
PHONE: 865-524-9411
WEBSITE: threeriversrambler.com
E-MAIL: form on website

John A. Craft

There are few perfect chances to ride a steam train in a beautiful part of the Appalachians, leaving from one of the more pleasant areas of a small city like Knoxville. But the Three Rivers Rambler offers just such an outing. From its departure point on the Tennessee River, it makes its way into the country to its namesake point: the confluence of the Holston and French Broad Rivers that creates the mighty Tennessee. The train bridges this point on a magnificent trestle that puts an exclamation point on the trip.

CHOICES: On the 90-minute round trip, you'll ride in a coach or an open-air car. Two steam engines or a diesel locomotive provide the power. No. 203 is a 1925 Baldwin steam engine and No. 154, an 1890 steam engine. The steam engines run mostly for special events.

WHEN TO GO: Excursions operate on Saturdays during summer and fall, and you can't beat autumn, especially for the colors. Special trains run for Easter, Christmas, and other occasions. A railfan weekend takes place in August with steam and diesel locomotives in action.

GOOD TO KNOW: Until its return to the rails in 2010, former Southern Railway steam engine No. 154, a 2-8-0 Consolidation built by Schenectady Locomotive Works, had been on display since 1953 in Knoxville's Chilhowee Park. It is oldest Southern Railway locomotive in operation.

WORTH DOING: The departure point on the Tennessee River is adjacent to the university in an area with several good restaurants. Sports fans could try and catch a University of Tennessee football or basketball game or visit the Women's Basketball Hall of Fame.

DON'T MISS: Along the way, feel free to ask the conductor or volunteer staff questions about the train or local history.

GETTING THERE: From I-40, take Exit 386B to Neyland Drive and turn left. Drive two miles to the parking lot on your left and look for signs. After parking, cross under Neyland Drive and proceed left down the riverwalk to the train at Volunteer Landing.

DISCOUNT: $2 off any summer season ticket.

Tennessee

TEXAS

Galveston Railroad Museum ❶

Located on Galveston Island, the museum was extensively damaged by Hurricane Ike in September 2008. Rebuilding projects continue and it is best to contact the museum for their operational status. The museum's collection includes three diesel locomotives that were operable before Hurricane Ike, three steam locomotives on static display, and numerous passenger and freight cars and cabooses of historical interest.

LOCATION: 2602 Santa Fe Place, Galveston
PHONE: 409-765-5700
WEBSITE: galvestonrrmuseum.com
E-MAIL: galvrrmuseum@sbcglobal.net

History Center ❷

The History Center features indoor and outdoor interpretive exhibits. Permanent displays include a 1920 Baldwin 4-6-0 from Texas Southeastern Railroad on which you can ring its bell and blow its whistle, a log car, and a caboose. The center contains a large number of photos on east Texas railroading and logging operations.

LOCATION: 102 N. Temple Drive, Diboll
PHONE: 936-829-3543
WEBSITE: thehistorycenteronline.com
E-MAIL: info@thehistorycenteronline.com

Houston Railroad Museum ❸

The museum features a unique collection of locomotives, freight cars, and passenger cars with a Texas flavor. At the museum, you can tour a *Texas Special* coach and a *Texas Eagle* sleeping car, view artifacts, and even blow a diesel's horn. It is open Saturdays April to November.

LOCATION: 7390 Mesa Road, Houston
PHONE: 713-631-6612
WEBSITE: houstonrrmuseum.org
E-MAIL: info@houstonrrmuseum.org

Lehnis Railroad Museum ❹

This railroad museum displays an AT&SF steam locomotive, a business car, and a caboose. It includes a collection of railroad china, lanterns, equipment, and photos. From the train-watching platform, you can look for passing BNSF trains. Located next to a Harvey House and Santa Fe depot, the museum is open Tuesdays through Saturdays.

LOCATION: 700 E. Adams Street, Brownwood
PHONE: 325-643-6376
WEBSITE: ci.brownwood.tx.us/LRM
E-MAIL: mirving@ci.brownwood.tx.us

McKinney Avenue Trolley ❺

McKinney Avenue Trolley operates a fleet of vintage streetcars built between 1909 and 1945. You can hop on and off a trolley and explore the city's Uptown area. Trolley rides are free, so you can hop all you want. Trolleys run daily, every 25 minutes on weekends and every 15 minutes on weekdays. A downtown loop down Olive Street connecting to St. Paul should be completed in 2012.

LOCATION: McKinney Avenue, Dallas
PHONE: 214-855-0006
WEBSITE: www.mata.org
E-MAIL: ask_mata@yahoo.com

New Braunfels Railroad Museum ❻

Housed in the restored 1907 International & Great Northern depot, the museum displays a 0-6-0 Porter oil-fired steam locomotive, a Missouri Pacific caboose, and numerous railroad artifacts. It is open Thursday through Monday.

LOCATION: 302 W. San Antonio Street, New Braunfels
PHONE: 830-627-2447
WEBSITE: newbraunfelsrailroadmuseum.org
E-MAIL: info@newbraunfelsrailroadmuseum.org

Railroad & Heritage Museum ❼

Housed in a 1910 Santa Fe depot, the museum features early Santa Fe and Missouri-Kansas-Texas station equipment, including a working telegraph. Outdoor exhibits feature a variety of cars, a steam locomotive, and a diesel engine. The museum is open Tuesday through Saturday.

LOCATION: 315 W. Avenue B, Temple
PHONE: 254-298-5172
WEBSITE: rrhm.org
DISCOUNT: 10% off gift shop purchase.

Railroad and Transportation Museum of El Paso ❽

A restored 1857 4-4-0 locomotive and other railroad exhibits are on display in the Transit Terminal of Union Plaza. One exhibit covers urban transit from the mule car through streamlined Art Deco streetcars. It is open Tuesday through Sunday.

LOCATION: 400 W. San Antonio Avenue, El Paso
PHONE: 915-422-3420
WEBSITE: elpasorails.org
E-MAIL: form on website

Railway Museum of San Angelo ❾

Located in a historic Kansas City, Mexico & Orient depot, which was completed in 1910, the museum highlights local railroad history. Static displays include two diesel locomotives, a boxcar, and a caboose. It is open on Saturdays.

LOCATION: 703 S. Chadbourne Street, San Angelo
PHONE: 325-486-2140
WEBSITE: railwaymuseumsanangelo.homestead.com
E-MAIL: form on website

Rosenberg Railroad Museum ⑩

The museum features Tower 17, the last manned interlocking tower in Texas, which was moved to the site. Inside the fully restored tower, you can work the interlocking machine. Other exhibits include signaling, station agent, and telegraph artifacts. The museum is also restoring an 1879 business car.

LOCATION: 1921 Avenue F, Rosenberg
PHONE: 281-633-2846
WEBSITE: rosenbergrrmuseum.org

Texas & Pacific Railway Museum ⑪

The museum is housed in a historic Texas & Pacific depot that was built in 1912. It contains artifacts and photos dating from the 1870s and a replica of an agent's office. For a panoramic view of the area, go to the depot's upper level and look out from the balcony. A Union Pacific caboose is also on the grounds. The Texas & Pacific Railway Museum is open Tuesdays through Saturdays.

LOCATION: 800 N. Washington Avenue, Marshall
PHONE: 800-513-9495 or 903-938-9495
WEBSITE: www.marshalldepot.org
E-MAIL: info@marshalldepot.org

Texas Transportation Museum ⑫

The museum displays a variety of railroad structures and equipment including two steam locomotives, two diesel engines, and rolling stock. It features a Southern Pacific depot built in 1913 that was moved from Converse. The two-room building contains memorabilia from the Southern Pacific and two other railroads that served San Antonio. The museum also operates a short train ride on weekends and fire truck rides when available.

LOCATION: 11731 Wetmore Road, San Antonio
PHONE: 210-490-3554
WEBSITE: txtransportationmuseum.org
E-MAIL: hugh@satx.rr.com

Wichita Falls Railroad Museum ⑬

The museum's collection includes a Fort Worth & Denver steam locomotive, a Missouri-Kansas-Texas switch engine, a 1913 Pullman all-steel sleeper, troop sleepers, cabooses, and other cars. Artifacts center on the railroads that served Wichita Falls, especially the Missouri-Kansas-Texas Railway. The museum is open Saturdays April through November.

LOCATION: 500 Ninth Street, Wichita Falls
PHONE: 940-723-2661
WEBSITE: www.wfrrm.com

Austin Steam Train 14

LOCATION: 401 E. Whitestone Boulevard, Cedar Park
PHONE: 512-477-8468
WEBSITE: austinsteamtrain.org
E-MAIL: info@austinsteamtrain.org

J. Parker Lamb

This tourist line was formed in 1989 to provide weekend service over a portion of a 167-mile route purchased from Southern Pacific. The train operates out of Cedar Park and rolls through the Texas hills—and history.

CHOICES: The railroad's operating hub is in Cedar Park, 19 miles from downtown Austin. The *Hill Country Flyer* makes a 70-mile round trip between Cedar Park and Burnet, and the trip includes a leisurely layover. On the 46-mile round trip aboard the *Bertram Flyer*, you'll leave Cedar Park, cross the South San Gabriel River, and arrive in Bertram. Rolling stock consists of six vintage Pennsylvania P70 coaches, along with three first-class parlor cars of AT&SF, NKP, and MP heritage. You have a choice of riding coach, excursion, or first-class. Coach cars have opening windows while the other cars are climate controlled.

WHEN TO GO: Excursions run weekends all year. Many visitors choose to ride during the spring and fall and bypass the summer heat. Special trains include murder mystery trains and the North Pole Flyer.

GOOD TO KNOW: Trains are pulled by an Alco RSD-15 in a black widow paint scheme until the restoration of SP Mikado No. 786 is completed.

WORTH DOING: Both Cedar Park and Burnet have numerous lodging and dining options for visitors, while Austin is famous for its museums, entertainment, and scenic drives.

DON'T MISS: In September, you can catch the *Oatmeal Flyer*, which takes you to the Oatmeal Festival in time to view the festival parade. complete with raining oatmeal.

GETTING THERE: Cedar Park can be reached from the north by leaving I-35 at Round Rock and using Highway 45 westward, while visitors arriving from the south will travel northward though Austin on I-35 and connect directly with Highway 183. Cedar Park is also served by Capital MetroRail, a commuter route from downtown Austin.

DISCOUNT: 10% off any *Hill Country Flyer* or *Bertram Flyer*; use code MEMBER.

Grapevine Vintage Railroad 15

LOCATION: 709 S. Main Street, Grapevine
PHONE: 817-410-3123 or 817-410-8136
WEBSITE: grapevinetexasusa.com

J. Parker Lamb

Grapevine operates the only 19th century steam locomotive in Texas, an 1896 Cooke 4-6-0 used for decades by the Southern Pacific in fire service on Donner Pass. With its home base at the restored 1888 Cotton Belt depot in downtown Grapevine, the railroad operates over 21 miles of ex-Cotton Belt trackage into the famous Fort Worth Stockyards Mall. It also includes a six-mile branch line running southward from the mall across the Trinity River.

CHOICES: The railroad's 90-minute ride takes you from Grapevine to the Stockyards, and the two-hour layover allows ample time for exploring the mall's many offerings. The Trinity River run passes through Trinity Park and the Fort Worth Zoo along a segment of the famous Chisholm Trail. Trains carry four 1925-era day coaches (19th century décor) plus a pair of open-air excursion coaches.

WHEN TO GO: Regular excursions run February through November. Between Memorial Day and Labor Day, they operate Thursday through Sunday. Frequency is reduced to three days (Friday to Sunday) during the rest of the season. The line offers numerous special events all season including train robberies, visits to historical frontier forts, Easter Bunny runs, and North Pole trains with a storytelling Santa.

GOOD TO KNOW: Grapevine is close to the Ballpark at Arlington (Texas Rangers) and Six Flags Over Texas. The Fort Worth Stockyards complex includes the Texas Cowboy Hall of Fame and weekend rodeo shows. Just north of the city is Grapevine Lake, a mecca for water sports.

WORTH DOING: True to its name, Grapevine is home to numerous wineries with regular tours and a special Grapefest celebration in September.

DON'T MISS: For maximum mileage, passengers can board at Grapevine, travel to the Fort Worth Stockyards, and then ride the Trinity River run, which connects with the return train to Grapevine.

GETTING THERE: The city of Grapevine is adjacent to the northwest corner of the DFW Airport, midway between the two hubs of the Metroplex. Three major highways (114, 121, and 360) intersect at Grapevine, with I-30 being only a few miles south of the airport.

Museum of the American Railroad ⑯

LOCATION: 6299 Cotton Gin Road, Frisco (or 1105 Washington Street, Dallas)
PHONE: 972-292-5658 (Frisco) or 214-428-0101 (Dallas)
WEBSITE: museumoftheamericanrailroad.com

Museum of the American Railroad

Founded in 1963, the museum features more than 35 pieces of vintage equipment. The museum contains an eclectic mix of all types of locomotives from both the United States and Canada. It features one of the nation's largest collections of pre-World War II heavyweight passenger equipment. It also has a variety of lightweight passenger cars, freight cars, and cabooses.

CHOICES: New to the collection is an Alco PA1 that was donated from the Smithsonian Institution. You can also find two of the Union Pacific's largest locomotives, a Big Boy and a Centennial DDA40X, and a Pennsylvania GG1. Other engines range in size from a Frisco 4-8-4 down to a diminutive 0-6-0 from the Dallas Union Terminal. Also on display are historic structures and a 1941 Ford truck used by the Railway Express Agency.

WHEN TO GO: The museum is open throughout the year and offers special events as well. They include a Whistle Fair that employs the Museum's steam calliope and its many steam engine whistles, a Day Out with Thomas in Grapevine, and Dinner in the Diner.

GOOD TO KNOW: During 2011, the museum should be in its new location in Frisco, 30 miles north of Dallas, having moved from Fair Park in downtown Dallas. Please check the museum's website for the most current information. In its new location, it will be able to display its entire collection.

WORTH DOING: While Dallas and all its attractions are a half hour away, Frisco has activities and attractions as well. You can visit the Texas Sculpture Garden, Sci-Tech Discovery Center, and Heritage Museum.

DON'T MISS: For a ride on a steam train, the Grapevine Vintage Railroad is 30 miles southwest of Frisco.

GETTING THERE: The easiest route to Frisco from Dallas is on the Dallas North Tollway. Although when traffic is bad, the 30-mile drive may take an hour.

Texas State Railroad 🔢

LOCATION: Highway 84 and Park Road 76, Rusk
PHONE: 888-987-2461 or 903-683-2561
WEBSITE: www.texasstaterr.com
E-MAIL: info@texasstaterr.com

Jonathan Gerland

Built in 1896 and operating excursions since 1972, the Texas State Railroad offers a relaxing, enjoyable ride through the piney woods region of east Texas at a leisurely pace between the small east Texas towns of Rusk and Palestine. Various steam and diesel locomotives with regional history pull the trains through tall stands of timber in the I.D. Fairchild National Forest, giving riders a glimpse into the railroad's origin of hauling agricultural and timber products in the early 20th century.

CHOICES: The Texas State Railroad offers visitors several options for trips on the 25-mile ride. You can ride in either open-air, general seating cars or in climate-controlled coaches (recommended during the summer months). Steam-powered trips alternate with diesel-powered trains at different times during the month. Round trips are available from either depot, and there is a 90-minute layover for lunch at the opposite destination. Box lunches are available for regular excursions.

WHEN TO GO: Trains currently operate year-round, mostly on weekends, but the schedule varies in frequency during non-summer months. Summers can be hot so book early for air-conditioned seating. The rest of the year is usually mild, so open-air seating then is very enjoyable. However, east Texas weather changes rapidly, so keep a jacket handy. Several times a year, various special events, photo excursions, and dinner trains are offered. Other events feature the Lone Ranger, Thomas the Tank Engine, the Polar Express, and Peanuts characters.

GOOD TO KNOW: Both depots are Victorian-styled stations and contain historical exhibits. Full-service camping and picnic sites are available adjacent to each depot.

WORTH DOING: Palestine features many restored Victorian homes, historic buildings from the early 1800s, and the Dogwood Trails Festival.

DON'T MISS: RailFest takes place on Labor Day weekend at the Palestine depot and includes a steam excursion to the Maydelle turntable, a shop tour, motor-car rides, and entertainment.

GETTING THERE: Major airlines to Dallas or Houston provide the closest air transportation. From there, a leisurely three-hour drive is required to reach the two east Texas towns.

UTAH

Western Mining and Railroad Museum ❶

Museum exhibits feature the Denver & Rio Grande Western and other railways. Located in the old Helper Hotel, which was completed in 1914, the museum contains four floors of artifacts. The third floor contains a railroad office and two rooms of railroading artifacts. A 100-year-old caboose is also on display. Other exhibits, including a simulated coal mine, focus on the mining industry and its workers. It is open year-round.

LOCATION: 296 S. Main Street, Helper
PHONE: 435-472-3009
WEBSITE: wmrrm.org
E-MAIL: helpermuseum@helpercity.net

Golden Spike National Historic Site ❷

LOCATION: Golden Spike Drive, Promontory
PHONE: 435-471-2209
WEBSITE: www.nps.gov/gosp
E-MAIL: form on website

Jeff Terry

The construction of the transcontinental railroad is one of the pivotal events in the nation's history. Completed May 10, 1869, at this remote spot northwest of Ogden, the National Park Service does justice to the event by running replica locomotives and conducting reenactments.

CHOICES: Reenactments of the Last Spike Ceremony, complete with dignitaries in period dress, take place on Saturdays and holidays May through Labor Day. The two steam locomotive replicas, the coal-burning Union Pacific No. 119 and the wood-burning Central Pacific *Jupiter*, are accurate reproductions and fully functional. The visitor center offers informative films and exhibits.

WHEN TO GO: Except for Thanksgiving, Christmas, and New Year's Day, the visitor center is open. Between May and Labor Day, the steam locomotives are on display and conduct demonstrations. During winter, when the locomotives are being maintained, engine house tours are available. Steam demonstrations and photo runs also take place during the annual Winter Steam Festival.

GOOD TO KNOW: The correct name for the location of Golden Spike National Historic Site is Promontory Summit, not Promontory Point, which is 35 miles to the south. The summit is the highest point of Promontory Pass. For some reason, the wrong location was reported in some records in 1869 and perpetuated throughout history.

WORTH DOING: Drive through Brigham City and view the interesting Box Elder Tabernacle, and stop at the restored early 20th century train depot.

DON'T MISS: The Big Fill Loop Trail (1.5-mile round trip) takes you out on the original Central Pacific grade and back on the Union Pacific grade. You'll see the site of the Union Pacific's trestle, go through cuts, and see drill marks where workers blasted away rock.

GETTING THERE: Golden Spike National Historic Site is in northern Utah, 32 miles west of Brigham City. From Brigham City, take Highway 83 to the entrance, which is Golden Spike Drive. The area is still very rugged and sparsely populated. Food and fuel are available in Brigham City.

Heber Valley Railroad 🔳

LOCATION: 450 S. 600 W, Heber
PHONE: 800-888-8499 or 435-654-5601
WEBSITE: www.hebervalleyrr.org
E-MAIL: reservations@hebervalleyrr.org

Jeff Terry

This railroad offers a scenic ride beside Deer Creek Reservoir and down Provo Canyon in unspoiled country with the Wasatch Mountains as a backdrop over a line that began operating in 1899.

CHOICES: Heber Valley offers two regular excursions in the shadow of 12,000-foot Mount Timpanogos aboard vintage coaches. The *Provo Canyon Limited* is a three-hour round trip that runs to Vivian Park and back. Along the way, you'll hear about the history of the area. The 90-minute *Soldier Hollow Express* goes to Deer Creek Reservoir and returns. Summer excursion packages combine river rafting, horseback riding, or bike riding with a train ride. In winter, you can train to a 1,000-foot hill and tube down. Numerous special events take place throughout the year, from sunset barbecues to cowboy poetry excursions.

WHEN TO GO: The railroad operates year-round. Each season has something special to offer, but summer is especially beautiful in Utah.

GOOD TO KNOW: Trains are currently operating under diesel power, and steam operations are scheduled to return in 2012 with the restoration of 2-8-0 No. 75.

WORTH DOING: Take a scenic drive along the Provo Canyon Scenic Byway (Highway 189) that runs between Heber Valley and Provo. A short side trip on the Alpine Scenic Loop (Highway 92) takes you past Robert Redford's Sundance Resort.

DON'T MISS: If you can, ride the caboose. It's the first steel caboose that belonged to the Union Pacific.

GETTING THERE: The railroad is located between Salt Lake City and Provo. From Salt Lake City, take I-80 east to Exit 148 and then follow Highway 40 into Heber. Turn right on W. 300 S and then left on S. 600 W to the station.

DISCOUNT: $5 off each adult ticket, scenic excursions only.

Ogden Union Station ❹

LOCATION: 2501 Wall Avenue, Ogden
PHONE: 801-393-9886
WEBSITE: theunionstation.org
E-MAIL: diana@theunionstation.org

Jim Wrinn

Built in 1924, Ogden Union Station now houses a variety of museums and galleries, including the Utah State Railroad Museum and Eccles Rail Center. The museum contains artifacts of Utah railroading, and the rail center displays historic pieces of equipment. Other museums in the station focus on history, firearms, gems, classic cars, and the arts.

CHOICES: You can browse an extensive collection of rolling stock that is displayed outside the station or go inside. You'll see locomotives and cars from the big Class I railroads that served Utah, including Union Pacific, Southern Pacific, and Rio Grande. Interactive exhibits bring to life the story of the first transcontinental railroad, which was completed nearby at Promontory Summit, just west of Ogden. You'll also pass under timbers used to construct the historic Lucin trestle across the Great Salt Lake. A model railroad depicts scenery from across Utah.

WHEN TO GO: The museum is open Monday through Saturday year-round, but the outdoor railroad exhibits are accessible anytime. Many special events take place at the station, some relating to railroading.

GOOD TO KNOW: UP 4-8-4 No. 833, representing the zenith of steam passenger and freight power, was one of the last big steam locomotives built in America.

WORTH DOING: There are numerous hiking trails in and around Ogden, on which you can see mountains, waterfalls, forests, and wildlife. In scenic Ogden Valley, you can ski on the same slopes as Olympic skiers did or just enjoy the scenery. In Ogden, you can take in a show or film at Perry's Egyptian Theater, with its restored Egyptian style.

DON'T MISS: View the Union Pacific cauldron car, which carried the Olympic flame during the 2002 Winter Olympics that were held in Utah and based in Salt Lake City. The unique car carried the flame more than 3,200 miles across 11 states.

GETTING THERE: From Salt Lake City, take I-15 north to Exit 341 and follow Highway 79 East. Turn left onto Wall Avenue. The museum is in downtown Ogden and directions are well marked.

VERMONT

New England Institute and Transportation Museum ❶
The centerpiece of the museum's railroad exhibit is the renovated Boston & Maine
No. 494. The museum also celebrates the railroad with its annual Glory Days of the
Railroad festival. Other exhibits are dedicated to aviation and river commerce. It has
winter and summer hours.

LOCATION: 100 Railroad Row, White River Junction
PHONE: 802-291-9838
WEBSITE: newenglandtransportationmuseum.org
E-MAIL: netim@myfairpoint.net

Shelburne Museum ❷
Outside the museum, you'll see the 1890 Shelburne passenger station, locomotive
No. 220, which pulled the trains of four presidents, and an 1890 private luxury car.
Other historic buildings, a steamship, and more than 200 horse-drawn vehicles are
displayed at the museum.

LOCATION: 6000 Shelburne Road, Shelburne
PHONE: 802-985-3346
WEBSITE: shelburnemuseum.org
E-MAIL: info@shelburnemuseum.org

Green Mountain Railroad ▪️3

LOCATION: 54 Depot Street, Bellows Falls
PHONE: 800-707-3530 or 802-463-3069
WEBSITE: rails-vt.com
E-MAIL: railtour@vermontrailway.com

Kevin Burkholder

Green Mountain Railroad operates excursions on three separate routes that allow you to see three different areas of the state: White River Junction to Thetford, Bellows Falls to Chester Depot, and Burlington to Middlebury.

CHOICES: On its two-hour round trip (White River Junction to Thetford), the *White River Flyer* rolls along the Connecticut River and provides a view of the White Mountain foothills. It also pauses at the Montshire Museum. The *Green Mountain Flyer* operates between Bellows Falls and Chester Depot. The ride follows the Connecticut and Williams Rivers, taking you past two covered bridges and a deep gorge at Brockways Mills. The *Champlain Flyer* travels between Burlington (Vermont's largest city) and Middlebury with special trains that include fireworks, historical runs, and fall foliage dinner trains.

WHEN TO GO: The *White River Flyer* runs Thursday through Sunday during July and August with service expanding to Tuesday to Sunday in September and October. The *Green Mountain Flyer* operates Fridays May through October. Both of these trains offer special events throughout the year.

GOOD TO KNOW: Former Rutland Railroad Alco RS1 405, which has operated in Vermont since it was built in 1951, makes regular appearances on Green Mountain passenger trains.

WORTH DOING: Spend some time to enjoy Burlington's Lake Champlain waterfront and the city's many diverse restaurants. The historic Hotel Coolidge operates across from the White River Junction depot, and Calvin Coolidge's boyhood home is preserved in a state historic site in Plymouth Notch.

DON'T MISS: Boston & Maine 4-4-0 steam engine No. 494 is on display by the active White River Junction depot.

GETTING THERE: Bellows Falls is reached from I-91 Exits 5 or 6. White River Junction is near the interchange of I-91 and I-89. Burlington is accessed from I-89 Exits 12, 13, and 14. Amtrak's *Vermonter* serves Bellows Falls, White River Junction, and Essex Junction.

VIRGINIA

C&O Railway Heritage Center ❶

A restored 1895 C&O freight depot exhibits the history of the Chesapeake & Ohio Railway. The center also displays a restored 1949 C&O caboose, dining car, and combination car. You can also climb into a replica signal tower and watch trains roll by.

LOCATION: 705 Main Street, Clifton Forge
PHONE: 540 862 8653 or 540-862-2210
WEBSITE: candoheritage.org
E-MAIL: cohs@cohs.org

Crewe Railroad Museum ❷

Housed in a rail station, the museum features memorabilia from the Norfolk & Western Railroad and a display of the Crewe roundhouse. The yard contains a steam locomotive, diesel engine, caboose, and several boxcars. The museum is open year-round.

LOCATION: Virginia Avenue and Meade Street, Crewe
PHONE: 434-645-9868 or 434-645-9146
WEBSITE: www.crewerailroadmuseum.org

Eastern Shore Railway Museum ❸

The museum is housed in a restored 1906 Pennsylvania Railroad passenger station. On the siding are two cabooses, a baggage car, a Pullman sleeper, a Budd dining car, and a touring car. The museum also includes an 1890s maintenance-of-way tool shed, a crossing guard shanty, and various railroad artifacts. It is open year-round.

LOCATION: 18468 Dunne Avenue, Parksley
PHONE: 757-665-7245
WEBSITE: www.parksley.com/seeus.shtml

Fairfax Station Railroad Museum ❹

At the Fairfax museum, visitors can learn about the Orange & Alexandria Railroad and Civil War history. Stations on the site played a role in several Civil War battles, and Clara Barton tended to wounded soldiers here. The current building is a restored 1903 station, and a Norfolk Southern caboose is also on display. The museum is open Sunday afternoons.

LOCATION: 11200 Fairfax Station Road, Fairfax
PHONE: 703-425-9225
WEBSITE: fairfax-station.org
E-MAIL: fxstn@fairfax-station.org

Old Dominion Railway Museum ❺

The Old Dominion Railway Museum tells the story of Virginia's railroading heritage through artifacts, videos, displays, equipment, and an HO layout. Located near the birthplace of Virginia railroad operations, this newly renovated Southern Railway station is open Saturdays and Sundays year-round.

LOCATION: 102 Hull Street, Richmond
PHONE: 804-233-6237 or 804-231-4324
WEBSITE: odcnrhs.org
E-MAIL: wrgoodie@henrico.k12.va.us

Suffolk Seaboard Station Railroad Museum ❻

The restored Victorian Seaboard Air Line passenger station features items from Seaboard, Virginian, Norfolk & Western, and Atlantic & Danville railroads. It is also home to a two-room HO scale model of Suffolk in 1907 and a caboose built for the Nickel Plate Line. It is open daily.

LOCATION: 326 N. Main Street, Suffolk
PHONE: 757-923-4750
WEBSITE: suffolktrainstation.org
E-MAIL: trainstation@exis.net

O. Winston Link Museum ⑦

LOCATION: 101 Shenandoah Avenue NE, Roanoke
PHONE: 540-982-5465
WEBSITE: linkmuseum.org

O. Winston Link Museum

Only two photographers in the United States have their own museums. One belongs to noted landscape photographer Ansel Adams. The other is O. Winston Link. A commercial photographer, Link was fascinated with steam locomotives and made a pilgrimage to record the last of these on the Norfolk & Western in the late 1950s.

CHOICES: The museum is housed in the former Norfolk & Western passenger station in downtown Roanoke. The station was the departure point for many of the trains Link photographed, making it an excellent departure point for a world of Link's photography. More than 300 of Link's photographs are on display. The museum includes interactive exhibits, Link's photography equipment, and his railroad sound recordings. Be sure to watch the documentary film on Link's life. It's an excellent look at the man and his work through his voice and those of many others.

WHEN TO GO: The museum is open daily except for Easter, Thanksgiving, Christmas, and New Year's Day. Fall and spring in the Blue Ridge Mountains are magnificent and wonderful times to explore the area.

GOOD TO KNOW: Famous for his nighttime scenes that record the passing railroad as well as slices of rural life, Link took many photos of the region in the late '50s and early '60s. For years, Link's work languished, but in the 1980s, his career rebounded as the art world discovered his genius of capturing steam at night in (mostly) black and white.

WORTH DOING: The Hotel Roanoke, directly behind the museum, is a former railroad hotel and a great place to spend the night. Spend some time on the front lawn and watch the coal trains lumber by as they have for more than 120 years.

DON'T MISS: The former station is a Virginia Historic Landmark and is listed on the National Register of Historic Places. It is one of several renovated railroad buildings in the area. Another is the Virginia Museum of Transportation, which is a short walk away. The two museums offer a combined admission.

GETTING THERE: Roanoke is about 190 miles west of Richmond and near West Virginia and North Carolina. To reach the museum from I-81, take I-581 south and exit at Williamson Road and turn right on Shenandoah Avenue.

Virginia Museum of Transportation ⑧

LOCATION: 303 Norfolk Avenue SW, Roanoke
PHONE: 540-342-5670
WEBSITE: www.vmt.org
E-MAIL: info@vmt.org

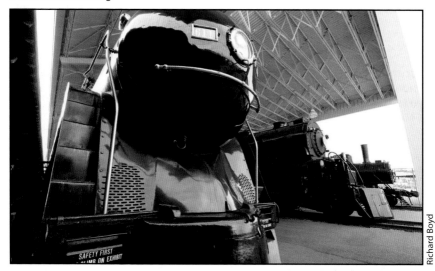

Richard Boyd

Roanoke was once synonymous with the best steam locomotives in the land. The Norfolk & Western built many of them right here, just a few blocks away. While the museum's scope is the broad subject of transportation, its heart is in railroading.

CHOICES: The museum is housed in a historic rail setting, the city's old N&W freight station. Through exhibits and rolling stock displays, you'll learn a lot about how people got around in the Old Dominion State. It displays steam and diesel locomotives, antique automobiles, trucks, and even a post office bus. The museum also includes several ongoing exhibits dedicated to railroading and a model railroad.

WHEN TO GO: The museum is open daily, except for some holidays and during inclement weather, throughout the year.

GOOD TO KNOW: Joint admissions are available with the O. Winston Link Museum and the History Museum of Western Virginia. Discounts are also available for members of several other rail-heritage organizations in western Virginia.

WORTH DOING: Stroll along the rail walk that connects the museum with the O. Winston Link Museum and Hotel Roanoke. The walk parallels the Norfolk Southern's mainline track and features displays and interactive exhibits along the way.

DON'T MISS: Climb into the crew cab of the streamlined Norfolk & Western 4-8-4 Class J. Built in 1950, No. 611 is the last of its kind, one of 13 that pulled the railroad's named trains. Capable of sprinting faster than 100 mph or climbing the mountains of West Virginia, these locomotives were considered to be among the best in the nation. You can stand in the cab and see the gauges, handles, and levers that made it all happen. Next door to No. 611 is No. 1218, a Class A. Built in 1943, this articulated locomotive features two sets of drivers and cylinders.

GETTING THERE: Situated in the Blue Ridge Mountains, Roanoke is served by a regional airport and several major highways. The museum is located downtown on Norfolk Avenue between Second and Fifth Streets.

WASHINGTON

Camp 6 Logging Museum ❶

Located in 14 wooded acres in Point Defiance Park, Camp 6 provides a first-hand look at the steam era of logging in western Washington. The re-created camp includes historic buildings, railroad equipment, and indoor exhibits. Rides aboard logging trains are available on weekends April through September.

LOCATION: 5400 N. Pearl Street, Tacoma
PHONE: 253-752-0047
WEBSITE: camp-6-museum.org/c6.html
E-MAIL: camp6museum@harbornet.com

Cashmere Museum ❷

The museum features a pioneer village with 20 historical structures, dating back to the late 1800s. Railroad displays include a Great Northern section house, ticket office, caboose, equipment, and artifacts. It is open March through October.

LOCATION: 600 Cotlets Way, Cashmere
PHONE: 509-782-3230
WEBSITE: cashmeremuseum.org
E-MAIL: pioneer49@frontier.com

Dayton Historical Depot ❸

Built in 1881, this is the oldest surviving railroad station in Washington. The stylish Stick/Eastlake building is now a museum of local history. It includes artifacts from the Union Pacific and the Oregon Railroad and Navigation Company, and a UP caboose is also on display. It is open year-round.

LOCATION: 222 E. Commercial Street, Dayton
PHONE: 509-382-2026
WEBSITE: daytonhistoricdepot.org
E-MAIL: info@daytonhistoricdepot.org

Lake Whatcom Railway ❹

This 90-minute train ride takes you from the shores of Lake Whatcom into the wooded countryside and back. The vintage coaches and diesel locomotive were all used on the Northern Pacific. A 100-year-old steam engine and wooden Great Northern freight cars are also on site. For a good workout, you can try your hand at riding a handcar. Excursions run during summer and for special events.

LOCATION: NP Road, Wickersham
PHONE: 360-595-2218
WEBSITE: www.lakewhatcomrailway.com

Northern Pacific Railway Museum ❺

The 1911 Northern Pacific Railway depot in Toppenish now serves as a museum to that railroad. The site's freight house has been converted to an engine house, where several steam locomotives are being restored. The museum offers caboose rides during special events throughout the year. It is open Tuesday through Sunday May through October.

LOCATION: 10 S. Asotin Avenue, Toppenish
PHONE: 509-865-1911
WEBSITE: nprymuseum.org

Ritzville Railroad Depot History Museum ❻

The brick mission-style depot was built in 1910. The building is on the National Register of Historic Places and retains many of its original features, including floor scales that you can try out. The museum contains railroad memorabilia, a telegraph machine, and local historical items. The museum is open Tuesdays through Saturdays during summer.

LOCATION: Railroad Avenue and Washington Street, Ritzville
PHONE: 509-659-1656
WEBSITE: ritzville-museums.org
E-MAIL: tloapo@centurytel.net

Washington State Railroads Historical Society Museum ❼

The museum features equipment, artifacts, and photos of the railroads involved in the state. Outdoors, it displays a variety of locomotives, passenger cars, freight cars, and cabooses. It is open on Thursdays, Fridays, and Saturdays.

LOCATION: 122 N. Tacoma Avenue, Pasco
PHONE: 509-543-4159
WEBSITE: wsrhs.org
E-MAIL: email@wsrhs.org

Yakima Valley Trolleys ❽

Yakima Valley trolleys have been operating for more than 100 years. You can ride along the historic line weekends and holidays from Memorial Day to Labor Day. Cars used on the line date between 1910 and 1930. Trolleys leave from the carbarn and museum.

LOCATION: S. Third Avenue at W. Pine Street, Yakima
PHONE: 509-249-5962
WEBSITE: yakimavalleytrolleys.org
E-MAIL: yakimavalleytrolleys@hotmail.com
DISCOUNT: Receive all-day pass for the price of a single ride ticket.

Chehalis-Centralia Railroad 🔟

LOCATION: 1101 Sylvenus Street, Chehalis
PHONE: 360-748-9593
WEBSITE: steamtrainride.com
E-MAIL: info@ccrandm.org

Dave LaClair

In the shadow of Mount Saint Helens, this relaxing train ride takes you into the forests of western Washington. You'll ride behind a steam locomotive that saw many years of service logging these very forests.

CHOICES: The railroad offers two different excursions. The 12-mile Milburn run takes you through forests and countryside. A longer 18-mile round trip to Ruth extends the ride by following the Chehalis River. The railroad's brunch and dinner trains follow the Ruth route and serve meals in a refurbished 1920s dining car.

WHEN TO GO: Summer steam train rides begin Memorial Day weekend and operate Saturdays and Sundays through September. Murder mystery trains, holiday trains, and other special events are scheduled throughout the year.

GOOD TO KNOW: For an extra fee, you can experience what it is like to ride in the cab of a working steam locomotive with a cab ride in No. 15, a 2-8-2 Mikado type steam engine.

WORTH DOING: Take time to visit Mount Saint Helens National Volcanic Monument and view the dramatic changes the area has undergone since the 1980 eruption. The 110,000-acre site contains hiking trails, several visitor centers, and an observatory.

DON'T MISS: On summer Saturdays, the railroad usually makes an early 12-mile run to Milburn and then follows up with an 18-mile run to Ruth later in the afternoon. You can catch the early run, take pictures with Mount Saint Helens as a background, and return on the later trip.

GETTING THERE: The railroad is about a 90-minute drive from either Portland or Seattle. From I-5, take Exit 77 (Main Street) into Chehalis. Turn left on Riverside Drive and then left again on Sylvenus Street. Nearby Centralia is also served by Amtrak.

DISCOUNT: $1 off each adult ticket, up to four adults; valid on regular runs only.

Chelatchie Prairie Railroad 🔟

LOCATION: 207 N. Railroad Avenue, Yacolt
PHONE: 360-686-3559
WEBSITE: www.bycx.com
E-MAIL: admin@bycx.com

Will Pickering

The train runs on a remote former logging railroad line in western Washington from Yacolt to Lucia. The five-mile route includes a 330-foot-long tunnel, a trestle over the Lewis River, and a half-hour layover at Moulton Falls.

CHOICES: You can enjoy the scenic ride by traveling in a coach car, open observation car, or caboose. Trains are powered by a diesel engine or steam locomotive. On the layover in Moulton Falls Park, you can have a picnic and take in two waterfalls and a tall arched bridge.

WHEN TO GO: The railroad operates May through December. It runs on various weekends and offers train robberies and fall color excursions as well as other specials throughout the year, including those for Mother's Day, Father's Day, Halloween, and Christmas.

GOOD TO KNOW: The railroad offers a unique Christmas tree and train experience for families. After taking the train to Moulton, you can visit with Santa, enjoy some cookies and hot chocolate, and pick out your Christmas tree. The locally grown tree is loaded into a 1912 heavyweight boxcar for the return trip to Yacolt.

WORTH DOING: A half hour may not be enough time to see Moulton Falls Park. The park contains a hiking trail and volcanic rock formations. It also connects to Lucia Falls Park and the Bells Mountain Trail. Mount Saint Helens is about an hour's drive north of Yacolt.

DON'T MISS: BYCX's coach car No. 60 has seen many changes since being built by the Pullman Company in 1918 as a 12-section sleeping car. It was later converted to a tourist sleeper and then in 1948 remodeled into a baggage car. No. 60 was put in maintenance-of-way service (and first painted mineral red and white) and in 1975, became a kitchen/bunk car. Now it is back in passenger service.

GETTING THERE: The railroad is located an hour's drive from Vancouver, Wash., and Portland. From I-5, take Exit 16 through Fargher Lake or Exit 9 through Battle Ground to Yacolt. In Yacolt, the station is on Railroad Avenue at Yacolt Road.

Mount Rainier Scenic Railroad ⑪

LOCATION: 54124 Mountain Highway East, Elbe
PHONE: 888-783-2611 or 360-492-5588
WEBSITE: mrsr.com

Jim Wrinn

Here's a chance to experience a real Pacific Northwest logging railroad at work. The locomotives, the setting, and the route all have the feel of a working railroad.

CHOICES: A pure steam experience, a 2-8-2T logging engine usually pulls the passenger coaches through the foothills of Mount Rainier on a two-hour round trip. You'll ride out over creeks, through forests, and across bridges to Mineral Lake. The railroad offers all three major types of geared logging locomotives as possible power: a Shay, a Climax, and a Heisler. You can choose to ride in a coach car, open-air coach, or open car.

WHEN TO GO: The railroad operates weekends May, June, September, and October, with daily excursions during the busy months of July and August. The Santa Express runs weekends during November and December.

GOOD TO KNOW: The railroad operates the only Willamette-type geared steam locomotive, No. 2. Built in 1929 in Portland, Ore., the engine was one of only 33 manufactured for use on logging railroads in the Pacific Northwest.

WORTH DOING: Mount Rainier National Park offers scenic drives and hikes around the 14,410-foot active volcano. Most roads are open from late May to October. Hiking, biking, and climbing are all fun activities.

DON'T MISS: Ride one trip and photograph another one, especially if you can get Mount Rainier to peek out from behind the clouds.

GETTING THERE: Elbe is located in western Washington near Mount Rainier National Park, approximately 75 miles south of Seattle and 125 miles north of Portland. From the Seattle area, take I-5 to Highway 512 and then exit on Highway 7, which is also Mountain Highway.

Northwest Railway Museum

LOCATION: 38625 SE King Street, Snoqualmie
PHONE: 425-888-3030
WEBSITE: trainmuseum.org
E-MAIL: info@trainumseum.org

Northwest Railway Museum

The museum is home to more than 70 pieces of rolling stock, the bulk of it from the Pacific Northwest. The museum also includes a collection of dining car china, tools, signs, and lanterns. It offers a short train ride from either Snoqualmie or North Bend.

CHOICES: The museum is headquartered at Snoqualmie depot, a restored 1890 Queen Anne-style building that is on the National Register of Historic Places. It features exhibits inside the depot and outdoor displays of restored equipment including steam locomotives, passenger cars, freight cars, and maintenance equipment. It offers 10-mile round trips to Snoqualmie Falls in restored heavyweight coaches pulled by first-generation diesel locomotives.

WHEN TO GO: The museum is open daily year-round except for Thanksgiving, Christmas, and New Year's Day. It offers train rides on weekends April through October, with special events scheduled during the year. Railroad Days takes place the beginning of August. Santa trains sell out quickly.

GOOD TO KNOW: The museum has restored a unique logging caboose. Built by White River Lumber Company in 1945, the caboose is just 24 feet long. Because of wartime shortages of raw materials, the caboose was made of wood and recycled parts.

WORTH DOING: View Snoqualmie Falls, one of the state's most popular attractions. The waterfall cascades down 270 feet, which is 100 feet more than Niagara Falls. You can see the falls from an observation platform inside Snoqualmie Falls park, but the park's hiking trail is closed until 2013.

DON'T MISS: Check out the nine steam locomotives in the collection, including the unusual Mallet engines that were used for logging—they're basically two locomotives under one boiler.

GETTING THERE: The museum is 30 miles east of Seattle on I-90. From I-90 east, take Exit 25. Heading north, follow Snoqualmie Ridge Parkway for approximately four miles to Highway 202. Turn right on Highway 202 and proceed a half-mile to the Snoqualmie depot on your right. To get to the North Bend depot, take Exit 31 off I-90. Follow Bendigo Street into North Bend and turn right on North Bend Way.

WEST VIRGINIA

Princeton Railroad Museum ❶

The museum is a replica of the Virginian Railway station that stood in Princeton for 70 years. It features exhibits devoted to the Virginian and Norfolk & Western Railways. It contains art, lanterns, and other artifacts. The museum is open year-round.

LOCATION: 99 Mercer Street, Princeton
PHONE: 304-487-5060
WEBSITE: cityofprinceton.org

Cass Scenic Railroad State Park ▪

LOCATION: Highway 66, Cass
PHONE: 800-225-5982 or 304-456-4300
WEBSITE: www.cassrailroad.com
E-MAIL: form on website

Jim Wrinn

The Cass Scenic Railroad is as close as you'll ever come to experiencing a mountain logging railroad—because it once was one. Leaving from the mill town of Cass along the beautiful Greenbrier River, trains climb steep grades out of the Leatherbark Creek area, negotiate two switchbacks, and hug hillsides to gain elevation. It was all about getting to the timber 100 years ago. Today, it's all about getting above it all. And Cass does that.

CHOICES: Got only a little time? Ride a two-hour trip to Whitaker station and back for a taste. Got plenty of time? Sink your teeth into a half-day trip to Bald Knob and back. At an intermediate point, trains pause for servicing, and you can inspect a re-created railroad logging camp. Continuing on, trains powered by unusual geared steam locomotives work their way to Bald Knob, which, at 4,880 feet, is the second highest point in West Virginia. The view there is spectacular, and the trains climb an 11 percent grade. There is also a half-day excursion to Spruce.

WHEN TO GO: The railroad runs Memorial Day through October, with heavy passenger counts during the colorful autumn. It schedules several special events during the season including a Fiddles and Vittles Train with dinner and bluegrass music.

GOOD TO KNOW: In spring, the railroad's support organization, the Mountain State Railroad & Logging Historical Association, holds a railfan weekend when all the Shay geared locomotives run. This event covers tracks not normally used by Cass trains.

WORTH DOING: Near Cass, there are several state parks and forests, including Droop Mountain Battlefield State Park, the site of the state's last major battle during the Civil War. The Greenbrier River Trail is a biking and hiking trail that runs along the river for many of its 78 miles.

DON'T MISS: Ticket price also includes admission to the logging museum, Cass Showcase diorama, camp tour, and shop tour. In the shop, look for Western Maryland No. 6, the last Shay built, and at 162 tons, the largest one left.

GETTING THERE: Cass Scenic Railroad is located in eastern West Virginia, and I-64 is the closest major road. From there, narrow, winding two-lane roads are the rule, so take plenty of time and watch for deer. Route 66 connects to Route 219 at Slatyfork.

DISCOUNT: $2 off standard fare Monday through Thursday, up to four fares.

Durbin & Greenbrier Valley Railroad **3**

LOCATION: 3 East Main Street, Durbin
PHONE: 877-686-7245
WEBSITE: mountainrailwv.com
E-MAIL: ticketinfo@mountainrail.com

Jim Wrinn

The Durbin & Greenbrier Valley Railroad operates three separate and distinct railways over 135 miles of scenic railroad through the Mountain State. The *Cheat Mountain Salamander* offers a ride into the high country of Cheat Mountain, the *Durbin Rocket* operates a 1910 Climax locomotive, and the *New Tygart Flyer* is a diesel-powered train that pulls coaches and first-class cars through the wilderness.

CHOICES: This railroad is all about choices. The *Salamander* provides rides of various lengths including a nine-hour round trip that features a stop at the High Falls of the Cheat, an impressive waterfall that puts an exclamation point on the journey. The *Rocket* is a peaceful ride aboard a caboose, coach, or open gondola behind a Climax geared steam locomotive along the unspoiled Greenbrier River. The *Flyer* provides a dramatic four-hour round trip through a curved tunnel, across a deep canyon, and over a rushing river. A dinner train also operates.

WHEN TO GO: The trains operate May through October, with some special Thanksgiving and Christmas trips as well.

GOOD TO KNOW: The *Flyer* boards in Elkins. The *Rocket* takes off from the restored C&O Railway depot in Durbin, and the *Salamander* departs from Elkins or Cheat Bridge (the three-hour trip). You can spend the night at a remote location aboard the *Durbin Rocket*'s Castaway Caboose, a restored Wabash caboose.

WORTH DOING: View the scenery in the Gaudineer Scenic Area in the Monongahela National Forest. Many of its trees are more than 300 years old.

DON'T MISS: The railroad's location is close to the Cass Scenic Railroad, enabling you to visit four great railroads in one impressive mountain setting.

GETTING THERE: Route 250 connects the railroad's locations. Durbin is 35 miles south of Elkins at the base of Cheat Mountain, and the *Rocket* leaves from the station on Main Street. Cheat Bridge is seven miles north of Durbin and 30 miles south of Elkins. The *Salamander*'s station is on Red Run Road. The *Flyer*'s station in Elkins is located at 12th Street and Davis Avenue, and the Belington station is a half-block west of Route 250 in town.

DISCOUNT: $1 off each adult ticket.

New River Train 4

LOCATION: Memorial Boulevard and 14th Street West, Huntington
PHONE: 866-639-7487 or 304-523-0364
WEBSITE: newrivertrain.com
E-MAIL: newrivertrain@aol.com

Chris Lockwood

The Collis P. Huntington Railroad Historical Society sponsors the New River Train, which runs all-day excursions during October to view autumn foliage. The society also maintains an outdoor museum.

CHOICES: The New River Train travels over the former C&O main line from Huntington to Hinton. You'll go under the New River Gorge Bridge, the largest arch bridge in the country, and enjoy a spectacular view of it. Other sights along the way include Kanawha Falls, Hawks Nest Dam, and Stretcher Neck Tunnel. You'll also roll past ghost towns and old mining sites. Seating choices are coach, premium, and private car (if available). Passengers can board the Amtrak-powered train at Huntington, St. Albans, or Montgomery. The outdoor museum, located in Ritter Park, displays ex-Chesapeake & Ohio Class H-6 articulated No. 1308, a saddle-tank switcher, a restored B&O section house, handcar, motor car, two cabooses, and several smaller items.

WHEN TO GO: The New River Train runs two October weekends during the peak fall foliage season. The museum is open Sundays June into September.

GOOD TO KNOW: Open by appointment, the society also maintains an indoor museum at its headquarters (1323 Eighth Avenue) in Huntington. It contains photographs, lanterns, china, models, and other rail-related artifacts. The town and society were named for Collis P. Huntington, who helped develop the transcontinental railroad and the Chesapeake & Ohio.

WORTH DOING: While in Huntington, stop by the Cabell-Huntington Convention & Visitors Bureau. The bureau is housed in a former B&O passenger station, and out front are two pieces of vintage equipment donated by the society: former Elk River Coal & Lumber Co. No. 10 and former Southern Railway sleeper *John W. Arrington*.

DON'T MISS: Huntington is two hours away from the New River Gorge National Park, which contains the bridge. You can plan a trip to the park by driving or by Amtrak's *Cardinal*. The third Saturday of October is Bridge Day, the only day you are allowed to walk across the bridge—or parachute from it.

GETTING THERE: To reach the outdoor museum, take I-64 to Exit 6. Follow Highway 52 north toward the Ohio River and get off at the first exit, Madison Avenue. Go east on Madison Avenue about three blocks to 14th Street West, turn right, and go south three more blocks and through the CSX underpass. The museum is on the right.

Potomac Eagle Scenic Railroad ▪

LOCATION: Route 28 North, Romney
PHONE: 304-424-0736
WEBSITE: potomaceagle.info

Mark Perri

Here's a three-hour train ride for the birdwatchers among us. After all, who doesn't enjoy the sight of a bald eagle floating on the currents. The Potomac Eagle goes in search of bald eagles down the remote South Branch of the Potomac just inside West Virginia.

CHOICES: All trains depart from the Wappocomo station, just north of Romney. The 40-mile excursion travels along the South Branch of the Potomac River and through the six-mile Trough, a narrow mountain valley where eagles are often seen. You can ride in open air coaches. Historic narration adds extra insight into the journey. EMD F units in striking C&O and B&O heritage schemes provide power for most of the trains.

WHEN TO GO: Trains run mid-May through the beginning of November. Departures are on Saturdays with a few Sundays sprinkled in. Autumn makes an especially great time to visit this railroad, and it offers trips almost daily during October.

GOOD TO KNOW: The railroad says eagles are spotted on 90 percent of its trains. As it enters the most remote and steepest portion of the South Branch valley, the train pauses, so you can find a seat in the open gondola for the best views.

WORTH DOING: Explore Romney, which includes numerous historic homes and buildings. Possibly the oldest town in West Virginia, it is said to have changed hands 56 times during the Civil War.

DON'T MISS: The railroad offers an occasional 70-mile, all-day trip down the length of the railroad; often this is a special photographer's trip usually the first weekend in November.

GETTING THERE: Romney is in the northeast corner of the state. It is about 25 miles from Cumberland, Md. Route 28 takes you to the station, which is 1.5 miles north of Romney.

DISCOUNT: $2 off each adult ticket, up to four adults.

WISCONSIN

Brodhead Historical Society Depot Museum ❶

This restored Chicago, Milwaukee & St. Paul depot, built in 1881, houses a permanent railroad display with rotating historical displays. Milwaukee Road switch engine No. 781 and caboose No. 01900 stand alongside the depot. It is open on Wednesdays, Saturdays, and Sundays between Memorial Day and Labor Day.

LOCATION: 1108 First Center Avenue, Brodhead
PHONE: 608-897-4150
WEBSITE: brodheadhistory.org
E-MAIL: info@brodheadhistory.org

Colfax Railroad Museum ❷

This museum includes a large collection of railroad memorabilia and an outdoor display of locomotives and rolling stock that features a Soo Line GP30 diesel engine, a wooden Soo caboose, a heavyweight coach, and other pieces of rolling stock. It is open May through September.

LOCATION: 500 E. Railroad Avenue, Colfax
PHONE: 715-962-2076
WEBSITE: colfaxrrmuseum.org
E-MAIL: form on website
DISCOUNT: 10% off gift shop purchase.

Historical Village ❸

The village features a restored C&NW depot and several other historical structures, including an octagon house. Built in 1923, the depot is authentically furnished and contains railroad artifacts. It also displays a 1941 diesel engine, a Soo caboose, and a C&NW caboose. The museum is open during summer and takes part in Heritage Days & Rail Fest.

LOCATION: 900 Montgomery Street, New London
PHONE: 920-982-8557 or 920-982-5186
WEBSITE: historicalvillage.org

Railroad Memories Museum ❹

This museum contains 12 rooms filled with railroad memories. Artifacts include lanterns, track equipment, photos, and other items. Housed in a former C&NW depot, it is located next to the Wisconsin Great Northern Railroad. The museum is open Memorial Day through Labor Day.

LOCATION: 424 Front Street, Spooner
PHONE: 715-635-3325 or 715-635-2752
WEBSITE: www.spoonerwi.com/railroadmuseum

Camp Five ▣

LOCATION: 5068 Highway 8, Laona
PHONE: 715-674-3414
WEBSITE: camp5museum.org
E-MAIL: info@lumberjacksteamtrain.com

Jeff Terry

Camp Five offers a steam train powered by a vintage 2-6-2 type logging locomotive. It takes you to the site of a timber company's 1914 farm camp, where you can tour a logging museum.

CHOICES: After boarding at an 1880s Soo Line depot, you ride the steam train 2.5 miles to the museum. You can ride in a passenger coach, an open-air car made from a boxcar, or a cupola caboose. At Laona, you can climb a set of steps to inspect the engine's cab. The tracks for the Lumberjack Steam Train, which dated to the early 1900s, have been recently rebuilt.

WHEN TO GO: Camp Five has a short season. It is open Monday through Saturday, starting in June and running through August. It is also open several days in fall.

GOOD TO KNOW: The railroad crosses the Rat River on a bridge. Lumber men who worked this river, floating giant rafts of logs together, became known as river rats. At the farm camp, the lumber company raised meat, produce, and horses to supply other camps as they set up in the forest.

WORTH DOING: Forest County is filled with lakes and covered by the Nicolet National Forest, so there are plenty of opportunities for fishing, hiking, and other recreational activities.

DON'T MISS: There is plenty to do at Camp Five. You can view exhibits on forestry, examine logging equipment, visit a nature center, or take an ecology walking tour.

GETTING THERE: Camp Five is located off Highway 8 west of Laona, about two hours north of Green Bay. From Green Bay, take Highway 141 north to Highway 64. Follow Highway 64 west to Highway 32. Continue on Highway 32 and turn left on Highway 8 past Laona to Connor Farm Road.

DISCOUNT: $2 off each adult ticket.

East Troy Electric Railroad 6

LOCATION: 2002 Church Street, East Troy
PHONE: 262-642-3263
WEBSITE: easttroyrr.org
E-MAIL: info@easttroyrr.org

Jim Wrinn

Interurban railroads once plied much of the Midwest, moving passengers easily from farm to city and vice versa. Today, a sprig of that heritage remains at the East Troy Electric Railroad, where electric trains run through the countryside.

CHOICES: On an 10-mile round trip, the railroad offers a variety of cars to ride, depending on the day, that include trolleys, electric freight motors pulling a caboose, and electrically powered traditional coaches from the famous South Shore line. Trains depart from both East Troy and Mukwonago. The railroad also offers dinner trains that run to Phantom Lake and back. After viewing the exhibits in the depot, you can walk two blocks to the shops and look at the equipment being refurbished.

WHEN TO GO: Regular weekend excursions run mid-May through October. From mid-June through August, trains also operate on Wednesdays, Thursdays, and Fridays (and Fridays in September and October). There is a slate of special events during the year including a Christmas Express.

GOOD TO KNOW: Sheboygan car No. 26 is a 1908 interurban built by the Cincinnati Car Company for Sheboygan Light, Power and Railway. No 26 later became a summer cottage until it was restored. Look for the railroad's newest additions, five Chicago South Shore & South Bend interurban cars, to enter service after restoration.

WORTH DOING: Regular excursions operate from East Troy to the Elegant Farmer near Mukwonago. What's an Elegant Farmer? It makes a great destination as the Farmer provides a deli, greenhouse, and market all in one. Be sure and try the award-winning baked apple pie in a bag.

DON'T MISS: You can explore the substation in East Troy, which is the heart of the operating gear for the electric railroad.

GETTING THERE: East Troy is located in southeastern Wisconsin, about 35 miles from Milwaukee and 15 miles from Lake Geneva. From Milwaukee, take I-43 south to Exit 38. Take Highway 20 to Main Street. Follow Main Street to Church Street and turn right to the museum.

Mid-Continent Railway Museum ⑦

LOCATION: E8948 Diamond Hill Road, North Freedom
PHONE: 800-930-1385 or 608-522-4261
WEBSITE: midcontinent.org
E-MAIL: inquiries@midcontinent.org

Mid-Continent Railway Museum

One of the best museums for the preservation of wooden railroad cars, Mid-Continent features a large collection of rolling stock, much of it kept indoors, and numerous exhibits. The museum also offers a train ride. It's all aimed at re-creating the experience of a branch or short line between 1885 and 1915.

CHOICES: Leaving from a restored 1894 C&NW depot, the seven-mile, 50-minute ride takes you through the rolling countryside. You can ride the restored 1915 steel coaches, but you can also get a ticket for the locomotive cab or the caboose.

WHEN TO GO: The railway operates from May into October and also includes a variety of special events. Between Memorial Day and Labor Day, it is open daily, other times on weekends only. Fall color, pumpkin, and Santa specials operate as does a snow train.

GOOD TO KNOW: More than 100 pieces of equipment are on display. One is an office car of Great Northern Railway founder James J. Hill's son that included space for hauling an automobile. Structures include a water tower, a crossing shanty, a section shed, a crossing tower, and a freight house.

WORTH DOING: Explore Devil's Lake State Park near Baraboo. This large park features 500-foot cliffs, hiking trails, and kayaking.

DON'T MISS: Make sure you go into the coach shed to see some of the finest wood craftsmanship around when it comes to railroad cars and also check out the engine house, where craftsmen are restoring three steam locomotives for operation.

GETTING THERE: The scenic route from Madison is along Highway 12 going north. Turn left on Highway 36 and then left again on Highway PF to North Freedom. In North Freedom, follow Walnut Street west to the museum.

DISCOUNT: Buy one coach ticket, get one of equal or lesser value free.

National Railroad Museum ⑧

LOCATION: 2285 S. Broadway Street, Green Bay
PHONE: 920-437-7623
WEBSITE: www.nationalrrmuseum.org
E-MAIL: form on website

Jeff Terry

Begun in 1956 by a group wishing to preserve a steam locomotive, the museum has grown to encompass more than 70 pieces of rolling stock, a seasonal train ride, and an unmatched collection of drumheads, the illuminated signs seen on the rear of many passenger trains.

CHOICES: Explore the museum on your own and then take a train ride. During the 25-minute train ride, the conductor provides information about railroad history and museum exhibits. Highlights include a Union Pacific Big Boy, a 1950s Aerotrain, and a Pennsylvania Railroad GG1 electric locomotive. The command train for General Dwight D. Eisenhower is also located at the museum in the company of a British Railways Pacific locomotive named for the World War II general. Group tours are also available.

WHEN TO GO: The museum is open daily year-round, except for Mondays January through April and several holidays. Train rides operate May through October, and numerous special events are scheduled during the year.

GOOD TO KNOW: The museum's new exhibit on Pullman porters, "From Service to Civil Rights" provides an excellent understanding of the role of these workers on board the rolling luxury hotels of their day. Using a computer generated porter, visitors can learn about all aspects of these workers' lives.

WORTH DOING: Take the kids to Bay Beach Amusement Park for some old-fashioned fun on classic midway rides. Football fans can visit the Green Bay Packers Hall of Fame and tour historic Lambeau Field.

DON'T MISS: Climb to the top of the 85-foot-tall observation tower for a bird's-eye view of the museum.

GETTING THERE: Green Bay is two hours north of Milwaukee. From Milwaukee, take I-43 to Exit 180. Take Highway 172 west and exit at Ashland Avenue. Bear right on Pilgrim Way and then turn left on Broadway Street.

Osceola & St. Croix Valley Railway ⑨

LOCATION: 114 Depot Road, Osceola
PHONE: 715-755-3570
WEBSITE: mtmuseum.org
E-MAIL: contact@mtmuseum.org

Steve Glischinski

The Minnesota Transportation Museum's Osceola & St. Croix Valley offers rides through the scenic St. Croix River Valley along the Wisconsin-Minnesota border. Trains are diesel powered, with a former Rock Island GP7 repainted in Soo Line's classic maroon and gold colors or a Burlington Northern SD9 pulling most trains. A recent addition is former Great Northern Railway SDP40 No. 325.

CHOICES: Two routes can be ridden from Osceola. One heads west 10 miles to Marine on St. Croix, Minn. This highly recommended trip follows the beautiful St. Croix Valley for its entire length. The other trip goes east to Dresser, Wis., a former Soo Line junction town that still contains its original wooden depot. Excursions offer both open- and closed-window coaches. If riding in the open cars during early spring or fall, be prepared to dress for cool weather. The railway also offers special trips that include brunch trains, pizza trains, and fall color trains.

WHEN TO GO: For the best views of the St. Croix River, May is the time to ride before the leaves have a chance to obstruct views of the river. The first or second week of October provide the chance to view the autumn colors before the long northern winter begins. There's nothing like a crisp, blue-sky autumn day in open-window coaches rolling through the St. Croix Valley.

GOOD TO KNOW: Osceola's downtown contains many examples of late 19th and early 20th century architecture. The St. Croix National Scenic Riverway includes 154 miles of the river and offers recreational opportunities on and off the river.

WORTH DOING: Take the train to Marine and ride over the Cedar Bend swing bridge across the river. While the bridge doesn't swing open any more, it's a classic steel structure complete with telltales on each end to warn brakemen of close clearances.

DON'T MISS: Watch ex-Northern Pacific Railway post office-baggage-coach combine No. 1102 pick up the mail on the fly from a mail crane at Osceola's restored depot, one of the few places where this once common occurrence can be seen.

GETTING THERE: Osceola is about an hour's drive from Minneapolis. For a scenic drive, follow Highway 95 along the east bank of the St. Croix from Stillwater north to Osceola. Once in Osceola, you'll come to Highway 35. Turn right and proceed under the railroad bridge and immediately turn right again onto Depot Road.

DISCOUNT: $3 off each adult ticket, up to four adults.

Wisconsin Great Northern Railroad 🔟

LOCATION: 426 N. Front Street, Spooner
PHONE: 715-635-3200
WEBSITE: spoonertrainride.com
E-MAIL: office@spoonertrainride.com

Steve Glischinski

The Wisconsin Great Northern Railroad operates excursion and dinner trains in the forested countryside along the scenic Namekagon River. The 30-mile round trip between Spooner and Springbrook takes you over former Chicago & North Western track.

CHOICES: In addition to sightseeing excursions, the Wisconsin Great Northern offers a variety of regularly scheduled dinner trains that include elegant dining, pizza, and Sunday brunches. The railroad runs special trains for Mother's Day, Father's Day, Thanksgiving, as well as a Pizza Party with Santa train in December. Former C&NW F7A No. 423 or ex-Milwaukee Road SW1 No. 862, both painted in a scheme resembling that of the former Great Northern Railway, pull the trains.

WHEN TO GO: Sightseeing excursions run late June through October, and dinner trains operate on a longer schedule, May through December. Summer and early fall are great times to ride. The cars are ex-Duluth, Missabe & Iron Range Railway heavyweights with windows that can be opened, and it's a delight to take in the sights during these times.

GOOD TO KNOW: For anyone wishing a unique wedding, the Wisconsin Great Northern offers the Great Wedding Train, the only such wedding train in the nation.

WORTH DOING: While Spooner is off the beaten path, there is much to do in the area, such as fishing, hiking, biking, camping, and tubing. Adjacent to the railroad's ticket office, the independent Railroad Memories Museum contains lanterns, track equipment, photos, and other railroad memorabilia.

DON'T MISS: Ride in the cab of the F7 or SW1 diesel. The railroad offers cab rides on most of its dinner and special occasion trains. Half-trip cab rides are available, and if you try a cab ride on the return to Spooner, the train backs up as it leaves Spooner for Springbrook.

GETTING THERE: The Wisconsin Great Northern is about 90 minutes from Eau Claire and two hours from Minneapolis and St. Paul. After you enter Spooner on Highway 70, turn left onto Front Street. Travel four blocks north on Front Street and then look for signs to the depot.

WYOMING

Cheyenne Depot Museum ❶

Cheyenne's architectural jewel is a major landmark in the city. Built in 1886, the Union Pacific depot houses a museum that details the history of the building, the operation of the railroad, and founding of the city. The museum may run a summer steam train excursion.

LOCATION: 121 W. 15th Street, Cheyenne
PHONE: 307-632-3905
WEBSITE: cheyennedepotmuseum.org
E-MAIL: info@cheyennedepotmuseum.org

Douglas Railroad Interpretive Center ❷

The Douglas Railroad Interpretive Center is housed in a restored 1886 passenger depot belonging to the Fremont, Elkhorn & Missouri Valley Railroad. It displays a 1940 Chicago, Burlington & Quincy steam locomotive and seven railcars. The building is listed on the National Register of Historic Places.

LOCATION: 121 Brownfield Road, Douglas
PHONE: 877-937-4996 or 307-358-2950
WEBSITE: douglaschamber.com
E-MAIL: chamber@jackalope.org

Union Pacific Roundhouse ❸

This complex includes a 28-bay roundhouse, a working turntable, and a renovated machine shop. Each year, Roundhouse Restoration, the group restoring the facility, holds a weekend festival in the roundhouse and gives yard tours. Nearby Depot Square includes a restored 1900 UP depot and other historic buildings.

LOCATION: 1440 Main Street, Evanston
PHONE: 800-328-9708 or 307-783-6320
WEBSITE: roundhouserestoration.net

Union Pacific Railroad ▪

LOCATION: UP Steam Shop, Cheyenne
PHONE: 307-778-3214
WEBSITE: www.uprr.com/aboutup/excurs/index.shtml

Jim Wrinn

This Class I mainline railroad maintains the only steam locomotive never retired, No. 844, a 4-8-4 built in 1944. Rebuilt between 1999 and 2004, it is used on occasional excursions and display tours.

CHOICES: Home for the locomotive is a nonpublic shop in Cheyenne, where the Union Pacific also maintains steam engine 4-6-6-4 No. 3985, believed to be the largest steam locomotive operating today. Departures occur from the UP rail yards as well as from the Cheyenne Depot Museum.

WHEN TO GO: Schedules and routes vary from year to year. One annual outing is the *Denver Post* Frontier Days excursion train from Denver to Cheyenne for the big rodeo event.

GOOD TO KNOW: The Union Pacific provides a GPS trace system for its steam train at www.uprr.com/aboutup/excurs/trace.cfm. Tours of the UP steam shop may be available by calling 307-778-3339 (in advance of your visit).

WORTH DOING: In July, you can take part in Frontier Days, a 10-day rodeo event that celebrates the West and features entertainment and other activities.

DON'T MISS: Visit the Cheyenne Depot Museum in the restored UP depot. Two historic engines are displayed in Cheyenne parks: a Big Boy engine in Holliday Park and the state's oldest steam locomotive, No. 1242, in Lions Park.

GETTING THERE: Cheyenne is in southeast Wyoming, about 90 minutes from Denver on I-25.

ALBERTA

Alberta Railway Museum ❶

The museum's collection of railway equipment and buildings focuses on the Canadian National Railway and the Northern Alberta Railway. It includes more than 50 locomotives and cars, three stations, and a water tank. Newly restored cars are a NAR engineering car and a CN combine car. The museum is open weekends from Victoria Day through Labour Day. You can take a guided tour, ride a speeder, and on select weekends, ride a passenger train.

LOCATION: 24215 34th Street, Edmonton
PHONE: 780-472-6229
WEBSITE: railwaymuseum.ab.ca
E-MAIL: form on website

Edmonton Radial Railway ❷

The Edmonton Radial Railway operates streetcars in Fort Edmonton Park and in Old Strathcona. At Fort Edmonton Park, the one-mile streetcar rides are included with admission. In Old Strathcona, the trolley crosses High Level Bridge over the North Saskatchewan River. The Strathcona streetcar barn contains exhibits on streetcar history.

LOCATION: 103rd Street and 84th Avenue, Edmonton
PHONE: 780-437-7721 or 780-496-1464
WEBSITE: edmonton-radial-railway.ab.ca
E-MAIL: info@edmonton-radial-railway.ab.ca

Fort Edmonton Park ❸

Nestled in Edmonton's river valley, Fort Edmonton Park is a living history museum that represents four historical periods between 1840 and 1920. It contains more than 75 buildings. A 1919 steam train takes you through the park, and caboose rides are available. A streetcar also travels along the historic streets.

LOCATION: Fox Drive and Whitemud Drive, Edmonton
PHONE: 780-442-5311
WEBSITE: fortedmontonpark.ca
E-MAIL: attractions@edmonton.ca

Alberta Prairie Railway Excursions ▪

LOCATION: 4611 47th Avenue, Stettler
PHONE: 800-282-3994 or 403-742-2811
WEBSITE: absteamtrain.com
E-MAIL: info@absteamtrain.com

Alberta Prairie Railway

A trip aboard the Alberta Prairie conjures up visions of what a central Alberta wheat line must have been like 100 years ago. Traveling from the well-developed community of Stettler, it passes through forests and fields before reaching Big Valley, where the ruins of a roundhouse and a restored depot remain.

CHOICES: The railroad offers an extensive schedule of excursions and specials throughout the year. All excursions include a buffet meal, which is served in Big Valley or Stettler, onboard entertainment, and possibly a train robbery. Specially themed rides include murder mystery, Christmas, family, and teddy bear trains. During winter, fine-dining trains provide a five-course meal and entertainment. The trains are pulled by Baldwin 2-8-0 steam engine No. 41 or by General Motors diesel No. 1259. Several times a year, usually for special events, such as on Canada Day, historic steam engine No. 6060 is in operation.

WHEN TO GO: Summer excursions begin in May and continue until mid-October each year. The winter fine-dining trains are offered November through April.

GOOD TO KNOW: The railway was once part of a vast grain railroad network belonging to the Canadian Northern. Be sure to chat with the train crew. Many of the veteran railroaders on this line have great stories. And if you get the right conductor, he might just sing you a song or recite a poem for you en route.

WORTH DOING: In Big Valley, the restored station and several railcars display railroad and local history artifacts. You can take a self-guided tour of the five-stall roundhouse remains and former rail yards, view a wooden grain elevator, and visit the Jimmy Jock Boardwalk, which is modeled after a frontier town's street.

DON'T MISS: For an added prairie experience, the railway offers two- or three-day packages that include a train ride and a 20-mile covered wagon trip along historic rail rights-of-way.

GETTING THERE: Stettler is about three hours northeast of Calgary on Highway 12.

Canadian Pacific Railway Steam Train 🔢

LOCATION: 401 Ninth Avenue SW, Calgary
PHONE: 403-837-0113
WEBSITE: www.cpr.ca
E-MAIL: form on website

Canadian Pacific

Based in Calgary, the CPR hosts Canada's only mainline, railway-operated steam train. Trips have operated across the CPR and Soo system from Delson, Quebec, to Vancouver and from Chicago to Portal, N.D. Often, passenger trips run in conjunction with a charity or special event, such as the Holiday Train that runs through parts of Canada and the United States during November and December.

CHOICES: The *Empress* steamed back into service in 2001 as a roving ambassador for the CPR. Built by Montreal Locomotive Works in 1930, it is the only surviving H1b Hudson. After a complete rebuild, the *Empress* was restored to original specifications with external details from the 1940s and '50s. Operating primarily in western Canada, it pulls passengers in former intercity coaches that feature reclining seats.

WHEN TO GO: Trips are not regularly scheduled so check the CPR website often. Look for trip announcements under the Steam Train link of the General Public section on the website or on Facebook.

GOOD TO KNOW: Make reservations early as seating capacity on the excursions is limited. While most departure and arrival locations are accessible via some form of public transportation, not all one-way trips include return transportation to the point of origin.

WORTH DOING: Many runs are made west of Calgary through the mountains, giving the engine a good workout.

DON'T MISS: Runs through Crowsnest Pass, which straddles the Alberta-British Columbia border, offer a good mix of engine noise and scenic highlights.

GETTING THERE: Departure and arrival locations vary by trip.

Heritage Park Historical Village ⑥

LOCATION: 1900 Heritage Drive SW, Calgary
PHONE: 403-268-8500
WEBSITE: www.heritagepark.ca
E-MAIL: info@heritagepark.ab.ca

John Godfrey

Discover what life was like in the Canadian West between 1864 and 1914 by visiting this re-created village framed by the Rockies. More than 150 exhibits, including many buildings transplanted from Calgary and other locations throughout Alberta, bring the past to the present.

CHOICES: The park includes a roundhouse and turntable along with more than 20 locomotives and cars. A train ride is an excellent way to see the park. Make a day of your visit and wander from building to building, paying particular attention to the transplanted railway stations, rolling stock, and re-created carbarn. If it's too hot, take a cruise on the water aboard the replica sternwheeler SS *Moyie*. Newly expanded, the park's latest attraction is Heritage Town Square, which represents a street scene from the 1930s to '50s, complete with automobile museum and replica train station.

WHEN TO GO: Heritage Park is open daily from the third weekend in May to Labour Day, and then only on weekends until Canadian Thanksgiving. Unlike the rest of the park, Heritage Town Square is open year-round.

GOOD TO KNOW: A short streetcar line connects the outer parking area to the main entrance. It's well worth it to park out there, view ex-CPR 2-10-4 No. 5931 and S-2 No. 7019, and then ride over to the gate in a replica Calgary or Winnipeg trolley. Many photographic opportunities are available around the park's railway loop.

WORTH DOING: Calgary's 10-day annual Stampede, which can draw more than one million people, is the world's largest rodeo. The event also features chuck wagon racing, agricultural exhibits, entertainment, and a parade.

DON'T MISS: During Railway Days, the park celebrates Canadian railways and rolls out much of its collection. Steam doubleheaders often operate for this event, and ex-CP Car 76, present at the driving of the last spike on the CPR in Craigellachie in 1885, may be rolled out.

GETTING THERE: Heritage Park is approximately a 20-minute drive southwest from downtown Calgary. A shuttle service operates during park hours from the Heritage light rail stop. Calgary is serviced by scheduled bus and air service.

Royal Canadian Pacific 🔢

LOCATION: 201 Ninth Avenue SW, Calgary
PHONE: 877-665-3044 or 403-508-1400
WEBSITE: royalcanadianpacific.com
E-MAIL: form on website

Royal Canadian Pacific

The Royal Canadian Pacific, an arm of the passenger department of Canadian Pacific Railway, offers periodically scheduled all-inclusive luxury-train ride packages on CPR's route through the spectacularly scenic Canadian Rockies. Restored vintage diesel locomotives haul a consist of about eight cars—all vintage, heavyweight CPR sleeping, observation, and dining cars with lavishly restored interiors. Cuisine in the dining room equals the finest on the continent.

CHOICES: The RCP's signature four-day, three-night Royal Canadian Rockies Experience tour heads west from Calgary into British Columbia, traversing Kicking Horse Pass and the railway's famous two spiral tunnels at the Continental Divide. At Golden, British Columbia, it heads south following the headwaters of the Columbia River and then turns east to surmount Crowsnest Pass back into southern Alberta, eventually turning north on the prairies to return to Calgary. The train stops each night while guests sleep in their wood-paneled rooms on board the train. Other themed experiences include golf, fly-fishing, and culinary excursions.

WHEN TO GO: The Canadian Rockies and the prairies have unpredictable weather with temperatures that can fall or rise quickly. The mountains offer spectacular scenery during every season.

GOOD TO KNOW: Calgary, Canada's largest city between Toronto and Vancouver, is a cosmopolitan city that still retains its western flavor and offers many cultural and entertainment opportunities. Calgary's C-Train light-rail system, with three routes radiating from downtown, is an efficient and fun way to see much of the city.

WORTH DOING: While in Calgary, you should visit Heritage Park, which in season features an operating streetcar, steam train, and other historic artifacts. Also worth visiting are the Glenbow Museum, Calgary Zoo, Calgary Tower, Canada Olympic Park, and Fort Calgary.

DON'T MISS: Along the way, watch for the fascinating rock walls and waterfalls of Yoho National Park and enjoy the views from an open-air vestibule as the train climbs through Kicking Horse Pass.

GETTING THERE: Calgary is served by many major airlines and the Rocky Mountaineer tourist train from Vancouver.

VIA Jasper-Prince Rupert Route 8

LOCATION: 607 Connaught Drive, Jasper
PHONE: 888-842-7245
WEBSITE: www.viarail.ca/en/trains/rockies-and-pacific/jasper-prince-rupert

VIA Rail

The VIA Rail Canada train between Jasper and Prince Rupert, British Columbia, is one of the scenic highlights of any trip to western Canada. The two-day, 725-mile trip, which includes an overnight stop in Prince George, takes you from the Rocky Mountains in Jasper National Park to the Pacific coast.

CHOICES: Travelers can opt for either economy or touring accommodation classes. Budget-minded vacationers can relax in the leg-rest seats found in economy class. Those with a voracious appetite for scenery may want to spend a little more for touring class which puts you in a dome car with its upper observation deck and panoramic views. Touring class also provides meals. During off-peak operation (mid-September to June), the dome car is accessible in economy class.

WHEN TO GO: The train operates Wednesday, Friday, and Sunday year-round. The shorter days and deep snows of winter give way to a plethora of spring flowers in May. Hot summer days morph into colorful, cool fall days by October. Economy class is offered year-round, and touring class is available only from early June to mid-September.

GOOD TO KNOW: Don't forget to book a hotel room for your overnight stay in Prince George. When arriving in Prince George, you may want to take a taxi, even though accommodations are a few blocks away as the area around the VIA station may be considered rough.

WORTH DOING: In Jasper, you can explore Jasper National Park, the northernmost park in the Rocky Mountains, and leave feeling hot or cold. You can experience a glacier close up and soak in a hot spring. In Prince Rupert, you can visit the Kwinitsa Railway Museum and the First Nation Carving Shed, where artists produce works in wood and metal.

DON'T MISS: Just west of Jasper, Mount Robson, the highest peak in the Canadian Provinces, is visible from the train for only a few cloudless days a year. You may also see moose, bear, elk, wolves, seals, and eagles along the way.

GETTING THERE: VIA Rail operates the Vancouver-Toronto *Canadian* three days a week through Jasper in each direction. Jasper is also served by bus from Edmonton and other points. Scheduled air service operates from Prince Rupert.

BRITISH COLUMBIA

BC Forest Discovery Centre ❶

The most relaxing, and most scenic, way to take in this 100-acre site is by riding the train, which is usually powered by a steam-powered 1910 locomotive. A gas-powered locomotive runs occasionally in its place. The centre's collection features Shay, Climax, and Vulcan locomotives. Other exhibits includes an operating sawmill, a lookout tower, and antique logging trucks.

LOCATION: 2892 Drinkwater Road, Duncan
PHONE: 250-715-1113
WEBSITE: discoveryforest.com
E-MAIL: info.bcfdc@shawlink.ca

Fort Steele Heritage Town ❷

Fort Steele Heritage Town is a restored 1890s pioneer town complete with railway. The railway operates during summer, and unlimited-ride tickets can be purchased. A Montreal Locomotive Works 2-6-2 prairie-type locomotive takes you on a 20-minute scenic ride. Rail equipment is displayed by the engine house, and roundhouse tours are available upon request.

LOCATION: 9851 Highway 93/95, Fort Steele
PHONE: 250-417-6000
WEBSITE: www.fortsteele.bc.ca
E-MAIL: info@fortsteele.bc.ca

Kwinitsa Railway Station Museum ❸

Located in Prince Rupert's waterfront park, this restored station house is an excellent example of the small stations once found along Canada's northern railway line. Photographs, videos, and detailed restorations depict the life of station agents and linemen who worked for the Grand Trunk Railway at the turn of the 20th century. It is open daily June through August.

LOCATION: Bill Murray Way and First Avenue, Prince Rupert
PHONE: 250-624-3207
WEBSITE: museumofnorthernbc.com
E-MAIL: mnbc@citytel.net

Railway & Forestry Museum ❹

The museum displays historic railway and forestry exhibits in a park-like setting. The extensive rail collection dates to 1899 and includes two stations and a turntable. It also contains both steam and diesel locomotives and more than 40 pieces of rolling stock.

LOCATION: 850 River Road, Prince George
PHONE: 250-563-7351
WEBSITE: www.railandforestmuseum.com
E-MAIL: trains@pgrfm.bc.ca

Revelstoke Railway Museum ❺

This railway museum focuses on the history of the Canadian Pacific Railway in western Canada. You can walk through Business Car No. 4 and view steam locomotive No. 5468, railcars, and artifacts. The museum also operates a small facility at Craigellachie, 28 miles west of Revelstoke, where the last spike of the Canadian Pacific Railway was driven. The museum is open year-round.

LOCATION: 719 Track Street West, Revelstoke
PHONE: 877-837-6060 or 250-837-6060
WEBSITE: railwaymuseum.com
E-MAIL: railway@telus.net

VIA Victoria-Courtenay Route ❻

This excursion runs between Victoria, at the southern tip of Vancouver Island, and Courtenay, at the northern end. Beside seeing the island's beautiful countryside, you can get off at other stops along the way and explore Pacific Rim National Park, hike the West Coast Trail, or discover towns such as Qualicum Beach and Chemainus.

LOCATION: 450 Pandora Avenue, Victoria
PHONE: 888-842-7245
WEBSITE: www.viarail.ca/en/trains/rockies-and-pacific/victoria-courtenay

Alberni Pacific Railway 7

LOCATION: 3100 Kingsway Avenue, Port Alberni
PHONE: 250-723-2118 or 250-723-1376
WEBSITE: alberniheritage.com
E-MAIL: info@alberniheritage.com

Alberni Pacific Railway

The Alberni Pacific offers passengers a chance to visit the former McLean Paper Mill, six miles east of Port Alberni over the former Canadian Pacific Railway Port Alberni Subdivision. The mill is a National Historic Site that now commemorates the history of logging and milling in British Columbia.

CHOICES: Trains to the mill are pulled by a 1929 Baldwin 2-8-2T steam locomotive, and passengers ride in converted former Canadian National transfer cabooses, three of which are open and two are covered. The 35-minute trips leave from a restored 1912 CPR station. Cab rides in No. 7 are also available. A diesel engine is also operational.

WHEN TO GO: Runs are made over this scenic trackage Thursdays through Sundays between the end of June until September. Special events occur throughout the year including wine trains, train robberies, and Santa trains.

GOOD TO KNOW: The McLean Mill is the only steam-operated sawmill in Canada. This historic site and the railway are part of the Alberni Valley Heritage Network that celebrates the area's history and culture. Also included are the Alberni Valley Museum and Maritime Discovery Centre.

WORTH DOING: Visit Port Alberni's quaint harbor, which offers a mix of restaurants, galleries, tours, and shops. You are also within minutes of numerous outdoor activities including seeing Delta Falls, the tallest waterfall in Canada.

DON'T MISS: At the mill, you can explore the site on your own or take a guided tour. It has been laid out as early 20th century logging camp with restored buildings and original pieces of logging equipment, including an operating steam donkey.

GETTING THERE: Bus service is available from Vancouver Island to Port Alberni. Scheduled air service is available from Victoria to the south. Ferry service operates between the mainland and various points on Vancouver Island including Port Alberni.

DISCOUNT: 10% off fare and gift shop purchase.

Canadian Museum of Rail Travel ⑧

LOCATION: 57 Van Horne Street S, Cranbrook
PHONE: 250-489-3918
WEBSITE: www.trainsdeluxe.com
E-MAIL: mail@trainsdeluxe.com

Canadian Museum of Rail Travel

The Canadian Museum of Rail Travel is a magnet for anyone interested in Canadian passenger rail travel as it once was. It is home to the only surviving train set of equipment from the 1929 *Trans-Canada Limited* as well as the beautifully reconstructed Royal Alexandra Hall.

CHOICES: Visitors can choose from several different guided tours that examine the trains in the museum's collection, including the *Soo-Spokane Train Deluxe, Trans Canada Limited, Pacific Express,* and *Chinook.* Various business cars, cars of state, and historic structures are also included. Guides explain the history of the equipment and bring to life the beautifully restored railcar interiors. Be prepared to walk. Depending on the tour, you could cover a half mile or more.

WHEN TO GO: The museum is open to the public daily from Victoria Day weekend to Canadian Thanksgiving in October. During the remainder of the year, it is open Tuesday through Saturday.

GOOD TO KNOW: Cranbrook is a gateway to the Canadian Rockies, which are a short drive away. Enjoy the sun and and a hot soak. Situated at an elevation of 3,000 feet, Cranbrook also is one of the sunniest spots in Canada. After a walking tour of the museum, you can soak in several hot springs in the area.

WORTH DOING: Fort Steele is less than 20 minutes away. Once a thriving mining town, Fort Steele became a ghost town when the railroad bypassed it for Cranbrook. It is now a heritage town, where visitors can experience its boom-town history.

DON'T MISS: Tour the exquisitely re-created Royal Alexandra Hall from the Canadian Pacific Railway's Royal Alexandra Hotel that once stood near that road's Winnipeg Station. The hall was the grand café of the hotel and features Edwardian architectural style.

GETTING THERE: Air service to Cranbrook is available with direct flights from Vancouver and Calgary. Greyhound also operates daily scheduled service to the city. It is about a 3.5-hour drive from Spokane, Wash.

Kamloops Heritage Railway 9

LOCATION: 6-510 Lorne Street, Kamloops
PHONE: 250-374-2141
WEBSITE: kamrail.com
E-MAIL: info@kamrail.com

Tammy Gibson

This steam-powered tourist line's regular excursion is a seven-mile round trip on the Canadian National's Okanagan Subdivision that features mountain vistas, lakeside scenery, and an occasional train robbery.

CHOICES: On the *Spirit of Kamloops'* 70-minute excursion, you can ride in an a restored 1930s air-conditioned coach or in an open-air car to take in the sounds of the railway's former CN 2-8-0 and the sights of mountain and lakeside scenery. The train departs from a restored 1927 CN station and crosses the South Thompson River on a 1927 steel trestle bridge. The railway also operates ghost trains, Railway Days, and other special events.

WHEN TO GO: The *Spirit of Kamloops* operates Mondays, Fridays, and Saturdays during July and August. Illuminated with hundreds of lights, the *Spirit of Christmas* is a one-hour special, complete with candy canes, hot chocolate, and caroling.

GOOD TO KNOW: Kamloops is a regional center that has a wide range of accommodations to choose from, as well as all the services one would expect in a small-sized city, including city bus service. The former courthouse, where train robber Bill Miner was tried and convicted, is now a popular hostel.

WORTH DOING: Bring your camera as the *Spirit of Kamloops* stops on the trestle bridge to allow passengers to photograph the scenic vistas.

DON'T MISS: On the *Spirit of Kamloops*, masked riders reenact the famous 1906 train robbery by the Bill Miner gang. Following the robbery, listen to Bill Miner's ghost tell his story.

GETTING THERE: Scheduled air service is located at Kelowna, two hours to the south of Kamloops. Daily bus service operates in the city, and VIA Rail's *Canadian* calls at Kamloops Junction three times a week in each direction.

Kettle Valley Steam Railway 10

LOCATION: 18404 Bathville Road, Summerland
PHONE: 877-494-8424 or 250-494-8422
WEBSITE: www.kettlevalleyrail.org
E-MAIL: kvr@telus.net

Doug Campbell

The Kettle Valley Steam Railway operates over a preserved portion of the famed Kettle Valley Railway between Faulder and the Trout Creek trestle. Passengers can enjoy the view across Okanagan Lake and the surrounding hills from a steam-powered train traveling over the remaining portion of the CPR's famed southern route through British Columbia.

CHOICES: The KVR offers conventional excursions over its 10-mile right-of-way. The two-hour trip winds through Prairie Valley and its scenic vistas. Former BC 2-8-0 No. 3716 or a backup diesel engine supply the power. You can ride in two 1950s passenger coaches or several open-air cars. Special events are scheduled throughout the year and include a Christmas train and a train robbery with barbecue.

WHEN TO GO: The KVR operates on a varied schedule mid-May through Canadian Thanksgiving in October. Spring and fall excursions run Saturday through Monday. In summer, Thursday and Friday excursions are added.

GOOD TO KNOW: Summerland is situated in the Okanagan Valley amid lush orchards and vineyards, and the valley is home to more than 50 wineries.

WORTH DOING: Take a side trip into nearby Penticton and tour the former CP ship SS Sicamous. This steel-hulled sternwheeler was built in 1914 as a multipurpose vessel that provided first-class passenger service as well as delivering cargo and daily mail.

DON'T MISS: The Trout Creek trestle, at the current turnaround point south of Summerland, sits 238 feet above the canyon floor and provides spectacular views.

GETTING THERE: Air service is scheduled into and out of Kelowna, less than an hour's drive to the east. The Prairie Valley station is located off Highway 97.

Rocky Mountaineer Vacations ⑪

LOCATION: 1755 Cottrell Street, Vancouver
PHONE: 877-460-3200 or 604-606-7245
WEBSITE: www.rockymountaineer.com
E-MAIL: reservations@rockymountaineer.com

Rocky Mountaineer

What many consider to be Canada's premier rail tour company offers a variety of rail outings through British Columbia and Alberta. In addition to its signature Vancouver to Jasper route, there are trips from Vancouver to Banff or Calgary, from North Vancouver to Whistler, and from Whistler to Jasper.

CHOICES: Rocky Mountaineer offers two-day (or longer) trips over four routes. On the First Passage to the West, you follow the route of early explorers over the Rockies from Vancouver to either Banff or Calgary in Alberta. On a Journey through the Clouds, you experience coastal mountains, Fraser Canyon, and Hell's Gate on the journey from Vancouver to Jasper, Alberta, with an overnight stop in Kamloops. The Rainforest to Gold Rush route takes you from Whistler through Gold Country to Quesnel for an overnight stay and then along the Fraser River to Jasper. These three routes offer a choice between GoldLeaf or RedLeaf service. GoldLeaf service features bi-level dome coaches with full-length windows, and RedLeaf service includes reclining seats, extended legroom, and at-seat food service. The Whistler Sea to Sky Climb is a three-hour trip between Vancouver and Whistler, British Columbia, that follows the Sea to Sky corridor, which provides scenic views of waterfalls, forests, and mountains. On this route, you have the choice of Whistler Classic or Dome service.

WHEN TO GO: Excursions run between April and October.

GOOD TO KNOW: The Jasper and Banff/Calgary trains are combined between Vancouver and Kamloops. Trains operating on the former British Columbia Railway north of greater Vancouver arrive and depart from the vicinity of the former BCR station in North Vancouver.

WORTH DOING: Go for the gold. You may as well take advantage of the fancy digs and pampering with GoldLeaf or Whistler Dome service. It is a cruise train, after all.

DON'T MISS: Except for the Whistler Sea to Sky Climb, trips run both eastbound and westbound, and either direction offers spectacular scenery.

GETTING THERE: Air service is available to Vancouver and Calgary. Scheduled motor coach service connects Jasper, Banff, and Whistler to the outside world. VIA Rail Canada provides service to Jasper and Vancouver.

West Coast Railway Heritage Park ⑫

LOCATION: 39645 Government Road, Squamish
PHONE: 604-898-9336
WEBSITE: www.wcra.org/heritage
E-MAIL: info@wcra.org

John Godfrey

Opened in 1994, the West Coast Heritage Park provides a home to the West Coast Railway Association's large collection of locomotives and rolling stock. Located in a beautiful 12-acre mountain valley setting, the museum offers visitors a chance to learn about railway history from 1920 to 1960 in Canada's westernmost province.

CHOICES: The park features a variety of railway stations and other buildings. You are also able to see railway equipment in various stages of restoration in the 1914 PGE car shop. The collection of more than 50 vintage railway cars and locomotives includes cabooses, snowplows, a restored 1890 business car, and the only surviving Pacific Great Western steam engine. A mini train ride circles the park.

WHEN TO GO: The park is open year-round, except for Christmas and New Year's Day. Summer months provide the least likelihood for an encounter with the area's famous "wet sunshine." The park holds various special events including Steamfest, Day Out with Thomas, and the Polar Express.

GOOD TO KNOW: The park's newly completed roundhouse is a 21,000-square-foot facility for displaying exhibits. Using a working turntable, Royal Hudson No. 2860 was the first locomotive moved into the roundhouse.

WORTH DOING: Incorporate a visit to the museum with a scenic drive along the Sea to Sky Highway for a nice day-long family outing. The Sea to Sky Highway travels through five different biogeoclimatic zones, from coastal rain forest to mountain forest. This predominantly two-lane road goes from Vancouver to Whistler.

DON'T MISS: Royal Hudson No. 2860 was one of the last Royal Hudson locomotives built for the Canadian Pacific Railway by Montreal Locomotive Works in June 1940.

GETTING THERE: From Vancouver, it is about an hour's drive north on Highway 99 along spectacular Howe Sound, North America's southernmost fjord, to Squamish. Turn left on Industrial Way until Queens Way and then turn right and follow the signs.

DISCOUNT: $2 off each adult ticket September-December; excludes special events.

MANITOBA

Prairie Dog Central Railway ⬛

LOCATION: Prairie Dog Trail, Winnipeg
PHONE: 866-715-2348 or 204-832-5259
WEBSITE: pdcrailway.com
E-MAIL: info@pdcrailway.com

Paul Newsome

This 36-mile round trip over the former CN Oak Point Subdivision from the north side of the Manitoba capital to the town of Warren offers a glimpse into prairie railroading of the past.

CHOICES: The train takes a leisurely trip through rural Manitoba, and you can choose to travel in either open-vestibule or closed-vestibule coaches. All the wooden coaches, built between 1901 and 1913, are fully restored and air-conditioned—when the windows are open. Power is provided by steam locomotive No. 3 or diesel locomotive No. 4138, which was built in 1958 for the Grand Trunk Western Railroad. Many options are available throughout the season including train robberies, historical trains, and Halloween trains. You can also ride in a caboose or be an engineer for a day.

WHEN TO GO: Trains operate on select weekends during May and June, and they maintain a regular weekend schedule July through September. Special runs also operate on Victoria Day, Canada Day, Labour Day, and other select holidays.

GOOD TO KNOW: Ex-Winnipeg Hydro 4-4-0 No. 3, recently rebuilt, was built in 1882 by Dubs in Scotland and is one of the oldest operable engines in North America. The railway's station, constructed in 1910 by the Canadian Northern Railway, is a Canadian Heritage Railway Station. It was moved from St. James Street to its present location in 2000 and renamed Inkster Junction Station.

WORTH DOING: During the stopover, take time to examine the displays of local crafts and home-baked goods. Grosse Isle is home to the 72-mile Prime Meridian Trail, a recreation and conservation trail built on an abandoned rail line.

DON'T MISS: Secure a ticket in either combine No. 104 (built in 1906) or coach No. 105 (built in 1901). These beautifully maintained relics are rolling time machines to another century.

GETTING THERE: The railway is located north of Winnipeg on Prairie Dog Trail. It is on the north side of Inkster Boulevard between Route 90 and Sturgeon Boulevard.

Winnipeg Railway Museum ②

LOCATION: 123 Main Street, Winnipeg
PHONE: 204-942-4632
WEBSITE: wpgrailwaymuseum.com
E-MAIL: wpgrail@mts.net

Mark Perry

The Winnipeg Railway Museum takes visitors back to the historical first days of railroading across the vast western Canadian prairies. The museum's two tracks, located under the train shed at VIA Rail Canada's Union Station, host a variety of equipment, exhibits, and displays for all to enthusiasts enjoy.

CHOICES: The museum operates in the train shed of the grandiose Canadian Northern 1911-built Union Station. It contains various displays of both vintage steam and diesel locomotives, rail buses, passenger coaches, freight cars, cabooses, and many other Canadian railway artifacts. A pair of restored vintage fire trucks that came from nearby railway shops are displayed. Various spreaders, snow dozers, and other equipment round out the collection.

WHEN TO GO: The museum is open February through October. During spring and fall, Winnipeg temperatures can dip below zero. While the train shed offers protection from the wind, a visitor should still be prepared to dress warmly.

GOOD TO KNOW: Located in the heart of downtown Winnipeg, Union Station is still actively used by VIA Rail Canada's passenger trains. The CN's busy two-track Rivers Subdivision runs right next to the train shed.

WORTH DOING: A historic gathering place for centuries, the fantastic shopping, dining, and entertainment development is Winnipeg's number-one tourist attraction. Formerly, The Forks was a CNR rail yard, and the remaining historic railway buildings have been well preserved and upgraded. Railway equipment is preserved on the grounds, and a pristine CNR F unit is displayed inside the Children's Museum.

DON'T MISS: The museum features some notable railway equipment on display including the first steam engine in Manitoba, Canadian Pacific's wood-burning Baldwin *Countess of Dufferin*.

GETTING THERE: Winnipeg is 85 miles straight north of the North Dakota border on Highway 75. VIA Rail Canada operates a cross-country passenger train from Vancouver and Toronto that stops in Winnipeg. James Armstrong Richardson International Airport makes it easy to fly in and out of the city.

NEW BRUNSWICK

New Brunswick Railway Museum ❶

The museum contains more than 20 pieces of rolling stock that includes locomotives, passenger cars, freight cars, maintenance-of-way equipment, and cabooses. Some of the cars are open for viewing. The museum also displays a speeder car, telegraph office, and smaller artifacts. It is open June through September.

LOCATION: Route 114, Hillsborough
PHONE: 506-734-3195
WEBSITE: www.nbrm.ca
E-MAIL: info@nbrm.ca
DISCOUNT: $1 off adult or senior admission during July and August.

NEWFOUNDLAND

Railway Coastal Museum ❶

The Railway Coastal Museum is housed in the restored 1903 Riverhead station and contains a large collection of items relating to Newfoundland's rail and coastal boat services. You can walk along the platform where passengers boarded the *Newfie Bullet* and examine the rolling stock displayed in the train park. The museum is open year-round.

LOCATION: 495 Water Street West, St. John's
PHONE: 866-600-7245 or 709-724-5929
WEBSITE: railwaycoastalmuseum.ca
E-MAIL: info@railwaycoastalmuseum.ca

Railway Society of Newfoundland Train Site ❷

The society maintains a collection of narrow gauge rolling stock from the Newfoundland Railway. Several trains are displayed including the *Newfie Bullet*, once Newfoundland's fastest passenger train. Steam locomotive No. 593 is displayed with a representative selection of cars. A snowplow train is also featured. You can walk through all the railcars. The museum is open daily during the summer.

LOCATION: Marine Drive and Station Road, Corner Brook
PHONE: 709-634-2720 (in season)
WEBSITE: cornerbrook.com

NOVA SCOTIA

Orangedale Railway Museum ❶

The museum was originally built in 1886 as a Queen Anne-style station. The ground floor retains the original appearance of the agent's bay and waiting rooms. The second floor has been restored as the station agent's living quarters. The museum also displays a diesel switching locomotive, snowplow, caboose, and several railcars. It is open late June through October.

LOCATION: 1428 Main Street, Orangedale
PHONE: 902-756-3384
WEBSITE: novascotiarailwayheritage.com/orangedale.htm
E-MAIL: orangedale.station@gmail.com

Sydney & Louisburg Railway Museum ❷

The museum features rolling stock, artifacts, and photographs relating to the Sydney & Louisburg Railway. Housed in an 1895 S&L station, the museum also contains historical exhibits about Louisburg. An original freight shed and roundhouse also contain displays. You can also view Nova Scotia's oldest passenger coach. It is open June through September.

LOCATION: 7330 Main Street, Louisburg
PHONE: 902-733-2720
WEBSITE: fortress.uccb.ns.ca/historic/s_l.html

ONTARIO

Chatham Railroad Museum ❶

Housed in a retired 1955 Canadian National baggage car, the Chatham Railroad Museum includes interactive exhibits and photos on local as well as national and international railroad history. Open May to Labour Day, it is located across from the VIA rail station.

LOCATION: Queen Street, Chatham
PHONE: 800-561-6125 or 519-352-3097
WEBSITE: www.chatham-kent.ca
E-MAIL: cktourism@chatham-kent.ca

CNR School Car ❷

Back in the good old days, you didn't have to walk miles through the snow to get to this school. Instead, it came to you. This car was one of seven railway schools that served children and adults along northern Ontario railways. Tour the car and see how teachers brought learning to isolated students. It is open Thursday through Sunday Victoria Day weekend through September.

LOCATION: 76 Victoria Terrace, Clinton
PHONE: 519-482-3997
WEBSITE: schoolcar.ca

Fort Erie Railroad Museum ❸

This museum site features the restored Grand Trunk's Ridgeway station, which houses historic furnishings, telegraph equipment, tools, and other artifacts. Canadian National Railway steam engine No. 6218, a 4-8-4 Northern type, is the museum's centerpiece. Also on display are a fireless engine, a CN caboose, and other equipment. The CN's B-1 station that monitored traffic over the International Railway Bridge is also on site. It is open June to August.

LOCATION: 400 Central Avenue, Fort Erie
PHONE: 905-871-1412 or 905-894-5322
WEBSITE: museum.forterie.ca/website/museumweb.nsf
E-MAIL: museum@forterie.on.ca

Komoka Railway Museum ❹

Kamoka's restored Canadian National station houses a collection of artifacts and photos dedicated to rail history in the area. It includes tools, lanterns, and a tiny flag stop station. Also on display are a 1913 Shay locomotive and a steel-sided baggage car. The museum is open Friday through Monday during summer and on Saturdays the rest of the year.

LOCATION: 133 Queen Street, Komoka
PHONE: 519-657-1912
WEBSITE: komokarailmuseum.ca
E-MAIL: station-master@komokarailmuseum.ca

Memory Junction Museum ❺

Memory Junction features several structures including an 1857 Grand Trunk station, a baggage shed, and an unloading depot. A rare N-4-a locomotive is on display along with a wooden, outside-braced 1913 boxcar and other railcars. The museum includes local historical and railway artifacts. It is open mid-May through mid-October.

LOCATION: 60 Maplewood Street, Brighton
PHONE: 613-475-0379
WEBSITE: memoryjunction.netfirms.com
E-MAIL: re.bangay@sympatico.ca

Muskoka Heritage Place ❻

Muskoka Heritage Place contains the Muskoka Museum, Pioneer Village, and *Portage Flyer*, a restored 1902 steam train that takes you on a short trip to the past. A diesel engine may also run. After boarding at the train station, you travel along the Muskoka River to Fairy Lake, where you can watch a turntable in action. You can enjoy the entire site or just ride the *Portage Flyer*.

LOCATION: 88 Brunel Road, Huntsville
PHONE: 705-789-7576
WEBSITE: muskokaheritageplace.org
E-MAIL: ron.gostlin@huntsville.ca

Northern Ontario Railroad Museum & Heritage Centre ➐

This museum emphasizes railroading history in northern Ontario and includes additional exhibits on mining and lumbering. Artifacts are displayed in the Museum House, which was used by the Canadian National as a superintendent's residence. In nearby Prescott Park, it displays a U-1-f bullet-nosed steam locomotive, a wooden CNR caboose, and other equipment.

LOCATION: 26 Bloor Street, Capreol
PHONE: 705-858-5050
WEBSITE: northernontariorailroadmuseum.ca
E-MAIL: normhc@vianet.ca

Port Stanley Terminal Rail ⑧

Excursion trains depart from a historic station next to the King George lift bridge. Early diesel locomotives pull open and closed coaches that have been converted from cabooses. Regular one-hour excursions run to Whytes Park. A variety of special trains run during the season, and some travel the entire line into St. Thomas. You can view the fleet of equipment in the yard just north of the station.

LOCATION: 309 Bridge Street, Port Stanley
PHONE: 877-244-4478 or 519-782-3730
WEBSITE: pstr.on.ca
E-MAIL: form on website

Railway Museum of Eastern Ontario ➒

This museum is housed in a restored 1914 Canadian Northern Railway station that contains artifacts relating to the Canadian Pacific, Grand Trunk, Canadian National, and other railways. The national historic site displays a 1912 steam locomotive, a CP diesel, passenger cars, and a unique dental car. It is open weekends and offers handcar rides.

LOCATION: 90 William Street West, Smiths Falls
PHONE: 613-283-5696
WEBSITE: rmeo.whereelse.ca
E-MAIL: rmeo_info@whereelse.ca

Toronto Railway Heritage Centre ⑩

The heritage centre features a variety of railroad components including the John Street roundhouse, an interlocking tower, and operational turntable. In addition to viewing historic rail equipment and displays, visitors can check out the cab of a steam locomotive, tour Roundhouse Park, and ride on a miniature railway.

LOCATION: 255 Bremner Boulevard, Toronto
WEBSITE: trha.ca
E-MAIL: trha@rogers.com

Waterloo Central Railway ⑪

The railway operates excursion trains through southern Ontario behind a 60-ton diesel locomotive. You can take the entire 12-mile round trip or detrain at St. Jacobs, where you can look around, and take a later train back. The railway also operates various special trains throughout the year.

LOCATION: 10 Father David Bauer Drive, Waterloo
PHONE: 519-885-2297
WEBSITE: steam-train.org
E-MAIL: form on website
DISCOUNT: Receive $1 off each regular round-trip ticket.

York-Durham Heritage Railway ⑫

The railway operates excursions and special trains between Stouffville and Uxbridge. Diesel locomotives pull passenger coaches built between the 1920s and the 1950s. The Uxbridge station, which was built in 1904, contains displays of rail artifacts. There are numerous special events, and extra trains run in fall. Caboose rides are also available.

LOCATION: 6176 Main Street, Stouffville
PHONE: 905-852-3696
WEBSITE: ydhr.on.ca
E-MAIL: ydhra@ydhr.on.ca

Algoma Central Railway 🔢

LOCATION: 129 Bay Street, Sault Ste. Marie
PHONE: 800-242-9287 or 705-946-7300
WEBSITE: www.algomacentralrailway.com

Algoma Central Railway/CN

The Algoma Central Railway offers the chance to ride into unspoiled Canadian wilderness from Sault Ste. Marie north into Ontario as far as the spectacular Agawa Canyon or to the end of the railroad at Hearst. Either way, you will not go away disappointed.

CHOICES: You can ride the tour train to Agawa Canyon and back, or you can ride the entire railroad—almost 300 miles one way—to the end of the line at Hearst. Or, best of all, you can do both: ride the canyon train out and then catch the regular passenger train to Hearst and back. Going to the canyon, you'll see mixed forests, mountain lakes, and streams, and past the canyon, there are boreal forests, muskegs, and moose. The railway also offers winter snow trains and wilderness adventure trains.

WHEN TO GO: The railroad runs year-round. Fall bookings can be intense so plan ahead. The average daily temperature stays below freezing during December, January, and February.

GOOD TO KNOW: The tour train is usually packed, but the regular passenger train is more relaxed. You'll stop at only the canyon on the tour train, but the regular train pauses to let fishermen, hunters, and other outdoor types get off at just about any point. It's a lot of fun to see what people will load onto the baggage car.

WORTH DOING: There is much to do in Sault Ste. Marie, such as strolling along the boardwalk, visiting a casino, and touring the locks. Winter activities include skiing and snowboarding.

DON'T MISS: For scenery viewing, ride one of the railroad's two dome cars. Find a good vantage point at mile post 19, where the railroad crosses the Montreal River on a huge curving trestle perched atop a dam. For a wilderness experience, you can camp out overnight in a caboose at Agawa Canyon.

GETTING THERE: Sault Ste. Marie is located at I-75 and Highway 17. Signs show the way to the depot, which is located downtown.

Canada Science and Technology Museum ⑭

LOCATION: 1867 St. Laurent Boulevard, Ottawa
PHONE: 866-442-4416 or 613-991-3044
WEBSITE: sciencetech.technomuses.ca
E-MAIL: cts@technomuses.ca

Canada Science and Technology Museum

The Canada Science and Technology Museum's rail collection contains 1,000 artifacts that range from photos to locomotives and dates back to the early days of Canadian railway history. The museum also operates a demonstration train ride. Other exhibits focus on Canadian inventions, communications, and space technology.

CHOICES: Locomotive Hall showcases four locomotives, but other equipment is displayed throughout the museum and outdoors in Technology Park. Technology Park also includes a lighthouse, radar antenna, and Atlas rocket. During the summer, on Wednesdays and Sundays, you can take a 10-minute ride in vintage railcars. Operated by volunteers of the Bytown Railway Society, the Shay locomotive usually pulls a century-old business car and a caboose.

WHEN TO GO: The museum is open year-round but is closed most Mondays during winter. It also closes down for about four days for its annual cleaning. Look for new exhibits and special events throughout the year.

GOOD TO KNOW: For a small fee, you can try museum's space simulator. Missions include trying to save a colony on Mars and flying toward a comet on a collision course with Earth.

WORTH DOING: In Ottawa, the country's capital, there are numerous attractions and activities. Sites to see include the Rideau Canal, Canadian War Museum, and National Gallery of Canada. You can even watch the changing of the guard at Parliament Hill.

DON'T MISS: In Locomotive Hall, you'll find four unique engines: CNR No. 40, built for the Grand Trunk Railway in 1872 and Canada's oldest mainline steam locomotive; Canadian Pacific No. 926, which spent 50 years hauling freight and passenger trains between Winnipeg and Calgary; CNR No. 6400 with its distinctive semi-streamlined design and painted olive green; and CP No. 2858, one of five preserved CP Hudsons.

GETTING THERE: The museum is located approximately 10 minutes southeast of downtown Ottawa. Exit Highway 417 at St. Laurent south and turn left on Lancaster Road. You can also reach the museum by the No. 85 or No. 86 city bus.

Credit Valley Explorer 🔢

LOCATION: Townline Road, Orangeville
PHONE: 888-346-0046
WEBSITE: www.creditvalleyexplorer.com
E-MAIL: info@creditvalleyexplorer.com

John Godfrey

The *Credit Valley Explorer* offers three excursion options on its round trip between Orangeville and Brampton over a route that was completed in 1879. The ride, aboard 1950s rail coaches, takes you through rolling hills and deep valleys, over the Credit River, and across a 1,146-foot-long trestle bridge.

CHOICES: The 46-mile, three-hour excursion departs Orangeville and travels through the Caledon Hills, Cataract, and the forks of the Credit River to Inglewood and Brampton before returning. Scenic excursions operate May to October. A casual dinner trains run from June to September, with special holiday runs in December. On February weekends, you can enjoy winter scenery on a snow train.

WHEN TO GO: Different times of year offer different experiences. Late spring and early summer give you a chance to see the countryside before the foliage becomes dense. Autumn is busy, and the trains are full, but the fall colors are spectacular.

GOOD TO KNOW: For a refreshing pre- or post-trip stop, walk a few blocks to the Old Train Station, a restaurant housed in a former CPR station. You can also take a walking tour through Orangeville's historic downtown or examine the unique Art Walk of Tree Sculptures.

WORTH DOING: The Hills of the Headwaters is a great area for experiencing the great outdoors, no matter what the season. Hiking trails abound, and you can also fish, golf, and ski in a variety of locations.

DON'T MISS: Just relax in reclining first-class seats, enjoy a complimentary refreshment, look through the large windows, and enjoy the scenic views.

GETTING THERE: Orangeville is about an hour's drive from Toronto in southern Ontario. Trains depart from the railway yard on Town Line Road. From Highway 10, take Broadway to Town Line Road and turn left. Follow Town Line Road to the entrance.

Elgin County Railway Museum ⑯

LOCATION: 225 Wellington Street, St. Thomas
PHONE: 519-637-6284
WEBSITE: ecrm5700.org
E-MAIL: thedispatcher@ecrm5700.org

John Godfrey

The railroad has been a part of life in St. Thomas since 1856. Over the years, a total of 26 railways have passed through town, helping it garner the moniker of the Railway Capital of Canada. Located in the former Michigan Central locomotive shops, the Elgin County Railway Museum helps preserve and display the railway heritage of St. Thomas and the surrounding area.

CHOICES: As a working museum, equipment restoration is ongoing, and you can occasionally catch a glimpse of the volunteers in action. The museum displays a variety of equipment including locomotives, cabooses, and passenger cars. Highlights are a CP diesel locomotive, a CNR Hudson, a Grand Trunk Western caboose, a Pullman sleeper, and an electric-powered car that transported children to school in the 1920s. In St. Thomas, the BX interlocking tower is available for touring by appointment.

WHEN TO GO: The museum operates daily between Victoria Day and Labour Day. Thomas the Tank Engine regularly stops by in July. It also hosts a Railway Nostalgia Weekend in June.

GOOD TO KNOW: A short drive from the regional center of London, St. Thomas is a small town with all services. Its Iron Horse Festival coincides with the museum's Railway Heritage Day.

WORTH DOING: Combining a visit to the museum along with a ride on the nearby Port Stanley Terminal Rail makes for an interesting day of exploring the preserved rails of southern Ontario.

DON'T MISS: The museum celebrates the Canadian railway on Railway Heritage Day, which is usually held in August. During the celebration, short train trips often operate within town.

GETTING THERE: VIA Rail offers scheduled passenger service through London to the north. In addition, scheduled air service is available to that city's airport. If you're tied to the rubber tire, the museum is two hours from Toronto, two hours from the U.S. border at Detroit, Buffalo or Niagara Falls, and one hour from Sarnia and Port Huron. Once in St. Thomas, you will find the museum on Wellington Street between Ross Street and First Avenue.

Halton County Radial Railway 🔟

LOCATION: 13629 Guelph Line, Milton
PHONE: 519-856-9802
WEBSITE: hcry.org
E-MAIL: streetcar@hcry.org

David Arthur

Canada's pre-eminent trolley museum brings the streetcar era to life with the help of the largest collection of operable streetcars in the country. Its streetcars, radial cars, and work cars operate over a rebuilt portion of a long-abandoned interurban railway.

CHOICES: Streetcars, such as Toronto Transit Commission No. 2894, travel over a short track on a 20-minute ride through a hardwood forest. The railway features four display barns filled with 75 pieces of equipment that, in addition to streetcars, includes freight cars, passenger coaches, buses, and a locomotive or two. Most of the streetcars were built in the early 20th century.

WHEN TO GO: Streetcars operate on weekends from May to October and daily during July and August. A number of special events are incorporated into the operating season and some center on spring wild flowers, autumn color, Halloween, and Christmas.

GOOD TO KNOW: Admission includes unlimited streetcar rides and access to the exhibits displayed in the carbarns and Rockwood Station, which was built in 1912 for the Grand Trunk Railway. You can also enjoy a picnic lunch on the railway's grounds.

WORTH DOING: On Labour Day weekend, steam fans can take in Milton's steam-era event that features steam-powered equipment in action, a parade of tractors and antique autos, and tractor pulls.

DON'T MISS: After a long day of streetcar riding, reward yourself with ice cream from the ice cream shop. Share a romantic streetcar ride under the stars and enjoy ice cream together on the Ice Cream and Starlight evening.

GETTING THERE: Milton is 25 miles west of Toronto on Highway 401. From Highway 401 take Exit 312 and go north on Guelph Line until you reach the museum. It is also the the terminus of Toronto's Milton commuter train line.

Polar Bear Express 🔢

LOCATION: 200 Railway Street, Cochrane
PHONE: 800-268-9281 or 705-272-5338
WEBSITE: ontarionorthland.ca
E-MAIL: tours@ontarionorthland.ca

Ontario Northland

Ontario Northland's *Polar Bear Express* transports you to the shores of James Bay and the edge of the Arctic. The company also offers two other passenger trains. Its *Dream Catcher Express* takes you on a brilliant fall foliage trip out of North Bay. The *Northlander* travels between northern and southern Ontario.

CHOICES: The *Polar Bear Express* provides passenger excursions between Cochrane and Moosonee on James Bay. You can take a day trip, with several hours for exploring the area, or stay over and return on a different day. The train features a family car to keep young travelers busy. It makes flag stops along the way. The *Northlander* passenger train operates between Toronto and Cochrane over the Canadian National south of North Bay. In fall, you can relax aboard the *Dream Catcher Express* between North Bay and Temagami and view the brilliant colors.

WHEN TO GO: Between late June and late August, the *Polar Bear Express* runs every day but Saturday, and the *Dream Catcher Express* runs on a limited schedule.

GOOD TO KNOW: In Cochrane, the Station Inn provides handy overnight lodging on the upper floors of the train station. The *Polar Bear Express* features a canoe car for storing canoes for anyone planning a paddling adventure.

WORTH DOING: On the *Polar Bear Express* layover, be sure to take one of the side trips to the island of Moose Factory, a former Hudson's Bay Company fur-trading settlement. If you want to see polar bears close up, you can visit the Polar Bear Conservation and Education Habitat, a polar bear rehabilitation facility, in Cochrane, where you can see the bears in natural habitat and even swim alongside them (with a window in between).

DON'T MISS: Aboard the *Polar Bear Express*, take in the scenic views from the dome car.

GETTING THERE: Cochrane, North Bay, and Toronto are connected by bus and train service. VIA and Amtrak service connects Toronto with southwest Ontario and New York. Scheduled air service is available to Toronto and to Moosonee.

South Simcoe Railway 19

LOCATION: Mill Street West, Tottenham
PHONE: 905-936-5815
WEBSITE: southsimcoerailway.ca
E-MAIL: info@southsimcoerailway.ca

John Godfrey

The South Simcoe Railway operates over four miles of former Canadian National trackage through rolling countryside approximately an hour north of Toronto. Most excursions are powered by a 1948 diesel locomotive or steam locomotive No. 136, which was built in 1883.

CHOICES: Regular excursions from Tottenham to Beeton and back take about an hour. As the train rolls through Beeton Creek Valley, the conductor provides an informative commentary. Passengers ride in restored 1920s steel heavyweight coaches. A Santa Claus Express operates weekends in December.

WHEN TO GO: The railway runs multiple trips on Sundays and on holiday Mondays, as well as some additional dates, between Victoria Day weekend and Canadian Thanksgiving.

GOOD TO KNOW: The town of Tottenham has a variety of quaint shops and eateries. Across the road from the railway is Tottenham Conservation Park, which offers swimming, camping, fishing, and hiking.

WORTH DOING: For a unique combination rail-water excursion, the RMS *Segwun*, the oldest operating steamship in North America, sails June through October on the Muskoka Lakes, about a two-hour drive north to Gravenhurst.

DON'T MISS: Take one rail trip and then follow one of the others for some great photos. The engine faces south into the sun, and the relatively slow pace of the train makes it easy to follow.

GETTING THERE: No public transit is available to this neck of the woods. From Highway 400, take Highway 9 west nine miles to Tottenham Road and turn right. Continue into downtown Tottenham and turn left onto Mill Street to reach the station.

PRINCE EDWARD ISLAND

Elmira Railway Museum ❶

The museum offers a look at railroading on the island in the early 1900s. It features re-created buildings representing the original wooden station house, platform, freight shed, and master's office. The station building contains two rooms of displays and artifacts. A miniature train operates around the museum, and a variety of special events take place on the outdoor stage, which was built from the base of a flatcar. The museum is open June through September.

LOCATION: 457 Elmira Road, Elmira
PHONE: 902-357-7234
WEBSITE: elmirastation.com
E-MAIL: elmira@gov.pe.ca

QUEBEC

Orford Express ❶

After boarding at the restored Sherbrooke station, this train takes you on a scenic trip along the shores of a river and several lakes, all in view of Mount Orford. Brunch, lunch, and dinner are dining choices for the 3.5-hour experience, and informative videos and narration add food for thought. L'Escapade is a non-dining option.

LOCATION: 720 Minto Street, Sherbrooke
PHONE: 866-575-8081 or 819-575-8081
WEBSITE: orfordexpress.com
E-MAIL: info@orfordexpress.com

Railway Interpretation Centre ❷

Housed in a 1917 station, this museum (Centre d'interpretation ferroviaire de Vallee-Jonction) relates the history of the Quebec Central Railway. On display are a CN 4-6-4T steam locomotive, a caboose, a tank car, and a boxcar. In August, the museum holds a railway festival.

LOCATION: 397 Rousseau Boulevard, Vallee-Jonction
PHONE: 418-253-6449
E-MAIL: garevalleejonction@globetrotter.net

Exporail ❸

LOCATION: 110 St. Pierre Street, St. Constant
PHONE: 450-632-2410
WEBSITE: www.exporail.org
E-MAIL: info@exporail.org

Exporail

The largest collection of railway equipment in the country is well worth a stop for anyone interested in Canadian railways and rail transit. Locomotives, rolling stock, and streetcars from many parts of the country tell of the evolution of both industries.

CHOICES: The museum's collection boasts 160 railway vehicles. A number of special events and exhibits are scheduled throughout the year and geared toward modelers, transit enthusiasts, and those with a love of railways. The museum has several train ride options. A streetcar runs daily. On select Saturdays and Sundays, you can ride on a demonstration passenger train pulled by a replica of an 1849 steam locomotive.

WHEN TO GO: The Canadian Railway Museum is open daily between late May and the beginning of September. During September and October, it is open Wednesday through Sunday. The remainder of the year, the museum is open on weekends, for spring break, and around Christmas.

GOOD TO KNOW: Wear good walking shoes and dress for the weather. The main building contains only a portion of the collection, and you can explore the rest of the site from stops along the streetcar loop. You'll be able to see Barrington Station, a restored, rural flag stop station from southwestern Quebec.

WORTH DOING: There is much to see and do in Montreal. You can discover centuries of history in Old Montreal and explore Olympic Park.

DON'T MISS: An observation pit in the Grand Gallery allows you to view the undersides of both a steam locomotive and diesel engine (CP No. 2850 and CN No. 6765).

GETTING THERE: The museum is located 12 miles from downtown Montreal. Montreal has extensive air, bus, and rail service. Amtrak's *Adirondack* connects the city with the rest of its network in Albany, N.Y. CIT Roussillon provides bus service near the museum. Several times a year, the Museum Express runs from Lucien L'Allier station in Montreal.

Hull-Chelsea-Wakefield Steam Train ▪

LOCATION: 165 Deveault Street, Gatineau
PHONE: 800-871-7246 or 819-778-7246
WEBSITE: steamtrain.ca
E-MAIL: info@steamtrain.ca

Raymond Farand

The Hull-Chelsea-Wakefield Railroad operates steam and diesel powered 35-mile round-trip excursions between Gatineau and Wakefield along the Gatineau River, using Swedish-made locomotives and rolling-stock.

CHOICES: You can ride a scenic excursion, enjoy a sunset dinner or Sunday brunch, or take in a fall foliage trip. You can choose to ride in a coach car or the luxurious *Riviera* club car. Scenic excursions are narrated, feature musicians, and include a two-hour stop in Wakefield. The railroad also offers special tour packages that include a train trip combined with other area attractions.

WHEN TO GO: Scenic excursions are offered May through September, with daily service in July and August. The Canadian Tulip Festival held in Ottawa and Gatineau each May draws many tourist, as do Canada Day celebrations. Early June or early September often see lighter passenger numbers. The sunset dinner train operates weekends June into September. The Outaouais Region is known for its fall colors, and fall foliage excursions begin in late September and continue through October.

GOOD TO KNOW: The HCW's equipment was imported from Sweden in 1992. Steam engine No. 909 was built in 1907 and the coaches are from the 1940s. Even the railroad's diesel engine was built in Sweden.

WORTH DOING: The region is home to most of Canada's national museums, including Canada's Science and Technology Museum, which houses a modest collection of railway equipment. Most of the former CPR right-of-way north of downtown Ottawa through Hull is now a recreational path, ideal for cycling or walking, and affords a great afternoon view of Parliament Hill.

DON'T MISS: Much of the route parallels the west side of the Gatineau River, making seats on the right side of the train northbound from Gatineau more desirable. In Wakefield, watch the engine turn around on the last manual turntable in Canada.

GETTING THERE: VIA Rail Canada operates into Ottawa from both Toronto and Montreal. Ottawa and Hull are also served by bus. Gatineau city buses operate across the Ottawa River into downtown Ottawa, making it possible to use public transit to get to the HCW station. It is also a short drive from Ottawa using Route 5.

SASKATCHEWAN

Rusty Relics Museum ❶

Rusty Relics Museum portrays pioneer life in Saskatchewan. Housed in Carlyle's 1910 station, its collection features several buildings, machinery, and artifacts. Railway items include a caboose, a jigger, a tool shed, and a working telegraph. It is open Monday through Saturday June to September.

LOCATION: 306 Railway Avenue West, Carlyle
PHONE: 306-453-2266 or 306-453-2363
WEBSITE: saskmuseums.org/museums

Saskatchewan Railway Museum ❷

This seven-acre museum contains more than 10 buildings, including a station, express shed, interlocking tower, and tool sheds, from the Canadian National, Canadian Pacific, Canadian Northern, and Grand Trunk Railways. On display are a variety of freight cars, passenger coaches, streetcars, cabooses, and a CPR S3 diesel locomotive. You can take a guided tour or explore the museum on your own.

LOCATION: Highway 60, Saskatoon
PHONE: 306-382-9855
WEBSITE: saskrailmuseum.org
E-MAIL: srha@saskrailmuseum.org

Reference maps

00 = train and trolley rides

00 = museums and other sites

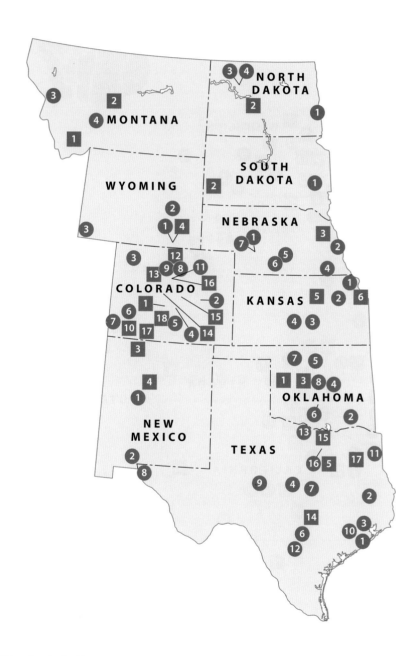

= train and trolley rides

= museums and other sites

⬛ = train and trolley rides

⬤ = museums and other sites

MICHIGAN

MICHIGAN

INDIANA

OHIO

KENTUCKY

TENNESSEE

00 = train and trolley rides

00 = museums and other sites

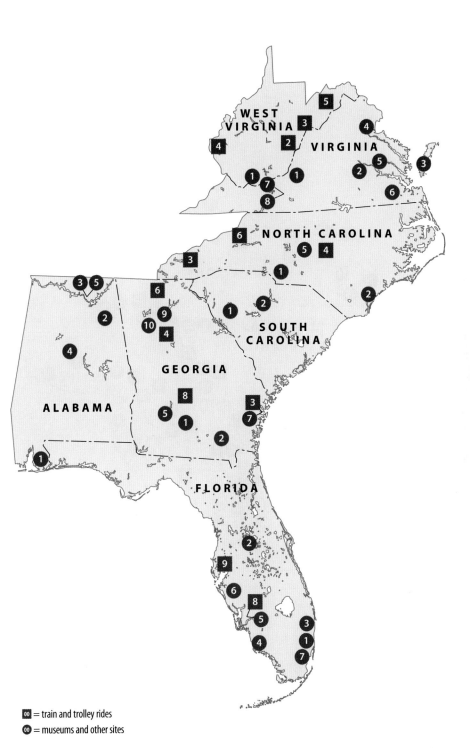

WEST
VIRGINIA

VIRGINIA

NORTH CAROLINA

SOUTH
CAROLINA

GEORGIA

ALABAMA

FLORIDA

= train and trolley rides

= museums and other sites

■ = train and trolley rides

● = museums and other sites

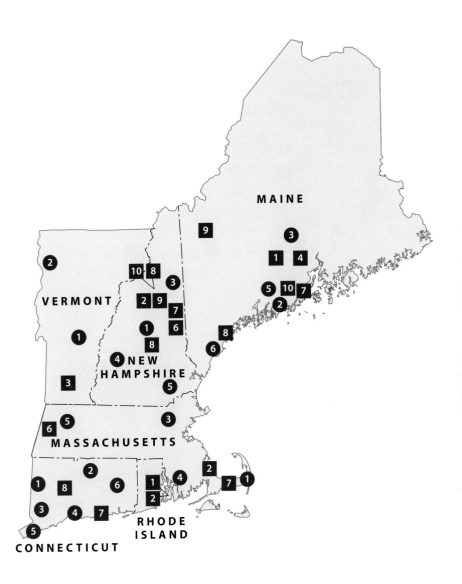

MAINE

VERMONT

NEW HAMPSHIRE

MASSACHUSETTS

RHODE ISLAND

CONNECTICUT

▪ = train and trolley rides

● = museums and other sites

= train and trolley rides

= museums and other sites

Index

Advertiser Index

EAST TROY RAILROAD

The East Troy Railroad is the last vestige of Wisconsin's once broad network of electric interurban railways. Concentrated in the southeastern quarter of the state, this network once totaled approximately 383 miles of track. Most of the interurban railway mileage in Wisconsin was built between 1890 and 1907; the last interurban passenger in the state was carried in 1963 by The North Shore Line. The East Troy interurban line, formerly a part of The Milwaukee Electric Railway & Light Company, carried passengers between East Troy and Milwaukee from 1907 until 1939. Since 1939 the six mile line has existed as a railroad freight connection for the Village of East Troy.

Ride Historic Electrics at East Troy

Operates May through October

browse **www.easttroyrr.org** for schedule

EAST TROY
ELECTRIC
RAILROAD

EAST TROY RAILROAD MUSEUM

Phone (262) 642-3263

2002 Church St.
East Troy, WI 53120

The only interurban electric dining car service in North America

PHANTOM WOODS

Colorado's Premier Rail Experience

Mountaintop Concerts

Historic Steam Rides

Wildlife Viewing

Historic Depot ~ 230 S. Broad St. Globe, AZ 85501

COPPER SPIKE
Train Excursion

ALL ABOARD

~ Luncheon and Dinner Service in premium dome cars

~ Appetizers and bar service in stylized club car

ARIZONA
ARIZONA EASTERN RAILWAY
www.copperspike.com ~ 866-979-RAIL (7245)

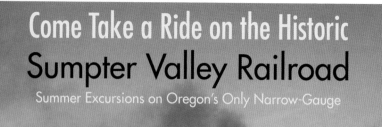

Come Take a Ride on the Historic
Sumpter Valley Railroad
Summer Excursions on Oregon's Only Narrow-Gauge

Located in northeast Oregon's beautiful Sumpter Valley, a half hour from Baker City, excursions operate every weekend and major holiday from Memorial Day weekend through the last weekend of September.

866-894-2268
www.svry.com - sumptervalleyinfo@yahoo.com

Black River Railroad Historical Trust

Come experience the charm of small-town railroading on the Black River & Western Railroad in beautiful Hunterdon County, New Jersey. Family-friendly trains and events operate on select dates throughout the year.

. . . .

Special events include the Easter Bunny Express, Great Train Robbery, Corn Maze at Pumpkin Junction, North Pole Express, Murder Mysteries, and more! Excursions are powered by one of our diesel-electric locomotives or steam locomotive #60.
Select trains feature rides in our open-air car or a caboose!

Groups can take advantage of discount pricing on most trains, or charter a coach or entire train for themselves!

Visit our website at **www.brrht.org** for our complete schedule, pricing, and other details.

Kids of All Ages Enjoy a Step into the Past

RIDE THE TRAIN!
FAMILY FUN

50-MINUTE DEISEL-POWERED TRAIN RIDE
Caboose and Cab Rides Available!

DOZENS *of* DISPLAYS
~ *Gift Shop in 1894 Depot* ~

OPEN DAILY
Memorial Day through Labor Day
OPEN WEEKENDS
May and September

Check out our rides like
Autumn Color,™ the Pumpkin
Special,™ the Snow Train™
and the Santa Express™ at:

www.midcontinent.org

MID-CONTINENT RAILWAY MUSEUM

Just 30 Minutes from the Dells at North Freedom, Wisconsin

Take Hwy. 12 south to Baraboo, then west on Hwy. 136 four miles, then left on County Hwy. PF 2 miles to North Freedom. Museum is 1/2 mile west of a 4-way stop in town.

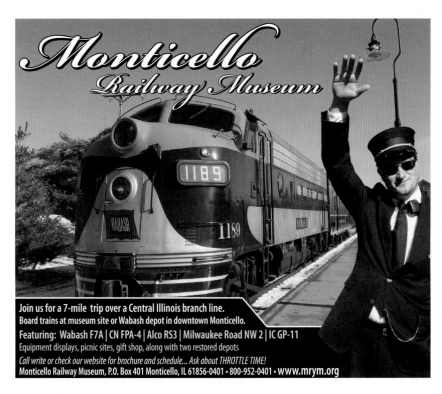

Join us for a 7-mile trip over a Central Illinois branch line.
Board trains at museum site or Wabash depot in downtown Monticello.
Featuring: Wabash F7A | CN FPA-4 | Alco RS3 | Milwaukee Road NW 2 | IC GP-11
Equipment displays, picnic sites, gift shop, along with two restored depots
Call write or check our website for brochure and schedule... Ask about THROTTLE TIME!
Monticello Railway Museum, P.O. Box 401 Monticello, IL 61856-0401 • 800-952-0401 • **www.mrym.org**

Every title is prepared to exacting standards and lithographed in full, rich color to closely match the prototype. Printed with fade-resistant inks and archival properties, these lithographs are designed with the serious collector in mind. Each print is 11" x 14" self-matted with title & description, a historical text is included on a separate document, the 5½" x 8¾" portrait cards include the description on the back. Available at select train shops and museums and online.

www.vanishingvistasonline.com

Vanishing Vistas
BY RICHARD E. COX

PO Box 1491T • ROCKLIN, CA • 95677-7491 • USA

The Train Where Eagles Fly

In 2005 through 2010 eagles were seen on every Train Ride

Historic Locomotives & Trains
in Romney, West Virginia

Regular 3.5 hour excursions & selected all-day trips available
Open window coach and observation car seating available on all trains

Excursions operate Saturdays & some Sundays May – September
Daily departures in October, check out our website for schedule

POTOMAC EAGLE®

Information and Reservations:
www.potomaceagle.info
304-424-0736

Potomac Eagle Wappocomo Station, Route 28 North, P.O. Box 657 Romney, WV 26757

West Virginia
State Parks and Forests

38° 27'N 79° 54'W

CASS SCENIC
RAILROAD
STATE PARK

The train to ride

In the heart of West Virginia is the foremost
roster of operating geared steam locomotives
in the world — Cass Scenic Railroad.
Find company houses to rent. The Last
Run Restaurant. Daily trips May–October.
Charter a train. Enjoy special evening trains
for murder mystery, bluegrass and more.

Time to climb aboard Cass Scenic Railroad —
"Preserving America's Past for the Future"

304-456-4300 • www.cassrailroad.com
Group contact: geraldine.e.bartels@wv.gov

HISTORIC MACHINERY SERVICES CORPORATION

36 Years Experience • *Museum Quality Restoration and Conservation*

- Repairs to Operating Equipment
- Extensive Rebuilding or Minor Repairs
- Steam Locomotives and Steam Engines
- Industrial Machinery - metal and woodworking
- Portable Crank Pin Turning
- King & Paxton-Mitchell Rod & Valve Stem Packing

- Boiler Work:
    - Form 4 inspections and calculations
    - Repairs and Alterations
    - ASME certified welders
- Part Replication:
    - From your drawing or old part
    - Injector Nozzles
    - Lever Operated Alemite Crank Pin Grease Gun
    - Washout Plugs, Bronze
    - SB-61 Pressure Part Bronze Castings

P.O. Box 856 • Springville, Alabama • SHOP PHONE AND FAX (256) 538-6938

www.HistoricMachineryServices.com

Enjoy California Wine Country in a Caboose B&B

LUXURIOUS, THEMED SUITES IN GENUINE RAILROAD CABOOSES
RELAXING, PARK-LIKE SETTING RIGHT ON CLEAR LAKE
IN-ROOM JACUZZI TUBS • BOAT LAUNCH • DOCK & PIER
FULL BREAKFAST • GREAT WEDDING & MEETING LOCATION

(800) 966-6322 • www.featherbedrailroad.com

340

Byesville Scenic Railway

Climb aboard the Byesville Scenic Railway and be transported back to a time when coal was king and whistle-stop train stations dotted the landscape. Enjoy a 1-½ hour-long round trip train excursion through scenic Southeastern Ohio. On board, passengers are greeted by our coal mining historians who share the life, heritage, and culture of our coal mining history.

An annual schedule is available detailing our train excursions and special events, we run rain or shine.

Special exclusive group trips may also be scheduled in advance during the day or in the evenings.

Learn more about our excursions at www.bsrw.org or call 800.933.5480.

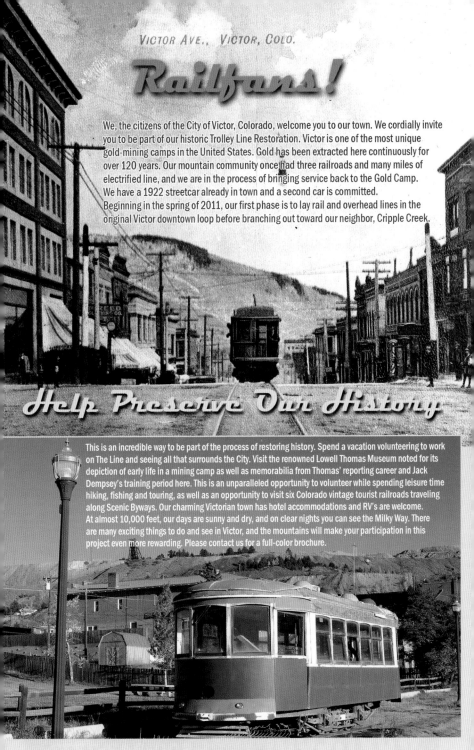

VICTOR AVE., VICTOR, COLO.

Railfans!

We, the citizens of the City of Victor, Colorado, welcome you to our town. We cordially invite you to be part of our historic Trolley Line Restoration. Victor is one of the most unique gold-mining camps in the United States. Gold has been extracted here continuously for over 120 years. Our mountain community once had three railroads and many miles of electrified line, and we are in the process of bringing service back to the Gold Camp. We have a 1922 streetcar already in town and a second car is committed.
Beginning in the spring of 2011, our first phase is to lay rail and overhead lines in the original Victor downtown loop before branching out toward our neighbor, Cripple Creek.

Help Preserve Our History

This is an incredible way to be part of the process of restoring history. Spend a vacation volunteering to work on The Line and seeing all that surrounds the City. Visit the renowned Lowell Thomas Museum noted for its depiction of early life in a mining camp as well as memorabilia from Thomas' reporting career and Jack Dempsey's training period here. This is an unparalleled opportunity to volunteer while spending leisure time hiking, fishing and touring, as well as an opportunity to visit six Colorado vintage tourist railroads traveling along Scenic Byways. Our charming Victorian town has hotel accommodations and RV's are welcome. At almost 10,000 feet, our days are sunny and dry, and on clear nights you can see the Milky Way. There are many exciting things to do and see in Victor, and the mountains will make your participation in this project even more rewarding. Please contact us for a full-color brochure.

The Victorious Society • PO Box 224 • Victor, CO 80860 • (719) 337-1954 • www.vrail.org
also visit www.victorcolorado.com

Middletown & Hummelstown Railroad Company

Enjoy an 11-mile train ride back into history aboard 1920's vintage passenger coaches.

Located near Hershey and Harrisburg PA. Regular schedule trains run May through October.

Middletown & Hummelstown Railroad Company
136 Brown Street, Middletown, PA 17057
717-944-4435, ext 0   www.mhrailroad.com

THE MILK & HONEY LINE

Come and ride the trains of the. . . . .

Boone & Scenic Valley Railroad & Museum

EXCURSION TRAINS
Sats. in May at 1:30 p.m.
Memorial Day weekend -
October 31
Sun. - Fri. at 1:30 p.m.
Saturday at 1:30 and 4 p.m.
DAY OUT WITH THOMAS™
Late September
SANTA EXPRESS™
Late Nov. - Dec.

DINNER TRAINS
Saturdays at 5:30 p.m.
April - November
Fridays at 5:30 p.m.
June - October
DESSERT TRAINS
Sat. at 12:30 p.m.
June - October
PICNIC TRAINS
Sun. at 12:30 p.m.
Late May - October

1-800-626-0319 • www.scenic-valleyrr.com

Boone & Scenic Valley Railroad & Museum
225 10th Street, Boone, IA

Colorado RAILROAD Museum ®

Lose track of time.

Depot Museum, exhibit galleries, General Store
and 15-acre railyard with over 100 narrow
and standard gauge steam and diesel locomotives,
passenger cars, cabooses and G-scale garden railway.
Open daily from 9:00am-5:00pm

TRAIN RIDES EVERY SATURDAY

www.ColoradoRailroadMuseum.org
303-279-4591 or 800-365-6263
17155 W. 44th Avenue,
Golden Colorado 80403

SCFD
Citizens of the
Scientific & Cultural
Facilities District
Making It Possible.

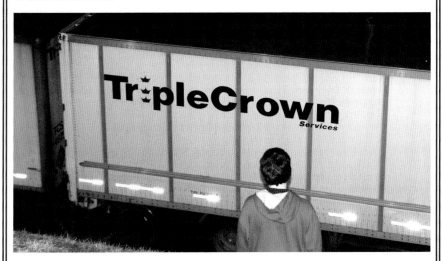

SILVER RRAILS
COUNTRY.COM

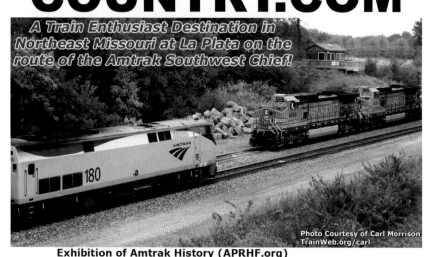

A Train Enthusiast Destination in Northeast Missouri at La Plata on the route of the Amtrak Southwest Chief!

Photo Courtesy of Carl Morrison
TrainWeb.org/carl

Exhibition of Amtrak History (APRHF.org)
Silver Rails Gallery & Memorial Library
Chris Guenzler Millionth Mile Rail Lookout Point
Restored La Plata Historic Santa Fe Depot
Chew Choo Cafe / Santa Fe Espresso / Santa Fe Lake
Amish Country Variety Store & Amish Country Bakery
Walt Disney Hometown Museum (& Santa Fe Steam Loco)
Moberly Historic Railway Museum & Depot Park
The Magic City Line Mini Train Ride at Rothwell Park
Bevier & Southern Railroad Co No 112 Steam Loco
Columbia Star Dinner Train
LocoVino railroad themed wines & 3 wine tasting rooms
Mark Twain Boyhood Hometown, Museum, and Caves
Tour TrainWeb.com & TrainParty.com Corp Headquarters
The Heartland Antique Ford Auto Museum, 50's Cafe,
& largest automated dairy carousel milking operation

DepotInnAndSuites.com &
SilverRailsEventCenter.com

Visit SilverRailsCountry.com